TECHNOLOGY'S CHILD

TECHNOLOGY'S CHILD

**DIGITAL MEDIA'S ROLE IN THE AGES
AND STAGES OF GROWING UP**

KATIE DAVIS

THE MIT PRESS   CAMBRIDGE, MASSACHUSETTS   LONDON, ENGLAND

The MIT Press would like to thank the anonymous peer reviewers who provided comments on drafts of this book. The generous work of academic experts is essential for establishing the authority and quality of our publications. We acknowledge with gratitude the contributions of these otherwise uncredited readers.

This book was set in Stone Serif and Avenir by Jen Jackowitz. Printed and bound in the United States of America

Library of Congress Cataloging-in-Publication Data

Names: Davis, Katie (Assistant professor), author.
Title: Technology's child : digital media's role in the ages and stages of growing up / Katie Davis.
Description: Cambridge, Massachusetts : The MIT Press, [2023] | Includes bibliographical references and index.
Identifiers: LCCN 2022010139 (print) | LCCN 2022010140 (ebook) | ISBN 9780262046961 (Hardcover) | ISBN 9780262370080 (epub) | ISBN 9780262370097 (pdf)
Subjects: LCSH: Internet and youth. | Technology and youth. | Child development. | Digital media.
Classification: LCC HQ799.9.I58 D38 2023 (print) | LCC HQ799.9.I58 (ebook) | DDC 004.67/80835—dc23/eng/20220831
LC record available at https://lccn.loc.gov/2022010139
LC ebook record available at https://lccn.loc.gov/2022010140

10   9   8   7   6   5   4   3   2   1

I dedicate this book to my son, Oliver.

CONTENTS

PREFACE

Research on kids and technology can be complicated, confusing, and inconclusive. Headlines and talking heads are even worse. This book brings clarity to the current state of knowledge related to technology's role in child development and provides guidance on how to apply the insights to individual children and adolescents so that their digital experiences will support rather than undermine healthy development.

The book examines the variety of ways that young people engage with technology across the course of their development, from toddlers who are exploring their immediate environment to twenty-somethings who are exploring their role in society. At its core, *Technology's Child* is about what happens when child development interacts with technology design and how this interaction is complicated by children's individual characteristics and their social and cultural contexts.

My research indicates that technology supports healthy child development when it's self-directed and community supported; it impedes development when it's not. By self-directed, I mean technology experiences that are initiated, sustained, and ended voluntarily, and that support a feeling of personal accomplishment and growth. By community supported, I mean technology experiences that are embedded in broader contexts of support. Sometimes the support is surrounding the technology use, like when a parent or sibling helps a child navigate the interface of a literacy app and reinforces the learning concepts during and after the app session. Sometimes the support comes from within the technology experience itself, like when a teen finds a supportive online community whose members affirm the teen's marginalized identity, or when a social media platform works out a thoughtful, effective approach to moderating hate speech.

Creating the best-case scenario isn't easy. It requires attention and work on the part of families and teachers, researchers, policymakers, and tech companies, and even young people themselves. The insights from this book will provide actionable guidance for each of these stakeholders.

So, what counts as "technology" for the purposes of this exploration? I focus my analysis on technologies that have one or more of the following qualities: *digital* (the 0s and 1s that undergird the pixels on your computer screen), *interactive* (the response you get when you make a swiping motion on your phone), and *networked* (the ability to consume and share content and connect with others across devices). Many of the technologies I examine have screens (phones, tablets, laptops), but not all (smart speakers, smart toys, and other devices powered by Internet of Things [IoT] technologies). For the most part, I focus on existing technologies that are already ubiquitous in the lives of most children in developed countries, but I'll also consider some emerging technologies, too.

WHO THIS BOOK IS FOR

This book is for anyone who is interested in and concerned about the impact of technology on children's development, from birth through emerging adulthood. I cover a lot of research terrain in these pages, which I've attempted to distill into a set of readily accessible and actionable ideas for:

- A parent who is trying to keep up with the technologies their children use daily, curious and perhaps a bit (or very) concerned about how these technologies are impacting their children's development, and who is seeking practical guidance on how to make good decisions when it comes to their children's technology use.
- A teacher who wants to understand the broader context of their students' digitally mediated lives outside the classroom and use technology to support meaningful, rich learning experiences inside the classroom.
- A policymaker—whether at the local, state, or federal level—who is seeking evidence-based insights to guide policy decisions aimed at mitigating the negative effects of technology while retaining its positive influences in children's lives.
- A design team, project manager, or executive at a tech company who recognizes the importance of drawing on research knowledge to inform their decisions about how technologies are developed, disseminated, and marketed to children of different ages and their families.
- A researcher or student who would like to inform their own thinking about and understanding of technology's role in child development.

As evidenced by this list, the solution to supporting children's positive technology experiences is not an individual one; it cannot and should not fall on individual parents, teachers, or tech developers. We must start looking at the broad conditions of children's technology use if we want to create an ecosystem of digital experiences that align with their developmental needs.

Ultimately, this book should give readers a way to think through and make sense of what's going on developmentally when a child interacts with a digital device, and what conditions are likely to make their experiences more self-directed and community supported—in other words, more supportive of healthy development.

One thing is clear from the disparate research studies addressing kids and technology: it's time to get specific. We need to look at specific technologies, specific children, and the specific contexts connecting the two if we want to truly understand what's going on with technology's role in child development.

WHY I WROTE THIS BOOK

Technology's Child is shaped by my knowledge and expertise as a researcher. I've studied children's and teens' technology use for more than fifteen years. It's also shaped by my experiences as a parent (chapters 2–4), a former elementary school teacher (chapter 5), and a sister (chapter 7). I use these personal experiences in the chapters following here to help bring aspects of the research I'll explore to life.

I don't intend my experiences to represent some sort of norm in children's technology—I intend the opposite. I use these personal experiences to call attention to the individual, personal dimensions of research on children and technology. Examining the when, why, and for whom of technology's impact on children requires paying attention to individual differences, instances when children and their circumstances don't conform to the average trend line.

My stance as a researcher is every bit as individual and specific as my role as a parent, teacher, and sister. I was trained by two developmental psychologists (Howard Gardner and Kurt Fischer) in an education school (Harvard Graduate School of Education). For the last ten years, I've worked at the University of Washington Information School, surrounded by colleagues whose work represents a broad range of scholarly disciplines, but I'm perhaps most influenced by those working in technology design. As a result, in my own work, and in this book, I bring together the fields of human development, education, and technology design.

This particular scholarly mix accounts for the two distinct questions that I explore in these pages. The first is an empirical question, something that a psychologist or other social scientist would ask: *What is the impact of different kinds of technologies on different kinds of children (experiencing different social, cultural, and economic contexts)?* If I had written the book after my doctoral studies, I would have stopped there (in fact that's exactly what I did with my first book, *The App Generation*, coauthored with Howard Gardner).

But my work for the last decade has been just as focused on exploring the design of new technologies as it has been on studying the impact of existing ones. So the second question guiding this book is a more action-oriented question, something that a design researcher would be more likely to ask: *How can technology be designed to support children's development?*

1

INTRODUCTION

At no other point in human history have we been so preoccupied with how we raise our children, and so concerned.[1] For the first several thousand years of our existence, the goal was pretty much survival. First, survive childbirth, then survive long enough to contribute to the survival of the human species.

The concept of childhood is a fairly recent invention; we used to perceive children as not-yet-grown adults. (Just take a look at some family portraits from the seventeenth century— the children are depicted as miniature adults, fully developed, and sometimes even with faces as lined as the parents seated next to them.) It wasn't until the field of child development was formed less than a century ago that we started to appreciate that children of different ages and stages think and experience the world in qualitatively different ways from adults.

This understanding overlapped with the shift in industrialized societies from human survival to human flourishing. Families who benefitted from the medical breakthroughs, technological advances, and increased economic prospects of the eighteenth and nineteenth centuries started turning their attention to raising children who would not just survive but thrive. We've been pursuing this holy grail ever since.

There's a lot about Western society that makes raising a child today particularly nerve-wracking for just about any parent: growing economic inequality in an increasingly winner-take-all society; civic unrest fueled by political and ideological polarization; a collective reckoning with the continued effects of racism, colonialism, and other forms of discrimination that marginalize groups of people; the herculean challenge of slowing down—let alone reversing—the effects of climate change and environmental degradation.

Add to this mix the speed of technological development, which seems to be shortening the length of generations to the point where older siblings look down at their younger, tech-savvier siblings, shaking their heads as they bemoan "kids these days." Parents have been living with the unease of raising digitally networked children for at least a generation now. The unease may feel more familiar, more par for the course during the many uncertainties associated with parenting, but that doesn't make it any easier. Research that's filtered through sensational headlines—which often contradicts the research published the week before—doesn't help.

I believe the coronavirus pandemic—in combination with other, concurrent events—has given rise to a new readiness to engage with the topic of kids and technology on a deeper level than the months and years prior to March 2020. Before the pandemic, the collective zeitgeist seemed focused on some variation of the following questions—*Screens: are they good or bad for children's development?* and *Screen time: how much is too much?*

This period of online school, work, playdates, happy hours, fitness classes, therapy sessions, music lessons, and much, much more taught us all that asking whether screens and screen time are good or bad are not the right questions. Technology has become too central to our lives.

For instance, the pandemic called attention to the fact that while we all may rely on technology, we don't all enjoy equal access to it. When school buildings closed and classes moved online, we learned about the stark differences between kids living in affluent homes—whose circumstances ensured they had access to high-speed internet, a dedicated computer, a quiet space to work, and a network of supportive people to help keep them on track—and kids living in low-income homes, who too often had none of these things. These marked differences in children's pandemic experiences exposed and amplified existing inequities in our educational system,[2] forcing us to ask: *Which children benefit most from technology, and why?*

In the last quarter of 2021, the leaking of internal Facebook documents by former Facebook employee Frances Haugen shone a light on the power of opaque algorithms to shape our experiences on social media platforms. Although this power had been well documented previously,[3] the media coverage surrounding the Facebook files helped bring it more directly into public consciousness. The public became more aware of how algorithms, designed to attract and hold our attention to platforms like Facebook and Instagram (and Snapchat, Twitter, TikTok, and YouTube, among others), can contribute to the spread of misinformation, hate speech, and the undermining of teens' mental health, preparing us to grapple with the question: *How does the design of a technology shape the way children use it and are affected by it?*

These developments show clearly that *relying on* technology is not the same thing as *thriving with* technology. We're ready now to go deeper into the when, why, and for whom of technology's impact on children. We're ready to explore the conditions that create technology experiences that are self-directed and community supported, which I argue are the two qualities that distinguish developmentally supportive use of technology.

WHAT IS DEVELOPMENT, AND WHAT IS HEALTHY DEVELOPMENT?

As a developmental scientist, I place front and center the understanding that the way children think about, interact with, and make sense of themselves and the communities they participate in is qualitatively different at different stages of development.

A two-year-old's way of interacting with their environment is clearly distinct from a twelve-year-old's, due in large part to differences in the complexity of the cognitive structures that process and interpret their experiences and how those structures interact with the people and cultural tools in their environment. The process of developing from a two-year-old to a twelve-year-old to a twenty-two-year-old is at its heart a process of changing the way one interacts with and participates in one's cultural communities.[4]

Children at different stages of development engage in different types of developmental tasks. Whereas toddlers are learning to regulate their emotions while interacting primarily with adult caregivers, teens are learning about who they are largely in the context of their peer relationships. To be sure, self-regulation is very much a work in progress throughout childhood and adolescence, but it's particularly central in early childhood. The same is true for identity development. Toddlers are doing important developmental work when it comes to differentiating themselves from the other people in their environment. However, grappling with who you are and how you fit into the broader world around you becomes more of a dominant focus during adolescence and emerging adulthood.

A developmental perspective also recognizes that there's considerable individual variation in the process of development, and, as a result, there exist many paths to healthy development. The process of development is going well when children experience a sense of initiative and ownership over their actions, a feeling that they can succeed and grow, and a sense of belonging and connection with the people in their communities.[5] This happens when children engage in experiences—including technology-based experiences—that are self-directed and community supported.

TECHNOLOGY'S ROLE IN HEALTHY DEVELOPMENT

Technology supports healthy development when it's self-directed and community supported; it impedes development when it's not. Self-directed technology experiences are voluntary—voluntarily started, sustained, and ended—giving young people a sense of initiative and ownership over their actions.[6]

Technology experiences that are externally controlled, by contrast, either through rewards or punishments, are less voluntary and therefore less likely to support healthy development. (Unfortunately, technology designers are very good at building incentives into their products to keep children and adolescents—and adults!—using them long beyond when they would otherwise have moved on to another activity.)

In many, but not all, cases, self-directed technology experiences are open-ended and flexible, allowing people to shape their experiences in a variety of different ways. Freehand drawing is open-ended; paint by numbers is not. It's easy to find examples of each in an app store. Complete open-endedness isn't always necessary, or even desirable. Sometimes external supports are appropriate, such as for young children who need help navigating the user interface of an app, or children with physical or cognitive disabilities whose use of assistive technologies greatly expands their range of actions. What's more important is that the technology experience supports children's feelings of mastery and personal growth.

Children and adolescents don't use technology in a vacuum. Their digital experiences are embedded in broader contexts of support—sometimes surrounding the technology, sometimes within it. Community support that surrounds technology use can come from family members, peers, teachers, and any other cultural community that children participate in, like a church group or afterschool club. Friends might work together to design a video game in the kid-friendly programming language Scratch. A trusted adult or sibling might help a teen process and navigate troubling or hurtful speech they experience online. These surrounding community supports make young people's technology experiences better.

Community support can come directly from the technology itself. As I'll discuss in chapter 7, online communities like Tumblr have provided support for many teens who feel marginalized in other contexts of their lives, whether due to their race, gender, and/or sexual orientation. Community support also relates to the way a platform is structured and governed. A platform's features, affordances, and moderation strategies can have a big influence on the kind of culture that evolves on it and whether that culture supports members' sense of belonging and connection to others.

THREE THEMES

Creating the conditions for self-directed and community-supported technology experiences is most likely to happen when we recognize and foreground the following: (1) the value of seeking a balance between average trends and individual children; (2) the importance of attending to the broader contexts of children's technology experiences; and (3) the need to consider the interaction between technology design and child development. Whether I'm focusing on early or middle childhood, adolescence, or emerging adulthood, these three themes recur throughout the book.

THEME 1: BALANCING AVERAGE TRENDS AND INDIVIDUAL CHILDREN

Research involving large numbers of children is valuable because it gives us an overall impression of general trends in a population. It's also a useful way to identify systemic differences that lead to common disparities among subpopulations in a society. For all the criticism that the No Child Left Behind Act generated when it was signed into U.S. law in 2001, even some of the legislation's strongest critics acknowledged the benefit of breaking down standardized test scores by race and income level, because doing so called attention to persistent inequities in the U.S. public school system.

But there's a limit to the value to be drawn from general trends. This is because the statistical models that form the basis of population-based research typically rely on averages.

Let's consider a hypothetical example involving the relationship between social media use and body satisfaction in teen girls. If you wanted to use the amount of time teen girls spend on social media sites like Instagram to predict how positively or negatively they feel about their bodies, you could generate a bunch of points on a graph, each one representing an individual teen girl's time spent on Instagram (a value on the x-axis) and their score on a measure of body satisfaction (a value on the y-axis). Next, you'd draw a line that goes through the middle of these points such that the distance between all of the points falling above the line and the line itself is just about equal to the distance between all of the points falling below the line and the line.

You'd use that line (not the points that generated it) to draw conclusions about the relationship between Instagram use and teen girls' body image. If it were falling steeply to the right, you'd conclude there's a generally strong, negative relationship between Instagram use and body satisfaction (not good). If it were dipping gently upward, you'd conclude there's a generally weak, positive relationship (better). These lines would allow you to make an informed guess about a specific teen girl's body satisfaction based on the amount of time they spend on Instagram.

The problem is, you'd probably be wrong—maybe not as wrong as pulling a value out of thin air, but wrong, nonetheless. Very few, if any, people ever land exactly on the trend line. It turns out, very few people are average! Averages are good at describing behavior on a group level, but considerably less so at describing the behavior of individual children.[7]

Thankfully, researchers who study the role of technology in the lives of children and adolescents are increasingly making use of methods that highlight rather than gloss over individual variation. In this book, I attempt to emphasize such research while treating population-based research with more skepticism.

At the same time, I'll discuss research that draws on averages, because it can provide a good starting point for understanding general trends within a group of children, and it's especially useful for identifying systemic disparities affecting particular subpopulations. But we should resist using this general understanding to draw conclusions about specific children.

THEME 2: TECHNOLOGY AND CHILD DEVELOPMENT TAKE PLACE IN CONTEXT

A criticism that's sometimes leveled at developmental scientists is that they overemphasize what's going on inside the head of a particular child (usually from a white, middle-class community in North America or Europe) without paying enough attention to the diverse social, cultural, economic, and historical contexts that children experience.[8] However, as cultural psychologist Barbara Rogoff has observed, "People develop as participants in cultural communities. Their development can be understood only in light of the cultural practices and circumstances of their communities."[9] In other words, understanding child development *requires* understanding the communities and cultural practices that children participate in.

Cultural communities shape our impression of what's considered dangerous and what's considered beautiful; what counts as intelligent or athletic or funny; and how intelligence, athleticism, and humor are expressed.

I spent much of my time while writing this book in Berlin, where many preschool ("Kita") teachers don't think twice about letting three- and four-year-olds use hammers, nails, and saws to work unsupervised with wood planks, something that would surely lead to a lawsuit in the Seattle neighborhood I had come from.

Children participate in a lot of different spaces, settings, and communities, each containing different configurations of people, practices, roles, and expectations. Sometimes the cultural practices across these contexts align, and sometimes they don't. Understanding how they relate—and how they connect to broader societal institutions and ideologies—is crucial.[10]

Let's return to the example of teen girls, social media, and body image. To do better than an average trend line at predicting the relationship between Instagram use and body satisfaction for a particular teen girl, it would help to have some understanding of her experiences with her peers and family members. What kinds of beauty ideals are promoted by each group of people, and how do they draw on, reinforce, or perhaps push back against broader cultural ideologies related to beauty? How do these dynamics influence what she sees and how she interprets content on Instagram? Does this teen participate in other communities, such as a church group, sports team, or afterschool club, that deemphasize physical appearance and elevate other qualities such as teamwork, spirituality, and community? How does this teen's racial identity, and the degree to which it's either marginalized or centered in the broader society, influence whether and how she compares herself to the images she sees on Instagram?

Questions like these highlight the importance of considering young people's varied social contexts, how these contexts relate to each other and the technologies used in them, and how all of these contexts are influenced by broader social, political, economic, and historical forces.

This book does not attempt to account for all possible contexts that affect children's development across the globe. In fact, with respect to geography, I focus primarily on the contexts in which I conduct my own research: North America and Europe. That leaves a lot of the world unaccounted for! Within this geographically and culturally narrow focus, I've incorporated research that addresses children with a wide range of intersecting experiences, such as those living in different socioeconomic circumstances, belonging to different racial and ethnic groups, expressing different gender and sexual identities, and possessing a range of abilities and disabilities.

THEME 3: DESIGN MATTERS

Technology is not neutral.[11] The autoplay feature on Netflix makes it that much easier for children to watch multiple episodes of a television show and that much harder for parents to avoid a confrontation when they seek to turn off the device. When a show ends, recommender algorithms on Netflix (and YouTube, Disney+, and other video-streaming platforms) determine what a child encounters next. Algorithms also determine the videos that show up on a teen's For You feed on TikTok and the pictures they see as they scroll through their Instagram feed. These algorithms are designed to draw and keep people's attention based on the information they've collected from their prior interactions with the platform.[12]

People design things like autoplay and social media algorithms. Their values, goals, assumptions, and worldviews are embedded in what they create. Designers, developers, product managers, and other employees of technology companies are disproportionately white, male, highly educated, liberal, or libertarian.[13] When they conjure a "typical user" that person is more likely to resemble them than not, increasing the chances that the resulting technology serves some people better than others.[14]

The companies that tech designers work for also have their own set of values, goals, assumptions, and worldviews. Most centrally, these companies are motivated by the bottom line, not a person's well-being. The bottom line does well when people are on the platform, and companies have figured out the kind of content that keeps people engaged: emotionally arousing posts typically win out over measured accounts of fact. This is why Facebook's algorithm prioritizes content with angry emojis over likes.[15]

I propose three layers for thinking about technology's influence on child development. The first is the *feature layer*, consisting of the 0s and 1s of digital experiences. These are specific features—autoplay, the like button, the disappearing photo on Snapchat, Instagram filters, Twitter's saliency detection algorithm, TikTok's For You feed algorithm—that allow people to do and see certain things and not others when they interact with a particular technology. An algorithm may seem cold and impartial, but many human decisions go into its creation and use.[16]

Next comes the *practice layer*, which addresses the relationship between people and the features they're interacting with. Here, we talk of the affordances or "possibilities for action" of a technology as people engage with it.[17] Features such as the retweet button on Twitter and the reblog button on Tumblr give rise to certain actions, making it easy for people to circulate content widely. *Spreadability* therefore represents an affordance of platforms like Twitter and Tumblr.

Other affordances that characterize social media platforms include *interactivity* (people can interact with each other's content and ideas), *reactivity* (people can also simply react to content by clicking a heart, or a like or angry emoji button), *persistence* (the digital traces created by posts, even after they've been deleted), *searchability* (the ease of locating information quickly), *replicability* (the ease with which content can be copied), and *anonymity* (some platforms make it easier to create identities other than one's government-issued identification).[18]

This list is by no means exhaustive for social media platforms or for the wider array of technologies that children interact with. What's important to keep in mind at the practice layer is the interaction between features and people and the kind of behaviors that emerge as a result. Certainly, the individual design decisions that go into a technology matter here, but so do the motivations, skills, and values of the people engaging with it.

The final layer is the *culture layer*. Here we ask: what kind of culture emerges in the context of a technology's features and affordances, and the way it's governed? Spend an hour each on Instagram and Tumblr, and you'll no doubt experience distinct cultures (there are many subcultures within each platform, so your experiences will likely be different from mine). Both Instagram and Tumblr are social media platforms, but they're designed and governed in quite different ways, giving rise to different user interactions, topics of discussion, norms of behavior, and so on.[19]

Here are just a few examples: Unlike Instagram, Tumblr isn't profile-based or linked to a person's legal name, making it much easier to experience a degree of anonymity, or "pseudonymity," which in turn makes people feel they can communicate more openly and about sensitive topics.[20] Tumblr places more emphasis on interaction than reaction through features such as reblogs and replies. In contrast, the heart button on Instagram lends itself to quick reactions as people scroll through their feeds (and it represents a source of stress for many teens who monitor closely the number of likes their posts receive). Instagram's primary mode is visual.[21] People post, like, and comment on their own and each other's photos, which has helped give rise to a culture of self-presentation and promotion. Tumblr content, by contrast, comes in many different forms, including text, image, GIF, meme, and link, helping support a community based on shared interest.[22]

What goes on at the feature, practice, and culture layers of technology use combine to shape young people's digital experiences in distinct and important ways. I'll use these layers throughout the book to explore the different ways that technology interacts with and influences child development.

THE CHAPTERS IN THIS BOOK

Technology's Child traces the arc of development from early childhood to middle childhood and adolescence and ends in emerging adulthood.

At each stage, I highlight one or two developmental tasks that are particularly salient, such as executive function and emerging literacy skills in early childhood, and peer relationships and identity formation in adolescence. This approach helps me scope a sprawling and complex topic while shining a spotlight on the key factors at play when it comes to technology's impact on child development.

Chapter 2 explores the constellation of skills that form a person's executive function ability, including the all-important skill of self-regulation, whose successful development in early childhood helps place children on a path to personal well-being, positive relationships, and academic success. We'll consider how carefully designed digital content can support executive function development, as well as the design abuses that too often undermine it. We'll also take a look at parents' technology use, and I'll introduce the concept of the "good enough" digital parent.

Chapter 3 continues to focus on early childhood as we consider another key developmental task of this period: early literacy development. As we explore literacy apps, conversational agents, and video chat platforms, we'll identify the qualities of self-directed, community-supported digital experiences that can support early literacy skills such as vocabulary development and letter recognition.

In Chapter 4 we'll explore the world of child's play and the many forms it can take in analog and digital contexts. We'll consider the value of "loose parts" in children's play experiences and identify the kinds of digital experiences that enable loose parts play and those that make it difficult. We'll also take a look at the affordances of video games (such as interactivity, low cost of failure, and clear and immediate feedback) that interact in complicated ways with individual children and their surrounding contexts.

Chapter 5 examines technology's current and potential role in learning during middle childhood. When designed carefully, learning technologies can encourage children to pursue their interests; they can address children's diverse ways of learning; and they can be meaningfully integrated into the cultural contexts and communities that children participate in. Unfortunately, as we'll see, several barriers prevent this potential from being realized for all children, including unequal access to learning technologies and the supports needed to use them and inflexible institutional structures that make it difficult to introduce new technologies into school settings.

With its focus on early adolescence, chapter 6 marks a shift away from adult-selected and adult-directed technology experiences to those that are more youth-driven. We'll consider how these technology experiences directed by young people can complicate the evolving relationship between parents and their tween children. We'll also explore how the features and affordances of social media platforms (such as like counts and publicness) and smartphones (such as notifications and mobility) place pressure on tweens' changing peer relationships and sense of self, giving rise to digital stress and cyberbullying among some tween children.

Chapter 7 examines the vulnerability and resilience of adolescence, identifying when and how digital experiences magnify certain vulnerabilities (like anxiety and depression) and when they support adolescent well-being and identity development. We'll consider the cultural dimensions of teens' social media experiences and how they put pressure on some teens while marginalizing others. We'll also take a look at the ways teens are pushing back against these challenges by developing their own strategies for self-directed, community-supported digital experiences.

Chapter 8 addresses our oldest youth, emerging adults, examining how they use networked technologies to connect their developing sense of self to social issues they care about. We'll explore how networked technologies have changed the way young people engage in public discussions about social issues, centering their voices in unparalleled ways. We'll consider when online forms of activism can be empowering for these youth and when they can lead to feelings of psychological stress.

I conclude each of these chapters in the same way, by taking stock with the "three Ds." I pull out key ideas relating to what is going on *developmentally* when children at a specific age and stage interact with various technologies. I then go *deeper* by highlighting the nuance and complexity that's underneath the top-level headlines—addressing both individual children and their social and cultural contexts. Finally, I consider the *design* considerations that can and should guide strategies for users (especially parents and children) to identify developmentally supportive technology experiences and for technology developers to design at the outset with such experiences in mind.

In the final chapter, chapter 9, I present a model of developmentally supportive digital experiences that shows the major determinants of self-directed, community-supported digital experiences and how these experiences can support children's healthy development. I consider how different stakeholders can make these positive experiences the rule rather than the exception for technology's child. I offer a set of concrete suggestions for technology designers, technology companies, policymakers, parents and caregivers, teachers and school administrators, and academics and researchers.

2

EARLY CHILDHOOD: LEARNING SELF-CONTROL IN A TECH-SATURATED WORLD

Gaining control over one's emotions and behavior—also known as executive function—represents an important developmental undertaking during early childhood. This chapter examines the interplay between young children's developing executive function skills and their experiences with commonly used technologies, identifying those that can support executive function development and those that can undermine it.

First, let's look at how a child's executive function skills develop.

Executive function can be thought of as the brain's "air traffic control" system.[1] This constellation of skills manages the quantity and variety of information that comes at us during the course of a day, prioritizing and focusing on the important things, setting aside what is less important (though perhaps more enticing), making decisions, planning, and revising plans, and moving back and forth between various goals and demands. Executive function dictates much of how we go about our day and how we engage with the world.

Although executive function continues to develop throughout childhood and into adolescence and even emerging adulthood, early childhood represents a sensitive period (a period when children are particularly responsive to environmental influences).[2] Young children learn to regulate their actions and emotions (self-regulation), hold information in their heads for short periods of time (working memory), and switch gears and adjust their behavior according to situational changes (cognitive flexibility). These skills will influence how they act on, interact with, and react to the people and experiences they encounter through their lives.

When things go well at this stage, children are positioned for future school readiness, both academically and socially, and they're better able to cope with stress and frustration. If things don't go so well, there's a greater chance they'll have trouble following directions, display disruptive or even aggressive behavior, and encounter interpersonal challenges with peers and teachers. For adults, executive function is central to most aspects of daily life, from performing well at work to maintaining healthy relationships.[3]

Anyone who's spent time with a toddler knows that these skills take time to develop. Two-year-olds are much better at disrupting plans than making them. Children develop their executive function skills through experiences like engaging in family conversations at mealtimes, sharing and taking turns with friends at preschool, and waiting in the checkout line at the grocery store.

Parents and other adult caregivers play a key role in supporting and reinforcing these emerging skills, by offering praise not only when a child demonstrates some mastery, but also when they model executive function skills such as planning and making decisions, regulating their emotions, and resisting distractions. (However, we'll see later in this chapter that parents aren't always the best models.)[4]

Other factors that can support or undermine executive function development include the way a child's environment is arranged and the objects available in that environment. A chaotic environment full of distractions and stressors will make it harder for children to develop strong executive function skills. In this chapter, we'll explore what sort of environment children's digital experiences create for their executive function development.

"OLD" TV

Although television may seem passé in 2023, TV viewing still represents the dominant form of media engagement for children aged zero to eight whether on a traditional screen, tablet, or smartphone, via cable television, Netflix, or YouTube.[5]

For as long as TV has existed, people have worried about its effects on children. Indeed, there's something a bit unnerving about the rapt attention of a young child sitting motionless in front of a TV screen when in any other circumstance they'd be in constant motion. What's going on here?

The way children—and, really, all of us—pay attention to TV is different from the way we attend to other aspects of our environment. When something unexpected in our environment catches our eye without our conscious effort, we're using automatic, "bottom-up" processes of attention. When we sit down to read a book or write out a shopping list, by contrast, we're using "top-down" processes. TV relies mostly on bottom-up processes through its visual and sound effects, as well as the common inclusion of surprising or fantastical events. In other words, it captures our attention and leads us through a viewing experience without us having to put in too much effort. Executive function, by contrast, engages top-down attentional processes. With enough television viewing, the theory goes, we may start to rely more on automatic, bottom-up processes of attention, leaving our more effortful, top-down processes unexercised.[6]

Another line of reasoning connecting TV and executive function suggests that the processing power required to pay attention to and make sense of the fantastical elements of television depletes resources that would otherwise be used for executive functioning.[7] This may be particularly true for very young children who have limited processing power to begin with and whose sensorimotor stage of development (interacting physically with the world through looking, touching, tasting, etc.) means they'll gravitate to features in their environment that stand out to them.[8]

Yet another explanation proposes that watching TV may take away from time that would otherwise be spent engaging in executive function-enhancing activities, such as baking cookies with a parent or engaging in pretend play with a sibling or friend.[9]

Still other explanations include television's modeling of poor self-control (e.g., TV characters acting violently), interfering with children's arousal systems, and promoting a style of attention that's constantly shifting rather than sustained.[10] For each of these explanations, young children would be considered at greatest risk, since early childhood is a sensitive time for executive function development, young children are particularly susceptible to environmental influences, and they're less able to regulate their arousal levels.[11]

It's not difficult to find research showing a negative relationship between TV viewing and executive function such that the greater the TV viewing, the worse children perform on measures of attention and self-control.[12] It's also not difficult to find research showing no relationship between TV and executive function.[13] And, in both cases, these are relationships only, not proof that TV viewing does or doesn't cause a change in children's executive function.

Collectively, this research paints a confusing picture in part because it's capturing average population trends, masking important variation among individual children and their contexts. For instance, infants and toddlers with difficult temperaments (prone to fussiness and crying) are more likely to be exposed to high amounts of TV, and parents are more likely to give devices (smartphones and tablets) to young children with social-emotional delays and behavior problems to calm them when they're upset, especially if parents themselves experience stress from their child's behavior.[14]

So the relationship between television viewing and attentional problems is wrapped up in other aspects of a child's environment, including parent-child relationships.[15] Indeed, in a systematic review of research investigating the relationship between television exposure and children's cognition and behavior, psychologist Katarzyna Kostyrka-Allchorne and her colleagues noted the many individual, family, and social factors that the studies they examined did *not* account for.[16] Here are just a few: a child's temperament, the quality of their self-regulation strategies, and their neurological sensitivity to environmental stimuli, as well as parenting style, household income, and the presence or absence of environmental stressors.

Design matters, too. It's not just people who are complicated. TV itself is a complex phenomenon.

For instance, there's the matter of *what kind* of television programming children are watching. Researchers have investigated the impact of changing various aspects of television programming, such as fast vs. slow pacing, fantastic vs. realistic content, educational content vs. entertainment, violent vs. nonviolent content, and child directed vs. adult directed.

Educational is generally preferable to entertainment-focused content,[17] nonviolent is better than violent,[18] and child directed is better than adult directed.[19] Investigations of fast vs. slow pacing and realistic vs. fantastic content have produced mixed results.[20]

Are there *any* concrete insights we can glean? While no definitive guidebook exists, here's a checklist of considerations that parents can draw on as they make decisions about their children's TV exposure:

1. Does my child have preexisting attention and/or behavior problems? If yes, then I need to be thoughtful about how I approach their television viewing. Television might be helpful to calm my child down, and could be one of several strategies I use during challenging moments. However, I would be very careful not to rely on it as the *only* way to calm them and help them focus.[21] Over-reliance on TV might get in the way of my child learning to self-regulate without external aids.

2. What sort of content is my child watching? Am I seeking out content that's age appropriate and educational?

The research may by somewhat muddled here, but it does suggest that parents avoid violence and seek out child-directed programming that incorporates opportunities for learning. For instance, educational shows like *Sesame Street* can support children's literacy development, particularly children in low-income families.[22]

3. What would my child be doing if they were *not* watching television? It's possible that screen media is taking time away from other experiences that we know support executive functioning, including sleep and interactions with caregivers.[23] Alternatively, screen media could be providing a welcome—and potentially educational—alternative to an otherwise challenging situation. For instance, parents may use screen media to occupy their children while they're busy with domestic tasks.[24] For children living in violent or unpredictable neighborhoods, parents could use screen media as a strategy for protecting their children's safety by keeping them at home and indoors.[25]

"NEW" TV

Most published research on children's TV viewing involves traditional TV sets that one might find in the family living room—after all, TV research is much older than the iPhone, iPad, and all the subsequent devices they've inspired.

Today, of course, children are increasingly forgoing the TV set in favor of tablets and smartphones. Nearly all (98 percent) American families with a child age eight or younger have at least one mobile device in the house, and 83 percent of children eight and younger have used a mobile device at least once.[26]

What changes when children switch from watching their favorite show on a forty-eight-inch TV to watching it on an eight-inch tablet that's perched on their lap? For one, the viewing experience becomes more intimate and individualized as a child holds the screen in their lap, making it more difficult for others to share in the experience. When a child wears headphones, they are well and truly having their own experience. This shift is worth bearing in mind in light of research documenting the benefits of parents (and other family members) co-viewing television programming with their children.[27]

Mobility also increases the contexts and times when media can be consumed, such as in a stroller, on a bus, or right before bedtime. Giving a tablet to a child during transit or at a restaurant may take away opportunities for children to practice self-regulation in the context of a sibling or caregiver—but it may also provide caregivers a rare opportunity to have a conversation, or even close their eyes for a moment.[28] With respect to bedtime, research suggests that interference with sleep could underlie the identified negative relationship between mobile media and self-regulation.[29]

Another characteristic of modern-day TV viewing is children's increased likelihood to be watching programming through a networked platform like Netflix or YouTube.[30] Indeed, children's content is among the most-watched on YouTube, receiving more views on average than other video content.[31] In 2020, "Baby Shark," an animated song for young children, became the most-viewed video of all time on YouTube.[32] This was also the first year in which children under age eight spent more time watching videos online than on live TV or streaming services.[33]

The on-demand viewing offered by platforms like You-Tube theoretically gives parents more control over what their young children watch and for how long. But other aspects of the platform design can undercut this control. Recommender algorithms take the data a platform has collected about a particular child and other children deemed to be like them (for instance, same age and geographical location), and they use that data to suggest what a child watches next.[34] Because of the visual prominence of these suggestions, they're difficult to ignore. Parents can change settings and install filters, but these measures require some technical savvy and the control they provide is limited.

Another feature that both Netflix and YouTube share is automatic advancing to the next episode or video. If you're binge-watching a show on Netflix, you might eventually see a popup message asking if you're still there. But up until this (quite generous) viewing point, Netflix will keep on playing episode after episode without your prompting—unless you've disabled autoplay on your account.

Autoplay is pretty easy to disable when setting up a child's profile. Even with it disabled, I found that by the time my son Oliver was three, he had learned how to click the "next episode" button before I could reach the off button.

Any sort of transition from one activity to another can be difficult for small children, calling on them to exercise their emerging self-regulation skills. Transitioning away from screen-based activities with autoplay may be particularly difficult.[35]

Research conducted by my colleagues at the University of Washington has shown how autoplay can undermine the limits that parents try to set for their children around digital devices, reduce children's likelihood to self-limit or self-monitor, and generally increase the painfulness of transitions away from screen-based activities.[36] None of this is good for children's developing executive function skills.

Autoplay is one of several *dark patterns* in the design of commercial technologies.[37] Other examples include hidden costs (you download a "free" app only to find that most of the content is locked behind a paywall), overly complex privacy settings (designed to leave users exposed), and disguised ads, including "advergames" (particularly tricky for children who have difficulty distinguishing between types of content online).

Dark patterns are design features intended to keep users engaged with a particular device, platform, or application, without regard to how their engagement might impact their autonomy and well-being. These features are difficult enough for adults to navigate but may be particularly challenging for young children whose critical thinking skills and self-regulation abilities are still developing.[38]

INTERACTIVE MEDIA: IS SWIPING A SCREEN DIFFERENT FROM STARING AT IT?

Watching television may be the most popular tablet- or smartphone-based activity for young children, but it's certainly not the only one. Apps geared to toddlers and preschoolers have increased dramatically since the introduction of the iPhone, iPad,[39] and their non-Apple equivalents, and the vast majority of apps in the education category are targeted to children.[40]

There are apps for painting, playing music, sorting objects, counting, developing letter recognition, and learning to use the potty, among many others. All of these apps share the common feature of interactivity, so a good question to ask is whether interactivity has an impact on children's developing abilities to pay attention and self-regulate.

Emerging research suggests that interactivity, when combined with educational content, can support certain kinds of executive function skills in young children.[41] However, not all interactivity is created equal, even when children are engaged with educational content. Some interactive apps dictate the specific sequence and pacing of interactions, whereas others let children control how and at what pace they engage with them. This distinction proves to be important with respect to how children's attention is captured and sustained when playing a game on a mobile device.

Researcher Alexis Hiniker and colleagues compared how young children age four to six engaged in play with analog toys (e.g., Legos, books, board games) versus tablet-based games and apps.[42] The children displayed high levels of focus in both conditions, but the way their attention was held was noticeably different. The key distinction between the toy and tablet play sessions seemed to be in *who* was controlling the child's attention.

In the toy play session, children seemed in control of their attention, moving comfortably between play and chatting with their parents about their play. By contrast, in the tablet play session, the app seemed to control the children's attention, with children being more likely to trail off in the middle of a response to their parent's question or to ignore them altogether. Relatedly, children were less likely to include their parents in tablet-based play compared to toy play.

That said, there were instances when children successfully maintained control over their own attention while playing with their tablets. This happened when they were playing with user-paced apps instead of with apps that set their own pacing outside the user's control. (This distinction between user-paced vs. app-paced experiences recalls the distinction between top-down and bottom-up processing of environmental stimuli I discussed earlier in the chapter in relation to TV viewing.)

An important postscript to this research is the finding that the analog/digital toy distinction mattered less than the way parents and their children interacted with each other. Whether playing with analog toys or on a tablet, the relationship and interaction style that parents and children brought to their play session mattered the most. This result underscores the fact that children's technology use happens in a broader context, and this context may matter just as much—sometimes more—than the technology itself. It also underscores the particular importance of the parents' role in supporting their children's engagement with technology.

Returning to the topic of technology and attention, companies put a lot of effort into designing technologies that capture and hold children's attention for as long as possible. Researcher and pediatrician Jenny Radesky and her colleagues have enumerated a series of *design abuses*—features that prioritize continued app engagement over a child's well-being—that can be found in apps geared to preschool-aged children.[43] For instance, many apps engage children in parasocial relationships, whereby a character in the app pressures the child to play longer (for instance, a crying character who can only be soothed if the child keeps playing) or to make a purchase. Lures are another type of design abuse—tokens, rewards, or virtual toys that attract children's attention and keep them engaged with the app. Radesky and colleagues also found evidence that children from lower socioeconomic status families (lower income, lower parent education level) are exposed to more design abuses.

Even supposedly educational features can co-opt children's attention and distract them from the task at hand; this is especially true for young children with limited fine motor skills, information processing capacity, and symbolic reasoning skills.[44]

For instance, research on storybook apps suggests that certain embedded features such as dictionaries, word pronunciation assistance, games, and links to animation, sound, and music can distract young children from the central reading experience.[45] Although many of these features, such as dictionaries, are intended to augment the learning experience, they seem to function more as distractions that tax young children's executive function abilities by requiring them to switch tasks and process extra information.

So, is swiping a screen better than staring at it? Emerging research indicates that interactivity can be beneficial for certain executive function skills and under certain conditions.[46] However, it's important to consider who is driving the interactivity: the child or the app. Design abuses that co-opt children's attention, like parasocial relationships and lures, are easy to find in apps geared to young children.[47] Supposedly educational features like hyperlinks, animations, and music play a role, too; whether they help or hurt depends on their alignment with the activity, the developmental readiness of the child, and the surrounding context of app use.

TURNING THE TABLES ON PARENTS

There have been too many times than I care to remember when Oliver has caught me checking my phone during play- . time with him. When he was two, his typical reaction was to bat the phone out of my hand and shout "Stop, Mummy! No do that!" It soothes my guilty conscience a little (but only a little) to know that this tech-based form of parental distraction is common enough that researchers have given it a name: technoference.

Although the term *technoference* isn't limited to parent-child relationships—any interpersonal interaction can be disrupted when one person breaks eye contact to look down at their phone—it's used frequently by researchers who study the effects of parents' technology-driven distractions in the presence of their children.[48] As newer technologies such as voice interfaces (e.g., smart speakers like the Amazon Echo) are introduced into more and more households, opportunities for technoference may only increase.[49]

Parental distraction isn't a new phenomenon, and it certainly predates smartphones and social media. When I think of my own childhood in the 1980s, my parents' attention was frequently pulled away by newspapers and magazines, the latest news or weather update on the radio (immediate and full silence was essential or we'd have to wait until the next update an hour later), cooking and housework, and other grown-ups (I was an only child for many years, so there were no other children to contend with). These disruptions were minor irritants to me, but also just part of the normal rhythm of daily life at home. (I'm told they produced some guilt in my parents, but it was trivial in comparison to the guilt engendered by stealing a look at a phone while playing with a child.)

Expectations around parenting have changed since the 1980s and earlier decades. (The word *parenting* itself is a relatively recent addition to common vernacular, gaining familiarity only in the 1970s).[50] Especially within highly educated households, today's working mothers spend just as much— and often more—time interacting with their children than stay-at-home mothers of the 1970s did.[51] And this parenting time is expected to be *quality* time. It's not good enough simply to be with your children; you should be reading to them, playing with them, and teaching them to read, write, count, and code.[52] In light of today's "intensive parenting,"[53] any sort of distraction from our kids seems to border on child neglect.[54]

There's also a strong case to be made that the nature of parental distraction is qualitatively different today than it was before we all started carrying around smartphones. Brandon McDaniel, a leading scholar studying technoference in families, observes that there's something new going on with parents and their mobile devices.[55]

Unlike a magazine or the radio, our smartphones are attached—or in very close proximity—to us at all times. In fact, we start to panic if we lose track of their exact location, even for a few moments. So much of our lives happens on our phones that it's as though they've become extensions of ourselves.[56] If we don't have access to them for whatever reason, many of us experience a fear that we're missing out on the latest happenings in our social circles.[57] This phone-specific fear even has its own name: nomophobia (NO MObile PHone PhoBIA).[58]

For new parents (often mothers) at home with their infant children, smartphones can feel like lifelines to the adult world, offering companionship and reassurance amid the insecurities, stress, and loneliness that can sometimes accompany parenthood.[59] Our phones also do their part to remind us of their presence and perpetual source of stimulation by sending us regular notifications whenever we receive a message, reminder, or news headline. We invariably respond to these pings and vibrations, looking down at our phones in the hope (whether consciously or not) that one of them will provide us with some sort of informational or social reward.[60]

At the same time they're holding themselves to unparalleled standards of parental engagement and responsiveness, today's parents are carrying around with them a constant and powerful source of distraction from those standards. It's little wonder that so many parents feel guilty about using their devices around their children.[61] But should they?

Let's start with the development of children's executive function skills, the primary focus of this chapter. There's a group of child behaviors—such as restlessness, becoming easily frustrated, and temper tantrums—that are known as *externalizing behaviors*. These behaviors are negatively related to executive functioning, meaning children with strong executive function skills are less likely to display them.[62]

Emerging research suggests that parental technoference and child externalizing behaviors are tied together in a reciprocal relationship. That is, parental technoference can lead children to behave disruptively out of frustration with their parents' phone use and in order to capture their attention. Children's disruptive behavior can, in turn, lead parents to turn to their phones to manage the stress associated with their children's behavior.[63]

There's another, less direct way that technoference could interfere with young children's executive function development. As I noted at the beginning of the chapter, parents play a crucial role in supporting the development of their children's executive function skills.[64] In fact, I sometimes feel as though most of my parenting energy goes into helping (some might call it cajoling, pleading, or bribing) Oliver to make a smooth transition from one activity to another, or to delay the gratification of watching his favorite TV show until he's done something less gratifying, like taking a bath or brushing his teeth. This support requires me to be highly in tune with and responsive to the cues he's giving me on a moment-to-moment basis. If I misinterpret a wriggle as defiance instead of his intended playfulness, I'll miss an opportunity to connect with my son and channel his playfulness into a positive behavior (like putting on his pajamas without a fuss).

Parental sensitivity is needed not just to support children's executive functioning but also more broadly—and fundamentally—to help them develop positive, secure attachments to their primary caregivers. These attachments will influence the quality and success of the intimate relationships they experience throughout their lives.[65]

Although there's no published research (at the time of writing this book) showing that parental technoference negatively affects children's attachment to their parents, there is research showing that parents who are distracted by their mobile devices display less sensitivity to their children. This research shows that parents whose attention is focused on their phones engage in less conversation with their children, show less responsiveness to their children's bids for attention, and sometimes display greater hostility when their children do get their attention.[66]

In addition to the direct support I give him, another way I help Oliver develop his executive function skills is to model the behavior I want to see him develop. I'm pretty good at remembering to take a shower and brush my teeth, as well as to wait my turn in a game and stand patiently in the checkout line at the grocery store. My modeling starts to break down when I turn instantly to my phone if it pings or vibrates, and place whatever I was just doing on hold. Several studies have accumulated in recent years showing evidence of this type of parental distraction around children while at playgrounds, restaurants, and museums.[67] What sort of a stance to technology are we modeling for our children when we allow our phones to so easily and frequently pull us out of an experience with them?

But let's not get too far ahead of ourselves. In this discussion, I've used a lot of words like *could* and *might*. Research on parental technoference brings with it all of the same cautions as research on children's TV viewing and tablet use. Most of it relies on observational and cross-sectional data, which cannot establish any sort of causal connection between two phenomena. A lot of it also relies on the self-report of parents, who, it turns out, are not very good at estimating their mobile phone use.[68]

And then there's the ever-present fact of individual and contextual variation that will inevitably require us to look beyond average patterns of behavior in large groups of people and examine how individual children and parents incorporate technology into their specific family contexts.[69]

THE "GOOD ENOUGH" DIGITAL PARENT

Now that I've added to your guilt as a parent, grandparent, or other caring adult in a child's life, let me try to bring back some balance.[70]

In the middle of the twentieth century, pediatrician Donald Winnicott proposed the concept of the "good enough" mother.[71] Let's update it for the twenty-first century to the good enough *parent*. Winnicott argued that it's actually *good* for children to experience instances when their parents aren't there for them 100 percent of the time to fulfill their every need or desire. By experiencing and working through the frustration that accompanies these moments of disappointment, children are able to build resilience that will prepare them for the challenges they'll inevitably encounter throughout their lives.

Good enough parenting isn't about making excuses for failing to live up to one's ideals as a parent. It's about recognizing that we should not even attempt to be the perfect parent.

First, and most obviously, perfection isn't possible; or, at least, it cannot be sustained throughout the long and often unpredictable course of childhood. More importantly, according to Winnicott, it's not in a child's best interest for their parents to be always attentive, because this attentiveness doesn't allow room for personal growth. I see the concept of the good enough parent as a call to parents not to settle for imperfection but to embrace it, both as a way to support their children's resilience and as a way to stay sane during the exhilaration and exhaustion of parenthood.

When it comes to technology, good enough parents will feel confident that occasionally being distracted by a screen or other device isn't the end of the world (and not the end of their child's prospects for a happy, fulfilling life). Good enough parents also recognize that their distraction isn't all their doing: tech companies have designed their products deliberately to grab our attention.

Distraction could even sometimes be a good thing, both for parents and for children, provided the concept of good enough parenting isn't distorted and used as an excuse to shirk parenting duties in the name of responding to emails or monitoring one's social media feed (and this is by no means an attempt to let tech companies off the hook for their persuasive designs!). The occasional distraction could provide an opportunity for parents to call attention to their behavior and create a teachable moment: "Oh, look, I've let myself get distracted by my phone! Let me put that away, and let's get back to where we were."

With Oliver, I do my best to limit my phone use around him, but I'm also trying not to place too much guilt on my shoulders when I sneak a peek at news headlines, exchange messages with a friend, or check my email inbox. These interactions sometimes feel like a lifeline, a way to connect with the outside world, the *adult* world, and maintain my sense of self beyond my role as a mother.

TAKING STOCK WITH THE THREE *D'S*

What's going on *developmentally*: Early childhood is a critical period for the development of self-regulation and other skills associated with the brain's "air traffic control" system (a.k.a. executive function). There's a lot to learn, and none of it is easy. Elements of children's environment—including support and modeling from parents, and interactions with technology—all play a role.

In this chapter, I focused a lot on "old" TV given its continued dominance among young children and the resulting high degree of overlap between TV viewing and screen media use. Some researchers have found a negative link between TV and executive function development, and there are legitimate reasons to be cautious based on what we know about how executive function develops and the way television works: TV's emphasis on bottom up rather than top down processes of attention; the information processing required to make sense of the speed and fantastical elements of many shows; and TV's potential displacement of other activities that are more supportive of executive function development.

When it comes to the broader category of screen media use, which typically incorporates the use of devices like phones and tablets, there's far less research addressing effects on young children's executive function skills.[72] Likely due to the high overlap between TV viewing and screen media use, much of this research tracks the larger body of research on television (i.e., mostly correlational research showing small negative or neutral relationships). Research that looks more specifically at children's *interactive* experiences with screen media devices suggests that carefully designed (more on that to follow!), educational content can support executive function development.[73]

I also considered parents' own media use in the context of children's developing executive function skills. Parents play an important role in supporting their children's self-regulation by modeling self-regulation themselves and by tuning into their children's cues to give them just-in-time support. Each of these things is difficult to do when a parent's eyes gravitate to a pinging phone during playtime, mealtime, or bath time. Although research on technoference can be cause for considerable parental guilt, I believe the goal we should be aiming for is not perfection, but rather "good enough" digital parenting—not sweating the occasional glance at your phone (which research suggests is pretty harmless),[74] while trying to balance those glances with stretches of focused attention on your child.

Going *deeper*: It's difficult to distill a clear set of guidelines when faced with population trends that sometimes show a negative relationship, sometimes a positive relationship, and still other times no relationship at all between screen media use and young children's executive functioning. Indeed, there are no one-size-fits-all answers because screen media use is too wrapped up in the particulars of individual children and their surrounding contexts.

The checklist I presented earlier in the chapter can help parents navigate this tricky terrain by calling attention to the specifics of their own circumstances: Does my child have existing attention and/or behavior problems (pay attention to the specific *child*)? What sort of content is my child watching or interacting with (pay attention to the specific media *content*)? What would my child be doing if *not* using screen media (pay attention to the specific *context* surrounding the media use)?

In short, while there's certainly reason for wariness and setting limits on children's (and parents'!) technology use, there are also many individual and contextual factors that will cause those limits to look different from one household to the next, including parents' attitudes toward screen media more generally.[75]

Design considerations: This chapter has revealed a variety of ways that screen media can tax and even undercut children's executive function skills. However, these challenges also point to a set of best practices for designing technologies that support executive function in young children, including:

- Minimize unnecessary bells and whistles, even if they're intended to be educational.
- Avoid outright design abuses, such as parasocial relationships and lures, that prioritize engagement over well-being.
- Make sure that navigating the interface isn't too cognitively or physically challenging.
- Promote top-down rather than bottom-up forms of attention by letting children dictate the pace of their interactions.
- Make it easy for children to involve others (parents, siblings) in their screen media use.
- Give children and their parents control over how and when they end an interaction.[76]

You can see from this list an emphasis on putting children (and their parents) in the driver's seat of their technology experiences. Designs that follow these best practices are more likely to engage young children in self-directed, community-supported (especially caregiver-supported) technology experiences.[77]

Design can also be used to help parents in their own efforts to support their children's executive function development. For instance, researchers are exploring the possibility of using the information that our smartphones are constantly collecting from us (such as the apps we're using and our location)—called passive sensing—to give parents "nudges" when it seems they've become distracted by their phone while spending time with their children.[78] In another example, some parents are using smart speakers to augment their existing parenting practices, such as by setting timers to help children transition from one task to another.[79] (For these parents, using the family smart speaker rather than their personal phone is more effective because their children perceive Alexa as a neutral third party.)

I began this chapter by noting that executive function is such an important skill to develop in the early years because it's implicated in just about every other skill that children develop throughout the course of childhood, adolescence, and into adulthood. In chapter 3, I'll turn to one of those skills, early literacy development, which develops in tandem with self-regulation during the first few years of life.

3

THE DIGITAL FEATURES OF EARLY LITERACY DEVELOPMENT

In one of my favorite pictures of Oliver, he's sitting on the kitchen floor, brow furrowed, legs outstretched in front of him, deeply absorbed in a book. He's not yet one, so he's not actually reading the individual words on the page. Still, this photo captures an early literacy experience that researchers say is preparing him to read and write later on.[1]

What if Oliver had been looking at an e-book on a tablet instead of a print book? Would that also count as a valuable early literacy experience?

This chapter explores the kinds of early literacy experiences that young children have as they read books and play games on a tablet, video chat with their grandparents on a laptop, and ask Siri, Alexa, or Google Assistant questions about their favorite animals. This exploration includes the specific qualities of self-directed, community-supported digital experiences that can support early literacy development.

First, let's agree on the definition of early literacy skills. There's solid consensus that these are skills children develop before they learn to read words and sentences in a book and write their own sentences and paragraphs on paper (or a computer). Holding a book upright, turning its pages, and pointing at and reacting to the pictures are all evidence that a young child like one-year-old Oliver is starting to understand basic literacy concepts and conventions.

Other important early literacy skills include letter recognition, basic word recognition (like pointing out a familiar word in a book or on a street sign), vocabulary development, the ability to tell coherent narratives, and phonological awareness (the ability to manipulate oral language, such as rhyming and clapping out syllables in a word).

The people, materials, and tools in children's environments are influential in shaping early literacy development.[2] Parents read storybooks aloud to their children, engage them in conversations about topics of interest, share stories, sing songs, and make observations about the print they encounter during daily activities like looking at billboards and scanning food labels for familiar letters or words.[3]

Starting somewhere between the ages of two and three, young children can also learn from people and characters on a screen.[4] However, as with executive functioning, the content of what they watch matters (such as simple and familiar storylines, a simple and consistent narrative structure, and age-appropriate content and vocabulary level)[5] as much as the distinct characteristics of the child who's watching that content and the broader environmental contexts surrounding the child's media use.[6]

Documenting the particulars of TV's impact on children's early literacy development is well-trod territory in research on children's TV viewing,[7] so this chapter focuses instead on the less understood impacts of interactive digital experiences such as literacy apps, conversational agents, and video chat applications.

I've built the chapter around some specific experiences Oliver had with a literacy app and a picture book when he was three. I'll describe what those experiences were, what I thought they meant, and how my observations dovetail with the current research.

It's worth noting here that most commercially available apps and e-books have zero rigorous research to back up the educational claims they make (and they make a lot!).[8] Still, though research on specific apps may be sparse to nonexistent, academic research can speak more generally to the role of interactive technologies in young children's early literacy development.

ENDLESS ALPHABET VS. BEST FIRST BOOK EVER!

I discovered *Endless Alphabet* one morning as I was getting ready for a (pre-pandemic) day of travel with Oliver. This trip involved two plane rides and a lengthy layover in between. I googled "best apps for toddlers" and clicked on a YouTube video of a mother talking about her son's favorite apps and why he (and she) liked each one. *Endless Alphabet* looked both fun and potentially educational, so I downloaded it. It was, and continues to be, a huge hit.

Here's how it works: There's a library of words to choose from, big words like *vegetable* and *umbrella*, and what would generally be considered sophisticated words for toddlers, like *scrumptious*, *timid*, *gargantuan*, and *famished*. When a child selects a word, a voice states it clearly, and a colorful version of each letter disperses across the screen leaving a greyscale outline behind. If the child places their finger on a dispersed letter, the letter sprouts googly eyes or a mouth and starts to wriggle and say its sound over and over ("wuh wuh wuh" for W, "tuh tuh tuh" for T) as it's dragged across the screen.

The idea is to drag the letter and place it on top of its outline, after which the narrator states the name of the letter. When all the letters have been placed correctly, several animated monsters act out the meaning of the word while the narrator provides a definition. All of this is set to cheerful music.

When I first saw the app, I thought it was brilliant. What a fantastic way to call attention to each letter in a word, its name, and the sound it makes. And what creative, sophisticated words! Surely exposing my son to words like *miniscule* and *cooperate* would be a great way to build his vocabulary.

For the first couple of months using *Endless Alphabet*, Oliver seemed to get the biggest kick out of the funny sounds and movements that the letters made as he dragged them to the right place in a word. However, I noticed that he never repeated a sound out loud, nor did he ever name a letter that he was moving. When I occasionally asked him what sound a certain letter made, he was too preoccupied with dragging and dropping to answer me.

It was a similar situation with the word meaning. Oliver loved watching the animated videos of the monsters acting out the definition of a word, but he never gave any indication that he understood this definition, and he certainly never used words like *scrumptious* or *famished* to describe the taste of his food or how hungry he was.

Oliver's initial enthusiasm for *Endless Alphabet* coincided with his frequent selection of Richard Scarry's *Best First Book Ever!* to read with me. Printed in 1979, this large, foot-long book belonged to me as a young child. Oliver found it on a bookshelf containing a collection of my favorite childhood books when we were visiting my parents one Christmas.

The book follows the Cat family and Lowly Worm as they go about their day, starting with waking up and getting ready for the day, and ending with nursery rhymes before bed. It's a picture book rather than a storybook, with each page packed full of objects and actions related to the theme of that particular page.

"Breakfast in the Kitchen" shows the Cat family in the kitchen surrounded by every possible food and kitchen appliance that you can imagine. Oliver loved to point out and name the objects he recognized, particularly if he had a personal connection to them. For instance, in the kitchen, he would often point out the eggbeater, whisk, and measuring spoons and tell me that he used these things when making cookies with Grandma.

No matter how many times we read this book together, I still managed to find something new each time we examined and talked about a page—there's a lot going on in Busytown! Toward the middle of the book, there's an "Alphabet" page that lists each uppercase and lowercase letter with a picture next to it. There's an owl next to the "O," but I quickly gave up calling attention to it. Oliver was far more interested in the fact that "O" is for Oliver, something he would declare within seconds of turning to this page.

After celebrating the "O," I typically asked him if he could spot "M" for Mummy, "P" for Papa (the name he gives to my father, his grandfather), "N" for Nay Nay (my stepmother), and "G" for Grandma (my mother) and Grandpa (my stepfather). These were the letters we spent most of our time with, the ones he had a personal connection to. Indeed, Oliver's engagement with this page was far more personal and connected to his direct experiences than the way he interacted with the letters and words he encountered with *Endless Alphabet*.

There's also a matter of pacing. Technically speaking, *Endless Alphabet* lets you drag and drop letters at whatever pace you want. However, the music that plays in the background does give a feeling that it's waiting for you to do something, and individual letters will sporadically fidget, as if they're getting restless waiting to be moved. There's also the knowledge that you'll be rewarded with a funny video once you've completed a word. These features work together to make it feel as though the app is encouraging you to move at a certain pace.

Things felt quite different when Oliver and I were looking at the Alphabet page in the picture book. It was a quieter, slower, more static experience. There's no music, no animation, just twenty-six letters and their corresponding pictures sitting there, motionless, on the page.

Oliver could focus on any letter he liked, talk about it in any way that he liked, for as long as he liked. The pace was dictated only by his interest in pointing to letters, naming them (or asking me to name them), and talking with me about things and people we know whose names begin with those letters. There's no end goal to reach. The experience belongs to us and is shaped by us. There's a long history of research showing that such personalized experiences are the most effective way for children to learn anything, including early literacy skills.[9]

I did begin to notice a change in Oliver's interactions with *Endless Alphabet* after a few months. He started to refer to some of the words in contexts outside of the app. Sometimes, he'd say a word, like *yodel*, out of the blue, apparently because he liked the way it sounded. Other times, he'd say a word in a relevant context like the time he declared that his corn flakes were *scrumptious*. He even started to point out "O" for Oliver, especially in words that he had interacted with repeatedly.

It felt to me—as his mother attuned to his cues and an observer attuned to the research—as if Oliver had encountered the other features so often that they were no longer novel and, therefore, less distracting. He was also that much older and had developed increased information-processing and executive-functioning abilities, as well as fine motor skills for successful interaction with the app's features. At nearly three-and-a-half years old, he could now work with the letters in new ways and, importantly, in ways that *he* dictated.

At the same time, however, Oliver also started to pass the tablet to me more frequently, asking me to drag and drop the letters into position, after which he would take the tablet back so that he could watch the animated video acting out the word. The intent was unmistakable: "Mummy, get me past this boring bit so that I can watch the fun bit."

Does this preference for the videos mean that he's learning more vocabulary than letter recognition? I wish I knew for sure. As I've noted already, most children's apps—*Endless Alphabet* included—have zero rigorous research to back up the educational claims they make.[10]

While purely observational, it's clear that Oliver has had different experiences with *Endless Alphabet* and Richard Scarry's *Best First Book Ever!*. And while there's no research on the connection between apps like *Endless Alphabet* and early literacy development, there is meaningful research on children's early literacy development, both with and without digital technologies, which can help us answer this question and make sense of my observations.

In each of the sections that follows, we'll focus on one or more of the observations I made about Oliver's interaction with the literacy app and the picture book and see what research can tell us about how these two experiences compare in their ability to support Oliver's early literacy skills.

UNEQUAL INTERACTIONS: THE IMPORTANCE OF SOCIAL CONTINGENCY

Although Oliver interacted actively with both the *Endless Alphabet* app and Scarry's *Best First Book Ever!*, these two interactions differed in one critical way. With the app, he performed an action, such as dragging a letter across the screen, the letter responded by moving, and the app cheered if he moved it to the correct location. The fact that it was *Oliver* performing these actions made absolutely no difference to the function of the app.

This was not the case with *Best First Book Ever!* When Oliver and I pointed out the letters in the book and drew connections to our family members' names, the activity was very much tailored to Oliver and his particular relationships and experiences. This type of interaction is socially contingent: I was the social partner who responded to what Oliver said, and I helped connect elements of the book to his life.

In contrast, interactions with apps such as *Endless Alphabet* are non-socially contingent: there is no social partner behind the screen to recognize Oliver's distinct Oliver-ness.

(Note that without my participation in the picture book interaction, there would be no contingent interaction at all, social or nonsocial.)

Socially contingent interactions, whether online or offline, are particularly supportive of children's early literacy development.[11] Recall in the opening of this chapter that caregivers play an important role in supporting their children's emerging literacy skills. Knowing their children as well as they do, caregivers instinctively tailor their speech, observations, storytelling, and read-alouds to their children's distinct temperament, recent experiences, relationships, and preferences. These types of personalized, socially embedded literacy experiences are an important part of what makes parents' support so crucial to their children's early literacy development.[12]

VIDEO CHATTING WITH GRANDMA AND GRANDPA

One day when Oliver was about ten months old, I had the brilliant idea of using masking tape to stick my smartphone to the back of the passenger seat of my car, directly in front of his car seat. From that day, I would pick him up from daycare, put him in his car seat, turn on my phone and call my mother and stepfather, who lived in another time zone, via FaceTime.

They sang songs and read books to him, and made him laugh during our drive home. It was a perfect setup. Oliver was entertained, and my parents had a chance to be a part of his day before they went to bed. It became a special experience for all of us (perhaps a bit less so for me as I was driving, but I loved hearing the interaction.)

About a year later, Oliver and I moved to Berlin for my sabbatical from the University of Washington. We no longer had a car for post-daycare video chats, but I soon discovered that having one of his two sets of grandparents read a few books on my laptop was an effective way to keep a very wriggly toddler in his seat at lunchtime.

Besides making my life a bit easier, was Oliver actually getting anything from these video chat sessions?

In 2013, researchers Sarah Roseberry, Kathy Hirsh-Pasek, and Roberta Golinkoff conducted the first study to examine young children's word learning through video chat technology.[13] They brought children between the ages of two and two-and-a-half into their lab and taught them a series of new words in one of three different ways. Some children were taught by an adult via Skype, others were taught by an adult in person, and the third group was taught by watching a prerecorded video of an adult teaching another child.

The researchers had good reason to believe that the two-year-olds wouldn't have much success learning new words by watching a prerecorded video. This is because very young children typically learn better when information is presented to them live and in-person versus screen-based and prerecorded—a pattern researchers refer to as the *video deficit effect*.[14]

But what about interacting with an adult via Skype? Like the children watching the prerecorded video, children using Skype had a two-dimensional experience, which we know can be difficult for young children to translate back to three-dimensional space.[15] However, the Skype group also shared an important quality with the in-person group: back-and-forth, real-time, and personalized dialogue between an adult and the child.

Children using Skype learned new words just as well as children who interacted with an adult in person. In contrast, those children who watched the prerecorded video had considerably more difficulty. Skype turned out to be more like interacting with an adult in person than watching one on a screen. Social contingency proved key.

This and subsequent studies show how, under certain conditions,[16] the social contingency of video chat applications such as Skype, Zoom, and FaceTime enable young children to develop early literacy skills and even form social relationships.[17] By age four, children can learn equally well from video chat as they do from live interactions with an adult.[18]

So, it seems that Oliver was likely learning something (though maybe not so much at ten months[19]) and indeed, continues to learn something from his video chats with his grandparents, which became even more frequent during the pandemic. Also important is my role during these video chats as a supportive co-viewer who guides his attention and reinforces what his grandparents are saying.[20]

Whether or not parents of young children are familiar with this research, they seem to make a distinction—consciously or not—between video chat and other forms of screen media when it comes to their children's technology use. Even parents who are otherwise restrictive about the time their children spend with other types of media have been found to make an exception for video chat.[21] Notably, these parents aren't using video chat to replace face-to-face interaction with adults, but rather to maintain connections to remote family members, something that became more widespread and valued during the pandemic.[22]

There are challenges associated with video chatting with young children, of course. Their sensorimotor penchant for touching everything in sight means that keys are often inadvertently pressed and calls accidentally ended.[23] It may take children some time to understand that they need to restrict their movements to the computer's visual field in order to be seen by those with whom they are chatting. The camera's typical placement at the top of the screen also makes it challenging to make eye contact and to follow what a person is pointing to in the child's environment.[24]

And then there's the ubiquitous challenge of pixelated or frozen screens and audio lags, which frustrates children and adults alike. In light of these challenges, parents play a central role in facilitating and troubleshooting video chats with remote relatives. These challenges also represent opportunities for technology developers to design video chat tools with young children in mind.

For several years now, design researchers have been exploring innovative ways to facilitate and enhance remote interactions among family members.[25] In one example, design researcher Svetlana Yarosh developed *ShareTable*, a video chatting system that made use of projectors to create shared spaces between remote family members.[26] When a child placed a favorite book on the table in front of them, the book showed up as a projection on their relative's table. Family members could also draw together in the projection space and play games like tic-tac-toe.

ShareTable tackled the challenge of how two people who are physically separated can jointly view and engage with a single book without the strained necks and awkward perspectives that come from trying to read a picture book while centering it in front of the computer's camera for the other person to see. In addition to demonstrating the possibilities of using interactive technologies to support children's literacy experiences, examples such as ShareTable illustrate the value of incorporating children's developmental needs and social contexts into the design process from the start.

CONVERSATIONAL AGENTS: A NEW TYPE OF SOCIAL CONTINGENCY

If you have a smartphone, odds are you have the ability to interact with a conversational agent like Siri, Alexa, or the Google Assistant. You might ask this artificial intelligence (AI)-powered virtual assistant what tomorrow's weather forecast will be, or the lyrics to a favorite song, or perhaps, if you're with your four-year-old son, whether water dragons are real.

Conversational agents also power smart speakers like the Amazon Echo and Google Nest, which are quickly becoming prominent in U.S. households. In 2017, 9 percent of homes with young children (ages zero to eight) had a smart speaker; in 2020, just three years later, fully 41 percent did.[27] Young children use smart speakers to play music, find out information, get jokes, or "just to talk or fool around with."[28]

Like smart speakers themselves, research on children's interactions with this technology is still emerging, and far from conclusive.[29] Researchers have begun to explore whether and how the introduction of devices like the Amazon Echo and Google Nest affect family interactions,[30] support learning,[31] engage children in playful activities,[32] and even support therapeutic interventions for children with neurodevelopmental disorders.[33] Researchers are also investigating how young children think about conversational agents, including the extent to which children imbue these devices with human-like qualities, trust what they say, and form emotional attachments to them.[34]

Conversational agents provide young children who can't yet read or write with unprecedented access to information on the internet. Researcher Silvia Lovato and colleagues found that children age five and six used this access most frequently to find out about the world around them ("How are pillows made?" "What's the fastest animal in the world?"). They also asked practical questions about everyday topics such as the weather and recipes, personal questions about the agent ("How old are you?") and themselves ("What's my name?"), and language-based questions such as asking for the meaning or spelling of a word.[35]

Notably, Lovato's research showed that conversational agents were able to answer only about half of children's questions, mirroring other research showing child-specific challenges related to smart speakers.[36] For instance, although getting better,[37] conversational agents sometimes have trouble understanding children's speech, especially young children whose speech skills are still developing.[38]

In addition, the answers are often difficult for children to interpret, requiring vocabulary, prior knowledge, or inferential reasoning that young children lack.[39] Conversational agents also don't seem particularly well-equipped to handle the types of curiosity-based, sometimes magical questions that children like to ask.[40]

For instance, ask Google Assistant if water dragons are real (you know, the kind that fly and breathe fire and only come out of the water at night), and she'll tell you about Asian water dragons, bright green lizards found in Thailand, Vietnam, Cambodia, Laos, Burma, and southern China, that are adept climbers and strong swimmers.

This research suggests that, at least initially, smart speakers weren't designed with young children specifically in mind. However, this is beginning to change. You can now find smart speakers geared specifically to children, featuring parental controls, child-specific content, and even positive reinforcement for using the word *please*. Technology companies are also making progress with recognizing children's voices.[41]

As smart speakers become better at recognizing and responding to young children, what are the possibilities when it comes to supporting early literacy development? Researchers Ying Xu and Mark Warschauer have shown that it's possible to design conversational agents that engage children in guided storybook reading (think of the back-and-forth exchanges between Oliver and me while reading *Best First Book Ever!*).[42] Moreover, they've demonstrated that these agent-based reading experiences can produce comprehension gains that are on par with reading with an adult.[43]

For commercial smart speakers to realize this potential, however, Xu and Warschauer observe that these technologies need to get much better at supporting open-ended dialogue and back-and-forth exchanges.[44] They need to encourage children to talk more and in as unconstrained a way as possible, asking children relevant questions and providing developmentally appropriate responses to their questions. These are all the things parents do regularly when reading to their children, and why such joint reading experiences are so supportive of children's early literacy development.[45]

WHEN THE DEVICE DOESN'T KNOW YOUR NAME

These discussions of video chat and conversational agents highlight the importance of social contingency when it comes to young children's ability to learn from their digital experiences. Engaging in a two-way exchange with someone who is trusted and responsive increases the personal relevance of information shared with children, making it possible for them to connect that information to their prior experiences and knowledge, and adapt it to their level of understanding. This is certainly good news for video calls with grandparents and other relatives, and the reason why the American Academy of Pediatrics makes an exception for video chat when it comes to their "no screens under the age of 18 months" recommendation.[46]

But what about the more common forms of digital experiences that engage children: mobile apps that are *interactive* but not *socially contingent*?

Let's return to Oliver's experiences playing *Endless Alphabet*. Like other toddlers, he spent more time in a typical week using such apps than video chatting with his grandparents. Apps like these provide highly interactive experiences, but they're not socially contingent, so what, if anything, are kids learning from them?

We know that starting somewhere between age two and three, children can learn from high-quality, educationally oriented television programs.[47] It seems plausible, then, that adding an interactive component—which many TV shows try to do by posing questions to the camera and pausing for children to answer—would likely support children's learning by making the experience more hands on and engaging. After all, children learn best by doing.[48]

Preschool-aged children are able, under certain conditions, to learn from contingent interactions on a touch screen, even if these interactions don't involve real-time interactions with a social partner.[49] And, by around age four, most children are able to learn equally well from interactive media as they are from live, face-to-face interaction.[50] They're also able to learn equally well—if not better—from interactive e-books as they are from print books.[51] This sounds like good news for the early childhood-focused apps available on mobile phones and tablets, which are responsive to children's actions (i.e., interactive) but don't rise to the level of the two-way, social interactions that are possible with video chat (i.e., social contingency).

Note, however, that I said "under certain conditions" young children can learn from interactive screen media. We can find some clues to these conditions in my earlier observations comparing Oliver's experiences playing *Endless Alphabet* to looking at the alphabet page of Scarry's *Best First Book Ever!*, also taking into account some of the insights from chapter 2.

One notable distinction between Oliver's app and print book experiences is the pacing—more precisely, who *controls* the pacing. When Oliver and I are looking at the alphabet page of *Best First Book Ever!* we might stay there for a few seconds or several minutes, depending on the letter or letters that catch our fancy and the conversations we have around them. Strictly speaking, *Endless Alphabet* does allow users to drag and drop letters at their own pace (which is notably different from many other apps that require users to keep up with a set pace). However, as I remarked earlier, the music and fidgeting letters impart a sense of externally imposed action forward.

Researchers think that self-pacing plays a role in supporting children's ability to learn new words from their tablet-based experiences.[52] Self-pacing, then, appears to be one factor in the learning potential of interactive media.

Related to self-pacing is the degree to which apps come with unnecessary distractions. As we saw in chapter 2, researchers have found that adding a bunch of "bells and whistles" to an app—no matter how educational they're intended to be—can end up distracting children from the central activity and interfere with their learning.[53] Features such as animation, sound, and music can distract young children from the central experience of following the narrative of a story.[54] This may be particularly true for young children, whose limited information processing and executive function skills (like selective attention and working memory) are easily taxed.[55]

Unfortunately, many educational apps—especially free apps—come with a lot of distracting bells and whistles, some of them intended to be educational, but most have nothing to do with the educational goals of the app (think of the design abuses discussed in chapter 2).[56] When I watched Oliver with *Endless Alphabet*, I noticed that he was absorbed in the funny animation and sounds that occurred as he dragged and dropped letters onto a word. When I first saw these features, I thought they were a clever way to call attention to individual letters and the sounds they make. However, Oliver seemed simply to enjoy them for their entertainment value, showing little evidence of understanding—or caring—that each letter was making a specific sound and that sound was the same every time (forget about making the next connection, that each sound has a role to play in the larger word).

Adding features such as sound, animation, and games should be done carefully, in a way that's closely related to the story rather than used primarily to keep children engaged for as long as possible.[57] If such features are used to scaffold the learning experience (for example, by reinforcing words and concepts through repetition) rather than distract from it, there's evidence that preschoolers can learn from e-books and other educational apps.[58]

Still, returning to the importance of focusing on individual children, researchers have found variations in children's learning based on their executive function skills, fine motor skills, gender, and socioeconomic status.[59] And, for very young children, around age two and under, existing research indicates that, at least for neurotypical children, reading and talking about print books with an adult is still the best way to develop their early literacy skills.[60]

Another tax on children's ability to attend to the educational content of an app is how easy or difficult it is for them to interact with its user interface. With *Endless Alphabet*, I noticed that it became considerably easier for Oliver to drag letters into their correct position between ages three and four. Young children are still developing their fine motor skills, which can make motions such as dragging objects across a screen more challenging than tapping on them.[61] Also challenging are features that require symbolic understanding, such as a progress bar, a visual element that lets users view their progress through an app.[62]

One last factor to consider is the extent to which an interactive media experience supports joint engagement with an adult.[63] By now, it should be apparent that parents (and other adults working with young children) play a critical role in executive functioning and early literacy development. Parents are able to respond to children in a highly individualized way based on their knowledge of and ability to tune into children's distinct personalities, abilities, and social cues. If a task is too difficult, a grownup can add just enough—and just the right kind of—support in order for a child to experience success—this is called "scaffolding."[64] Over time, the adult gradually removes the support until the child can perform the task independently—this is called "fading."[65]

Although interactive media can respond to children's actions to a certain extent, the typical apps one finds in the App Store and Google Play Store cannot respond yet in such a highly individualized and calibrated way. It therefore follows that apps that allow for and, even better, *encourage* adult participation are likely to result in a greater degree of learning among young children.[66]

The flip side of parents' supportive involvement in their children's media use is parental distraction at the hands of their own devices. Researcher Jessa Reed and colleagues conducted an experiment in which mothers brought their two-year-old children to a research lab and were asked to teach them two new words. One of the teaching periods proceeded uninterrupted, but the other one was interrupted by the mother receiving a cell phone call.[67] Children were able to learn the new word when teaching was uninterrupted but not in the interrupted condition. This study joins a growing body of research on the negative effects of parental technoference (see chapter 2), in addition to a well-established knowledge base underscoring the importance of responsive and consistent caregiver-child interaction.[68]

WHY NOT STICK WITH FACE-TO-FACE INTERACTIONS AND PRINT BOOKS?

This discussion suggests that the more you make a screen-based experience resemble a face-to-face one—or even a print book—the better. So why not stick to face-to-face interactions and print books?

If you're a parent, you can probably point right away to two compelling reasons: your kids love interacting with phones and tablets, and you appreciate the time it gives you to do the dishes, change the laundry, or just breathe. I think these are perfectly valid reasons and sufficient to justify moderate daily use of interactive media among young children.[69] There are also trends from emerging research that would seem to support children's occasional use of screen media.

For example, different populations of children have different kinds of early literacy experiences and different kinds of digital experiences. Researchers have documented disparities in children's early literacy experiences across demographic categories such as race and socioeconomic status (a combination of education, income, and occupation).[70] With respect to digital experiences, as of 2020, Black children and children living in lower income households tended, on average, to spend about two hours more per day with screen media than white children and children living in higher-income households.[71]

This same survey showed that these children spent considerably more time per day reading in 2020 than they did in 2017 (about a 70 percent increase for Black children and a 65 percent increase for low-income children).[72] In contrast, white children and children living in higher-income households read about the same amount in 2020 as they did in 2017.

This meant that by 2020, Black and low-income children were spending more time reading per day than other groups of children. What tipped the scales was the greater amount of time they spent reading e-books.

These are only trends, and they say nothing about the context or quality of children's screen media experiences. Without that context, we don't know whether they reinforce, narrow, or have no impact whatsoever on existing disparities in children's early literacy development. They are indications of a potential that needs to be explored further when it comes to leveraging technology to support literacy development among different populations of children.[73]

TAKING STOCK WITH THE THREE *D'S*

What's going on *developmentally*: It's generally difficult for children to learn much from watching content on a screen before the age of about three due to challenges such as developing attentional abilities, limited information processing capacity, and the nontrivial task of translating content presented in a two-dimensional format back to three-dimensional space.[74] High-quality educational pro-grams might lower this age a bit,[75] and interactive media experiences can lower it even further.[76]

We identified two different kinds of interactivity: the back-and-forth, socially contingent interactions children experience when talking to their grandparents (or other close adults) over video chat, and the responsive but not person-alized (i.e., non-socially contingent) interactions children engage in when playing with an educational app on a phone or tablet. Although socially contingent interactions provide the richest early literacy experiences—closest to the child-focused speech that occurs during mealtimes and bedtime reading with a parent—educational apps can be designed to support early literacy development.[77]

By around age four, typically developing children can learn under all of these screen-based conditions—noninteractive, interactive, and socially contingent—just about as well as from face-to-face interactions, provided the content is high quality.

Going _deeper_: However convenient it would be, there doesn't appear to be a precise age or developmental stage when a proverbial switch is flipped and children can be depended on to learn from television, video chats, smart speakers, or apps. Technology—and children—are too com-plicated for that.

In considering how technologies may interact with other aspects of a child's life to produce differential effects, we saw that young children's ability to learn new words from interactive apps varied depending on factors such as their executive function skills, fine motor skills, gender, and socio-economic status.[78] Considerations of physical and cognitive disabilities among children are also relevant, and more research is needed to understand the distinct possibilities and challenges.[79]

We discussed as well variations in the amount of time that children from different demographic groups spend each day with screen media—about two hours more per day for Black and low-income children compared to white and high-income children.[80] I suggested the potential value of leveraging these differences to support early literacy development among different populations of children.[81]

Design considerations: There are concrete strategies to be gleaned from existing research when it comes to designing technologies that support children's early literacy development.[82] These strategies follow on from the best practices identified in chapter 2 and align with the overarching call of this book to design for children's self-directed, community-supported digital experiences.

For instance, we returned to the value of designing *self-paced experiences* that allow children (and their parents) to dictate how they engage in a tech-based activity. Self-pacing can help children engage in an interactive experience in a way that matches their abilities, preferences, and goals. In addition, *minimizing features that distract* and employing features that reinforce target learning objectives can help children whose executive function abilities are still developing. Also important is making sure young children can interact with and *make sense of an application's formal features* (for example, dragging and dropping, pinching, progress bars) given their fine motor skills and symbolic reasoning abilities are still developing.

Our explorations of video chat and conversational agents demonstrated that socially contingent interactions can support the *back-and-forth, personalized* way that children learn to speak and read.[83] Although conversational agents present some user challenges for young children (e.g., understanding their speech), the potential is there for these technologies to support early literacy development provided they're designed in such a way that encourages *open-ended dialogue*.[84]

Even when technology experiences are non-socially contingent, they can be designed to *encourage the involvement of parents and other adults*, thereby introducing an element of social contingency. When parents are encouraged to join in with their children's tech experiences, they can provide the personalized, just-in-time support that's so valuable for early literacy development.[85] At the same time, parental distraction at the hands of their own devices can diminish their ability to provide this support.[86]

There's one important dimension of young children's interactions with apps and other interactive technologies that we haven't addressed in any serious way in this or the previous chapter: they're *fun*. Although fun and play don't seem terribly relevant to the serious tasks of executive function and literacy development, we'll see in chapter 4 that play is central to just about every aspect of child development, including things like self-regulation and vocabulary development.

4

LOOKING FOR "LOOSE PARTS" IN CHILDREN'S DIGITAL PLAY

"It is fun to have fun, but you have to know how."[1]

Like the Cat in the Hat, children know how to play and have fun. This is good news, because play provides an important context for the developmental milestones discussed in chapters 2 and 3—executive function and early literacy development.[2]

It goes without saying that these days, play comes in both analog and digital forms. Children can build fortresses with sticks or *Minecraft* bricks. They can chase after and roughhouse with their friends on the schoolyard, or they can hunt down and battle the boss in a video game.

In this chapter we explore the similarities and differences between analog and digital forms of play, whether there is room for both, and how adults and the surrounding environment affect children's play experiences. Throughout, I'll use the concept of "loose parts" to examine what it means to be in control of one's play, why this is desirable from a developmental perspective, and the circumstances under which children are in greatest control over their play.[3]

This chapter addresses a transition point between early and middle childhood. As such, I'll begin by focusing on young children's analog and digital play experiences and then move into middle childhood where I'll consider the role of video games in children's development.

THE FORMS AND FUNCTIONS OF CHILDREN'S PLAY

Play starts early in life. Even small babies enjoy playing games like pattycake and peekaboo with their caregivers.[4] As babies grow into toddlers and preschoolers and start to think symbolically, they make breakfast for their dolls and dinosaurs and pretend the stick they found in the bushes is actually a horse they can ride.

Play becomes more sophisticated and rule-based during middle childhood, but no less fun, and no less important to a child's development.[5]

Certain features cut across the different forms of children's play and distinguish them as *play*.[6] Most importantly, play is freely chosen and self-directed.[7] Children engage in play for its own sake, because it's fun, and not to earn any sort of reward at the end.[8] There's a sense in play that it's somehow separate from everyday life; therefore, the rules are slightly different, and children are freer to try out new roles and behaviors. In fact, experimentation is key to play. Children try out new actions and behaviors as they play, they observe the consequences, and adjust their future actions accordingly.[9]

For all the fun to be had through play, children are gaining important skills. The experimental nature of play helps children learn to adapt to new circumstances in their environment, a skill that remains valuable throughout the course of life and in just about any context. As psychologist Alison

Gopnik has observed: "The gift of play is the way it teaches us how to deal with the unexpected."[10] Play also teaches children about what to expect from their environment. Through play, children learn about the norms, rules, values, tools, and skills associated with their culture and society.[11]

Social play has particular benefits for children's development. Play among friends involves negotiating a sense of what's right and wrong, what's fair and what's not, learning to understand someone else's point of view, and managing your emotions when things don't go your way.[12] In the process, children develop their interpersonal skills, social understanding, and moral sensibility.[13]

In early childhood especially, a lot of young children's social play involves pretending. When children play house or dragon hunters with their friends, they're developing their ability to engage in symbolic and counterfactual "what if" ways of thinking, creating opportunities to imagine different possibilities for themselves and the world around them.[14] Pretend play also helps children develop their ability to understand what's going on in other people's minds. This is true whether children engage in pretend play with flesh-and-blood friends, or with their imaginary friends (like four-year-old Oliver's ten dragon friends, led by the head dragon, Lightning Fierce).[15]

WHAT PLAYGROUNDS CAN TEACH US ABOUT DIGITAL PLAY

Playgrounds may seem pretty far removed (both conceptually and physically) from playing games on a tablet or video game console. However, they provide a useful context for highlighting key qualities of children's play generally, which we can then apply to digital play experiences specifically. Playgrounds also offer a valuable setting for reflecting on the preconceptions we have about what makes for a quality play experience, whether online or offline.

As a parent of a young child, I've spent a lot of time at playgrounds. Thanks to the particular blend of my work and family life, I've had a chance to sample playgrounds in Seattle (where I work at the University of Washington), Bermuda (where my extended family lives), and Berlin (where I spent my sabbatical).

Berlin playgrounds are things of beauty, each one a unique gem of imaginative design and careful construction. They often have a theme, such as a dragon or a pirate ship, or something more prosaic like a post office. Whatever the theme, you can be sure the principal material used to craft a Berlin playground is wood—the more hand-chiseled and weathered looking, the better.

In contrast, the playgrounds I've frequented in Seattle and Bermuda pretty much all look alike, using the same brightly colored, durable plastic components to create the standard sliding, climbing, and swinging experiences for children. There are exceptions, of course, but the general pattern is unmistakable.

When I first returned to Bermuda after spending several months in Berlin, I remember noting the stark contrast. I admit to thinking that my childhood in Bermuda had somehow been impoverished by its lack of whimsical, wooden playgrounds.

But then I found myself one afternoon sitting with Oliver on the steps behind my childhood home. These steps are lined on one side by a stretch of long grasses, behind which sit a series of Match Me If You Can bushes. Oliver decided we would have a picnic, and began setting the table with two plates, each one a Match Me If You Can leaf. He foraged a dozen or so stones small enough to fit onto our leaves. These were our pancakes. Two straight, smooth twigs were our forks, which he laid carefully on the side of each leaf-plate. He poured the maple syrup (air) on our pancakes, and we enjoyed our picnic together.

I realized then that my childhood may not have included life-sized pirate ships or dragon-inspired climbing frames, but it *was* full of open-ended, self-directed play experiences. When we returned to Berlin in mid-March 2020, just before the first pandemic lockdown, Oliver was well prepared to create his own worlds with the materials he found on our walks and along the periphery of the playgrounds that were now closed throughout the city. It took a bit of coaxing him away from the cordoned-off play equipment at first, but after a few days he seemed to forget the playgrounds were even there. In fact, even when they reopened, I noticed that he often still chose to play in the grassy areas surrounding them, hunting for bugs and chasing imaginary dragons.

The aesthetic qualities of a toy or play experience may come to dominate our assessment of its intrinsic value, obscuring other important qualities, such as the availability of materials with which to exercise one's imagination and engage in different forms of self-directed play, from rough-and-tumble to fantasy play. We may perceive play on the "ugly" plastic playground as somehow inferior to play on the charming wooden playground. However, the quality of play isn't determined by the *aesthetics* of a toy or playground so much as by the *design* of the play experience.

THE VALUE OF PLAYING WITH LOOSE PARTS

We may not think of play experiences as having a particular design, but all this means is that the structure of play environments and the materials available in them make possible certain kinds of behaviors and prevent (or at least discourage) others.

In *The Design of Childhood*, architecture and design critic Alexandra Lange draws on the concept of loose parts to examine the quality of children's play in different environments.[16] The idea is as simple as its name: according to the late sculpture professor Simon Nicholson, children's play is enriched from the availability of open-ended play materials—"loose parts"—that they can use to create their own imaginary worlds rather than play within a world of someone else's design.[17]

In an environment filled with loose parts, children's play has the potential to be far more creative and sophisticated than, say, in a playground where each piece of equipment is typically designed for a single, specific purpose. The concept of loose parts is well aligned with a key feature of play: it's self-chosen and self-directed.[18]

To demonstrate the value of loose parts, researchers at Cornell University conducted a series of studies in which they observed preschool-aged children on a playground.[19] In the first study, they watched children play in a standard-issue playground context, focusing on how the design features of the play equipment influenced the children's play behaviors and social interactions.

They found that most of the children's play was "functional"—repetitive movements such as running, climbing, and jumping that engage gross motor skills. Dramatic play—considered a higher-order form of play because it engages more complex cognitive processes such as symbolic thinking—was observed less frequently and only in certain areas of the playground, such as enclosed spaces, nodes and connector spaces, and stage-like spaces. Another higher-order form of play—constructive play, such as building with blocks, sticks, and other found materials—wasn't observed at all since the equipment was static and children couldn't alter anything.

For their second study, the researchers introduced a variety of loose parts onto the playground: large Styrofoam and plastic blocks, pieces of fabric, tires, tree stumps, and PVC pipes.[20] They then watched as a separate group of children played on the transformed playground.

The children immediately gravitated to the areas of the playground that had the loose parts. They used these loose parts to engage in both constructive and dramatic play with each other. They created houses, forts, and towers (constructive play), which they used as settings for their dramatic play. In this way, the loose parts facilitated two forms of higher-order play, one of which (constructive play) had been nonexistent on the original playground.

The theory of loose parts tells us that the distinction between wood-crafted versus stock plastic play equipment isn't what counts when it comes to supporting children's play. Climbing up and jumping off a plastic frame is probably not much different an experience from climbing up and jumping off a frame made of wood. The imaginative stories that children invent within a plastic playhouse are likely just as creative as the stories they invent in a wooden one.

Wooden playground settings may look more idyllic and "pure" to us adults (and provide better backdrops for our photos) than plastic, but the types of play they inspire in children are probably comparable, especially when the underlying equipment differs only in the material used to construct it. More important than aesthetics is the fact that both playgrounds—the beautiful wooden one and the charmless plastic one—are highly, even *over*-designed by adults.

Play experiences that are designed by adults can limit the range of what children do on their own, particularly what they create and imagine.[21] Adults can also limit children's play by calling attention to certain features of a toy or play environment rather than letting children explore it for themselves.[22]

Play experiences that are less deliberately designed and directed tend to give children more freedom to come up with a greater range of actions and plotlines. Just think of all the ways children find to play with cardboard boxes versus the thing that was actually in the cardboard box.

Not always, though. There are times when play experiences can be painstakingly designed specifically to provide children with autonomy and agency to act on their environments. Lange points to a variety of highly designed playgrounds in the United States (such as the Hills on Governors Island off the southern tip of Manhattan) that deliberately incorporate a variety of loose parts and ambiguous equipment so that children can manipulate and act on their environment in creative ways.

And here's where I'll acknowledge that the charming Berlin playgrounds do tend to align better with loose parts theory than the plastic playgrounds one finds in Seattle and Bermuda. It's quite common, for instance, to encounter sand, water, movable parts, and abstract structures in a Berlin playground. Once I learned to dress Oliver appropriately, I enjoyed watching him get wet and sandy as he built sandcastles surrounded by winding waterways.

LOOKING FOR LOOSE PARTS IN DIGITAL PLAY

This discussion of loose parts and playgrounds can help us assess the quality and value of children's various digital play experiences.

First, as much as we might be tempted to value wood over plastic (or pixelated) toys, loose parts matter more than aesthetics when it comes to supporting children's play.

So when a child is engaged in digital play, it's probably less helpful to bemoan the fact that they're not playing with wooden blocks and instead consider whether there are tools and materials available for them to construct their own worlds. Once constructed, are they able to place themselves in that world and engage in fantasy play? And what about opportunities for social interaction?

Second, play experiences that are devised and designed by adults can sometimes undercut the freely chosen, self-directed quality of children's play. The norm in digital play seems to be highly designed experiences that structure children's play (and attention) in specific ways. We saw this in chapter 3 when I compared Oliver's engagement with a literacy app versus a print book, and in chapter 2 when I described a study comparing children's analog and digital play.[23] In that study, children seemed less in control over how and where their attention was directed when they were playing on a tablet versus an analog game.

In chapter 2 we also considered the dark patterns and design abuses, such as parasocial relationships, lures, and virtual trophies, found in many children's apps that can co-opt children's attention.[24] Such features make these digital play experiences extremely engaging, but less freely chosen and less child directed.

What are less easily identifiable (but by no means impossible to find) are digital play experiences that let children dictate the pace and shape of play, transform existing worlds, and maybe even create new ones. Perhaps somewhat counterintuitively to the theory of loose parts, these types of open-ended, user-paced digital experiences can be—perhaps even *should* be—carefully designed to support children's creative play.

One can find examples from design research to illustrate how intentional design can produce technologies that support children's play.[25] Researchers in Sweden collaborated with landscape architects to design a set of open-ended interactive play technologies, which they installed in a schoolyard environment.[26] For instance, the "tube" (a square-shaped wooden shaft outfitted with sensors) could detect certain qualities of objects that were placed in it, such as liquids, noise, and movement. The tube reacted in different ways to different materials that children put through it.

The researchers found that adding the tube and other inter-active elements to the outdoor environment invited chil-dren into playful explorations and supported a wider range of play activities than before.[27]

This kind of intentional technology design can also be used to support inclusive play experiences for children with disabilities.[28] For example, researchers have explored using augmented reality and tangible toys to facilitate pretend play and collaborative play in autistic children.[29]

Children with disabilities often require more direct sup-ports (typically from adults) to facilitate their play.[30] There-fore, designing interactive technologies for these children may require a slightly different approach from the open-ended, child-directed one I've emphasized so far in this chapter. Even so, designs for inclusive play should be flex-ible enough to adjust to a child's abilities, and they should encourage social interaction.[31]

THE LIMITS OF DIGITAL LOOSE PARTS

Even when designers take great pains to create virtual envi-ronments that encourage exploration and creative expres-sion, the added layer of inflexibility associated with the digital format can limit children's range of actions more so than in the analog world.[32] Two kinds of playful mixing—one with paints, one with toys—illustrate this point.

I'll use Oliver's play to illustrate the first kind of mixing. When he creates a picture on his tablet, the app he's using lets him draw freely, select colors, even erase and start over. It's a pretty open-ended experience that he directs. Simi-larly, when he creates a picture using paints, paper, and a paintbrush, Oliver decides what he wants to draw and the colors he'll use (although erasing isn't so easy).

The two painting environments start to diverge when it comes to mixing two or more colors together. In the analog world, Oliver can use the colors as they are right out of the paint tube, but he can also mix colors together and create different shades. There's really no limit to the variety of colors he can create. On his tablet, by contrast, he's limited to the colors that the designer has programmed into the app. If he's able to mix two colors together (which not all apps allow), the result is still a shade predesignated by the underlying code. The analog world allows for more texture and more nuance than the digital world of binary 0s and 1s.[33]

The second kind of mixing involves toys. Children frequently bring together toys made of different materials and on different scales, toys with different back stories, abilities, and intended functions, and they put them to work in new scenarios of their own invention. Just think of Andy (and later, Bonnie) from Pixar's *Toy Story* movies and the many stories he invents with his vintage pull-string doll Sheriff Woody, the plastic action figure Buzz Lightyear, and a variety of other toys including Mr. Potato Head, Bo Peep (a figurine once attached to his sister's bedside lamp), Slinky Dog, and Rex the dinosaur.

This type of toy remixing is much harder to do on a tablet, where each app is its own distinct environment that doesn't communicate with other app environments.[34] Other kinds of digital toys may be easier to mix and appropriate for different play scenarios, especially "phygital" toys that combine physical and digital play experiences.[35]

One example is *Purrble*, a worried pet who calms down when children stroke his soft fur.[36] Although Purrble was designed to help children manage their strong emotions through calming another being, Oliver had no trouble incorporating this smart toy into play scenarios with his other, nondigital toys (including Woody and Buzz Lightyear).[37]

LOOSE PARTS AREN'T EVERYTHING

Not all play experiences need loose parts. Even the playgrounds with immoveable, standard equipment have their place. Climbing, sliding, and jumping on stock play equipment are valuable activities for developing children's gross motor skills. No one toy, app, or piece of play equipment will give rise to all forms of play, nor need it, provided children have access to a variety of play experiences in their daily lives.

When considering the full range of children's play experiences—both analog and digital—it's worth considering how those experiences were designed. Do children have opportunities to exercise gross and fine motor skills? Do they have opportunities to play alone and with others (both peers and adults)?[38] Are there places and circumstances when they can build (and sometimes destroy) things, invent things, and dream up new worlds?

For the parents who just read this and started worrying that there's not enough variety in their children's play experiences, remember the good-enough digital parent from chapter 2! Aim for some mix of self-directed and guided play experiences, realizing there's no magical ratio or combination of play activities (that we know of yet).

And don't forget to let children figure this mix out for themselves, even allowing them the space to be bored as they decide what they're going to play next. Boredom—or more precisely, the ability to successfully navigate one's boredom—has its value, giving children the opportunity to practice managing their emotions, directing their attention, and setting and pursuing new goals.[39]

Lastly, supporting variety in children's play experiences isn't just a family issue, it's also a societal one. Concerns over neighborhood safety have increased in recent decades, making many families hesitant to allow their children to play outside unsupervised.[40] A parent who's worried about their child's physical safety may decide it's preferable for them to play on a phone rather than up in a tree.[41] Other societal-level challenges include external demands on parents' time, such as long work hours and shift work, which can limit their capacity to create and oversee quality play environments for their children.

FROM PLAYING TO GAMING IN MIDDLE CHILDHOOD

Play becomes less grounded in fantasy and more structured and rule-based in middle childhood (around ages six to ten).[42] Instead of playing house or pretending to be dragon hunters, children are more likely to engage in adult-organized activities (like team sports) or games that have formal rules (e.g., board games) and informal rules (e.g., tag). These forms of play offer children a greater variety of roles, including opportunities to engage in teamwork and practice their leadership skills.[43]

Video games represent the most popular form of digital play during middle childhood. In 2021, children between the ages of eight and twelve spent about an hour and a half per day gaming—approximately one-third of their daily screen time—though this average was much higher for boys (over two hours) and lower for girls (just under an hour).[44]

Our societal perception of video games and their effects on children is about as complicated and inconsistent as our views of technology and screen time more generally.

One the one hand, *Minecraft*—a game in which players explore, build, and find ways to survive in virtual landscapes—is extolled for its potential to teach a wide variety of skills and knowledge, from geometry, coding, and electronics, to digital citizenship, social skills, and collaboration.[45] In fact, Mojang, the company that created *Minecraft*, and Microsoft, which later bought it, developed *Minecraft: Education Edition*. According to the *Minecraft* website, this educational version of the game is being used in more than 115 countries to teach just about any skill you can think of.

On the other hand, it's common to encounter dire news headlines warning parents about the dangers of violent video games and video game addiction. Indeed, video games have been regularly singled out as a major contributor to America's gun violence over the decades.[46]

Little wonder that parents enthusiastically enroll their children in *Minecraft* camps, hoping they'll learn about geometry, coding, and electronics, at the same time that they try to limit how much time their children spend playing *Fortnite*, worried about the possibility of video game addiction.

These contradictions and mixed messages are mirrored in published research on the effects of video games on young people. Part of the challenge here is the unwieldy, amorphous group of activities we collectively refer to as video games. Video game scholar Daphne Bavelier and colleagues have warned: "One can no more say what the effects of video games are, than one can say what the effects of food are."[47]

But even when focusing on a narrower type of game—violent video games—scholars can't seem to agree on their effects. As with research on children's TV viewing, it's easy enough to point to research showing a positive relationship between violent video games and aggressive behavior,[48] but equally easy to find research showing no relationship at all.[49]

However, amid this murky research landscape and the heterogeneity of video games, it's still possible to identify concrete strategies for assessing the quality of children's video game experiences. To do this, we have to consider what video games offer and what children do with them.

With respect to what video games offer, recall one of the cross-cutting themes of this book: *design matters*. In chapter 1, I discussed the importance of considering how a technology was designed and how it's currently used, from the feature layer to the practice and culture layers.

Video games may be a gnarly construct, but they do tend to converge on a core set of affordances, or "possibilities for action."[50] Scholar Isabela Granic and colleagues identified interactivity as a core affordance of video games: "The most essential distinguishing feature of video games is that they are interactive; players cannot passively surrender to a game's storyline. Instead, video games are designed for players to actively engage with their systems and for these systems to, in turn, react to players' agentive behaviors."[51]

Interactivity gives rise to additional affordances, like a low cost of failure and immediate feedback.[52] If your player is defeated, no problem, just start the game over. You can do this as many times as you like until you've mastered the game. Video games also typically offer clear and immediate feedback to players, so that you always know where you are in the game and how well you're doing.[53]

Video games provide an optimal balance between challenge and frustration—often referred to as a *flow* state—so that you're never bored but also never feeling so frustrated that you feel like quitting the game.[54] This balance is tied to the fact that games can dynamically calibrate to a player's skill level, so that you're always being challenged just enough but never too much.[55]

Finally, many of the video games that children play today are inherently social, requiring complex coordination to accomplish specific goals.[56] Whether building structures and worlds in *Minecraft*, creating their own games and playing other people's games in *Roblox*, battling for survival in *Fortnite*, or going about their day in a village in *Animal Crossing*, video games engage children in a wide variety of social interactions, from collaborating and taking leadership roles within a team of players to engaging in outright competition.

There's also a layer of social interaction surrounding the immediate game environment, such as social viewings of gamers who livestream their game-play sessions. Indeed, many people point to these social dimensions when they talk about why they enjoy playing video games.[57]

Interactivity, low cost of failure, clear and immediate feedback, an optimal balance between challenge and frustration, and social interaction: these are the things that video games can offer children. Next, we need to consider whether—and when—these affordances lead to experiences that are self-directed and community supported—the key ingredients of developmentally supportive digital experiences.

WHO'S IN CONTROL, YOUR CHILD OR THE GAME?

There's a lot about video games that seems well aligned with the sense of initiative and ownership that exemplify self-directed digital experiences. Things like immediate feedback, low cost of failure, and just enough challenge make video games good at generating feelings of personal progress and even mastery. Such affordances are precisely why many scholars and educators are enthusiastic about modeling school learning experiences around children's video game play.[58]

However, these same affordances make video games extremely engaging and sometimes very difficult to put down. Remember, self-directed digital experiences are voluntary. Feeling compelled to earn more points, collect more rewards, and reach the next level can make video game play feel less than voluntary for some players.

In June 2018, the World Health Organization (WHO) determined that *gaming disorder* is a diagnosable condition and announced their intention to include it—alongside other disorders related to substance use or addictive behaviors—in the eleventh edition of their guide to diseases and mental health problems. The WHO defines gaming disorder as "a pattern of gaming behavior ('digital-gaming' or 'video-gaming') characterized by impaired control over gaming, increasing priority given to gaming over other activities to the extent that gaming takes precedence over other interests and daily activities, and continuation or escalation of gaming despite the occurrence of negative consequences."[59]

Although there's controversy over whether or not gaming disorder should be a formal diagnosis,[60] there are people—including young people—for whom the WHO's definition aligns with their behavior. They have difficulty controlling the amount of time they spend playing games; they prioritize gaming over other activities; and they continue to game even when they experience negative consequences (e.g., lower grades in school, loss of friendships). Although only correlational, there is evidence linking problematic gaming behaviors to psychological distress in some children.[61]

Behaviors like these warrant attention. They are an indication that the video game is in greater control of a child's attention than they are. This type of relationship to games is at odds with the qualities of play that support children's development: freely chosen and self-directed. Moreover, spending a disproportionate amount of one's time playing video games can take away from other development-enhancing play experiences, not to mention sleep, which is crucial to children's healthy development.[62]

At the same time, as I argue throughout this book, problematic behavior associated with video games should be placed in the broader context of a young person's life. For instance, what if a young person turns to video games as a way to cope with something stressful in their life, such as bullying or family conflict?[63] Focusing on their gaming behavior alone—and especially pathologizing it with labels such as gaming disorder—would fail to address the underlying cause and could even exacerbate the problem by stigmatizing or forbidding an activity that is helping that young person cope with a life challenge.

FINDING COMMUNITY IN AND AROUND VIDEO GAMES

I've already noted the social quality of many video games—the ability to collaborate and compete with friends and strangers plays a major role in their sustained popularity. Also key are the social interactions that take place on networked platforms surrounding the game, such as *Discord*, which lets players talk to each other while gaming, and *Twitch*, which lets players live-stream their game play to large audiences.

For many young people, these game-based social interactions are overwhelmingly positive and rewarding. *Minecraft*, still among the most popular digital games played by children, is one example of a game that gives children opportunities to collaborate, compete, or just have some silly fun with friends, whether sitting next to them on a couch or connected remotely through a server.[64]

They might even become part of a broader community of *Minecraft* players, such as the global community that researchers Katie Salen Tekinbas and Mizuko Ito have created through their Connected Camps. This nonprofit brings children together from around the world and, with support from teen mentors, engages them in *Minecraft* experiences that aim to develop their creativity, problem solving, and collaboration skills.[65]

Community-supported gaming isn't limited to peers; families can also come together around video games. Consider *Pokémon Go*, a location-based mobile game that uses the GPS on a player's phone to overlay a game world on top of the real world, allowing players to hunt for virtual monsters called Pokémon. Soon after its release in 2016, *Pokémon Go* became a popular game for families to play together as they went on "Pokéwalks" through their neighborhoods.[66]

Researcher Kiley Sobel and colleagues found evidence that playing *Pokémon Go* together provided a bonding experience for family members, strengthening common interests and creating topics for conversation between parents and their children.[67] The game offers many ways for families to play together—on their own phones, sharing a single phone, parents cheering their children as they hunt for Pokémon, or both parent and child hunting together as equal partners. There's even the potential for broader community engagement as families come together and interact around their interest in the game.

There are also dark sides to some game-related cultures, including games and surrounding online discussions that promote violence, profanity, racism, and sexism. An incident called Gamergate[68]—in which the misogynistic elements of gamer culture were on full display as online harassers targeted women in the video game industry with threats of violence—is a good example of how some gamers can experience the opposite of community support through their gaming experiences. Gamergate represents a very public, widely discussed example of game-based harassment, but even smaller-scale occurrences of bullying, trolling, and other negative social experiences in games can be harmful to children.

In such instances, the community support that children experience *surrounding* their game play becomes crucial. For instance, some parents have told me that their children seem agitated and revved up after playing games with violence, observations that are consistent with experiments showing increased arousal levels immediately following video game play.[69]

Tuning into these behaviors and engaging children in conversations around them is important; it creates an opportunity to discover how they're making sense of their gaming experiences and integrating them into the rest of their lives. Depending on their age, these conversations could even help children place video game content into a larger societal context, such as the underrepresentation of women and people of color in the gaming industry and sexist and racist encounters in online game spaces.[70]

TAKING STOCK WITH THE THREE D'S

What's going on *developmentally*: Children's play is serious work, central to virtually all aspects of development, from physical growth to social understanding. Play isn't a uniform construct, and the many types of play, from rough-and-tumble to fantasy play, each contribute in distinct and important ways to children's development. In light of this range, children should be given opportunities to engage in a variety of play experiences.

Play that's open-ended and child-directed is generally best, especially in early childhood. Young children are scientists who learn about their world by trying things out and seeing what happens.[71] Interactive technologies can support open-ended play, but it's not guaranteed, and many existing digital play experiences contain design abuses (like parasocial relationships and virtual trophies) that prioritize engaging children over supporting their self-directed play.

Going *deeper*: Variety and self-directed exploration in play experiences can be challenging for children to come by in the context of neighborhood safety concerns, parents' work demands, and social pressures to fill children's schedules with enriching activities.[72] These societal considerations inevitably interact with children's digital play experiences, making the optimal balance between digital and analog play (and variations within each) different across children. The challenge isn't—or at least, shouldn't be—left to families to figure out alone; societal-level dynamics call for societal-level attention.

Moving into middle childhood, we saw that many qualities of video games seem to align well with how children play and learn: their interactivity, low cost of failure, appropriately calibrated challenge, and opportunities for social interaction. And yet, research doesn't paint a uniformly positive picture—far from it.

Due to the variety of game genres and the conflicting research on their effects, it's possible to get lost in the weeds of research, news reports, and word of mouth, trying to figure out the different effects that different games can have on different children. To provide some direction, I showed how the dimensions of self-direction and community support are important factors in distinguishing video game experiences that are developmentally supportive and those that aren't.

Design considerations: There will always be limits to what children can do with the materials (analog or digital) they're using in their play. The red marker can't be green just because one wants it to be, and the fort one creates in the living room is limited by the size and weight of the pillows and blankets used to build it.

But current digital materials are a little less flexible, on balance, than their analog counterparts. The process of digitizing certain actions, encoding them in a series of 1s and 0s, necessarily constricts those actions, ruling out a range of possibilities that would otherwise be present in the analog world.[73] This places limits on how much agency can be transferred from designer to child once a digital tool has been created.

These limitations appear to be largest in the context of tablet- and smartphone-based apps. Right from the outset, one's choice of device (Apple or Android) directs you either to Apple's App Store or the Google Play Store, both of which maintain tight control over the apps they make available for download (Apple's control is notably tighter). Moreover, there's currently little to no opportunity to blend experiences from two or more different apps. In other words, these companies don't make it particularly easy to design for loose parts play.

In contrast, "phygital" toys, which combine physical and digital play experiences, offer children considerably more flexibility.[74] Smart toys like Purrble, the worried pet, and smart playground equipment like the "tube" show that it's possible to design loose parts into children's digital play by creating open-ended, flexible experiences that children direct themselves. Loose parts play doesn't mean zero support, however, especially for children with disabilities, who can benefit from structured support that matches their abilities.[75]

Consistent with our discussions of executive function and literacy development, design abuses like parasocial relationships, lures, and virtual trophies should be avoided, because they undercut children's ability to maintain control over their digital play experiences. These designs may look appealing, but remember, the quality of play isn't determined by a toy's aesthetics so much as the range of actions that its design allows.

Our discussion of video games surfaced several affordances—low cost of failure, clear and immediate feedback, an optimal balance between challenge and frustration, and social interaction—that have the potential to promote self-directed, community-supported digital play experiences. Realistically, technology designers may have limited control over whether these affordances meet their potential due to the complex ways that digital technologies interact with specific children and their surrounding contexts. But that doesn't mean designers have no control. And they certainly have a responsibility to try.

Designers, and the companies they work for, should weigh the extent to which their designs promote feelings of progress and mastery versus feelings of being compelled to keep playing in order to keep advancing in the game. Designs (in combination with moderation policies) should promote positive social interactions by aligning such interactions with success in the game and discouraging behaviors like bullying and trolling.

Designs should also give children opportunities to involve their family members in their digital play experiences. These efforts may not guarantee that all children experience self-directed, community-supported digital play, but they will make these experiences more likely.

We move now from playing to learning, which, under the right conditions, amount to the same thing. In chapter 5, we'll take a look at technology at its best and worst when it comes to supporting children's learning experiences during middle childhood.

5

THE "CURSE OF THE FAMILIAR" AND ITS IMPACT ON LEARNING

So much for play. Childhood is also a lot of work, especially as young ones move from the early to middle years. In contrast to the exuberant explorations of infants and toddlers, developmental psychologist Alison Gopnik observes: "There may be no saner and more sober creature on earth than your average eight-year-old."[1]

This chapter examines the current and potential role of digital technologies in children's learning during middle childhood (roughly ages six to ten) and how essential community is when it comes to promoting children's developmentally supportive digital experiences. Schools, families, neighborhoods, and the policies that structure them play an integral role in shaping how technologies are designed and used in the service of learning.

Above all else, the chapter addresses the discrepancy between technology's potential to support rich learning experiences and the reality of how existing technologies actually get taken up (or not) in schools, homes, and other learning contexts. We'll see that learning technologies can be—but too often aren't—designed to support self-directed, community-supported learning experiences during middle childhood (and beyond).

THE SANE AND SOBER EIGHT-YEAR-OLD

The turn toward the sober described by Alison Gopnik is reflected in theories characterizing middle childhood.[2] Freud called it the latency stage, when children repress their sexual preoccupations (we humans' fundamental motivation, according to Freud) and focus instead on developing their intellectual and social skills.[3] Developmental psychologist and psychoanalyst Erik Erikson described middle childhood as a period of industry, when children are busy learning to do new things and demonstrating their newfound abilities.[4] Developmental psychologist Jean Piaget defined middle childhood in terms of its central cognitive accomplishment: the ability to engage in logical thought.[5]

Latency, industry, logical thought—these labels evoke the child whose primary job is to learn.

As children's play changes its shape from early to middle childhood, which we saw in chapter 4, so too does children's approach to learning. Their focus narrows, and they start working on acquiring specific skills—whether reading, playing basketball, or mastering traditional family recipes. This kind of learning involves more practice and repetition than the discovery-based learning of early childhood.[6]

This transformation coincides with and is reinforced by children's transition to the highly structured environment of school. Considering its central role in most children's learning experiences—not to mention the sheer amount of time kids spend there—school will be a major focus in this chapter.

But school isn't the only place children learn, and so we'll consider some more informal learning contexts, too. Thanks to decades of research, we know a lot about how children learn best, in and outside of school. We know the value of tapping into children's interests to motivate and guide inquiry-based learning experiences;[7] providing supports—or scaffolds—that are appropriate to children's existing skills and ways of learning;[8] and recognizing, valuing, and incorporating the skills, knowledge, and experiences that children bring with them from other parts of their lives.[9]

These insights can be useful in identifying the types of technology experiences that are most and least likely to support learning. However, if I were to enumerate these tech-based experiences and call it a day, I'd be missing a crucial part of the story relating to technology and learning.

HIGH HOPES MEET STARK REALITY

A couple of months into the pandemic, I was an invited guest on *Silver Lining for Learning*, a weekly online discussion series about the future of learning. Launched at the start of the pandemic by a group of education researchers,[10] the series invites researchers and education leaders to share the work they're doing to reimagine and reinvent the processes of teaching and learning, often with digital, networked, and interactive technologies.

I was a guest with Cecilia Aragon, with whom I coauthored *Writers in the Secret Garden: Fanfiction, Youth, and New Forms of Mentoring*,[11] a book that explores the impressive amount of learning that takes place every day when young people (and adults) come together informally in online fanfiction communities to share and give feedback on their writing.

Cecilia and I waxed eloquent (or at least impassioned) about the pandemic being an unparalleled moment when we could really shake up the whole enterprise of schooling, creating in schools the kind of self-directed, intrinsically motivated learning that we had documented in our years-long investigation of fanfiction communities.

We were quickly proven wrong . . . and more than a little naive. By the end of the 2020 school year, it was evident that most teachers had turned to the same practices and technologies they'd been using to teach in brick-and-mortar schools, adapting them as necessary for online school.[12] Paper worksheets became digital worksheets. Demonstrations on a classroom whiteboard were transferred to a Zoom whiteboard.

These observations are by no means a criticism of teachers. Far from it. The pivot to online school that teachers managed in a very short time, with very few resources, was truly remarkable. In most cases, though, it was not transformative.

We also saw during the pandemic that existing educational disparities magnified and grew larger as children in rural neighborhoods and low-income households lacked the connectivity, equipment, and surrounding environment (such as a quiet space to study and an available adult to provide support) needed to log on and engage with online school.[13] There were certainly instances of transformation happening in some schools and classes, but they were the exception.

What happened during the first year of pandemic schooling largely mirrors the story of technology's role in schools and learning over the last several decades. It illustrates the discrepancy between the potential for technology to support rich learning experiences and the reality of how technologies actually get taken up (or not) in schools and other learning contexts.

WHEN TECH INNOVATION MEETS SCHOOL STATUS QUO

I started my career in education in the early 2000s, teaching the equivalent of fourth grade (nine- and ten-year-olds) in a school located just about a mile from the school I had attended as a child in Bermuda.

When I set foot in my first classroom, things looked pretty much identical to the way they had some fifteen years earlier, when I was nine. I'm sure part of the effect related to the fact that many of the teachers who had taught me were now my colleagues, and I was now teaching their children.

But it was also the classroom itself that felt familiar. Desks, placed in orderly rows, faced the whiteboard at the front of the classroom (the whiteboard was new, but the school still had its fair share of chalkboards). Chairs still had tennis balls wedged onto the legs to prevent the sound of metal screeching across a linoleum floor. Lining the walls were selections of student artwork, posters extolling the fun of reading, math, and geography, and a colorful tree cutout whose leaves were labeled with the names of weekly class helpers.

I recognized many of the same learning props used in my childhood, such as math manipulatives, flashcards, even an abacus. The school day was divided into roughly the same blocks of time, each corresponding to a distinct subject such as math or science or geography. There were weekly spelling and multiplication quizzes, math practice problems, and reading comprehension exercises.

One new item was a desktop computer that sat on a table next to the teacher's desk. My students and I loved using this computer. I used it regularly to communicate with my colleagues across classrooms (to share lesson ideas and school-related memes) and with the school administration (to receive notifications about upcoming events and disruptions to the daily schedule).

The students mostly used the computer to take reading and math quizzes. These quizzes were tied to the independent work they did after completing the main classwork assigned for that day. The idea wasn't much different from the leveled reading comprehension cards or math workbooks I had used when I was a child: work at your own pace, review your answers against an answer key, and go as far as you want to in the amount of time you have.

There were some distinct advantages to this digital approach to independent work. Once a student had completed a quiz, they printed out a report showing what they had answered correctly or incorrectly, as well as a cumulative report of their progress to date. The immediacy of the computer-generated grading saved time, and the visualization of a student's progress over time was useful. These were nice features, but they didn't fundamentally change what happened in my classroom.

What I didn't realize as a new teacher was that there had already been several cycles of excitement—and disappointment—in previous decades regarding technology's potential to transform teaching and learning.[14] It hadn't happened then, and it clearly hadn't happened over the span of me moving from a grade-school student to a twenty-four-year-old teacher.

Over the next twenty years, as I made the transition from elementary school teacher to graduate student to university professor, the number and variety of learning-related technologies increased considerably, from programmable robots and child-friendly programming environments to MOOCs (massive open online courses) and intelligent tutoring systems.

Yet even amid these innovations, school has managed to remain pretty much the same. There may be pockets of innovation here and there, but they're limited in number and typically found in the best resourced schools.[15]

Why have new technologies failed to reinvent children's learning experiences at school? It's the same reason school during the pandemic turned out to be an online version of brick-and-mortar school.

In his book *Failure to Disrupt: Why Technology Alone Can't Transform Education*, education researcher Justin Reich observes that "new technologies do not disrupt existing educational systems. Rather, existing educational systems domesticate new technologies, and, in most cases, they use such technologies in the service of the well-established goals and structures of schools."[16]

This is why, at the beginning of the pandemic, we saw paper worksheets turn into digital worksheets, and why the computer in my elementary school classroom was used for practice math problems and reading comprehension quizzes. In both instances, technology was used to replicate an existing pedagogical practice.

Reich refers to this phenomenon as *the curse of the familiar*: when new technologies are introduced, whether in school or in another context, they're invariably used at first to replicate old ways of doing things (albeit more efficiently) rather than to create new things to do.[17] The curse of the familiar may be even more entrenched in schools, which are notoriously conservative, regimented, and slow to change.

Technologies that are good at reproducing existing practices are the ones that typically find their way into schools. Newer technologies that encourage new ways of teaching and learning remain, for the most part, outside of the classroom. If they do find their way inside, they're typically "domesticated" to fit existing practices.

One example that Reich uses to illustrate this dynamic is Scratch, the online programming environment developed by Mitch Resnick and colleagues at the MIT Media Lab. Children use Scratch to design and program their own games, art, and interactive stories. They can share their creations with other Scratch users in the online Scratch community, and maybe even inspire others to remix their work into new projects.[18] Now in its third version, Scratch has become extremely popular. As of May 2022, the online community had more than ninety million registered users and one hundred million-plus shared projects.

Scratch is based on a theory of learning called constructionism, developed by Seymour Papert (who advised Resnick when he was a student at MIT). Constructionism depicts learning as an active, hands-on process that happens as children explore and create new artifacts in their environment.[19] Like other pioneers of progressive education (John Dewey and Maria Montessori, for example), Papert believed that children should be at the center of their learning, exploring what interests them about their environment, and, through their engaged exploration, learning far more than they ever could from a one-size-fits-all curriculum that emphasizes rote memorization of impersonal facts.

Most schools—especially public schools in under-resourced districts—aren't structured for these types of constructionist learning experiences. So, while Scratch is used in a lot of classrooms across the country and even around the world, these classrooms represent outliers rather than the norm. What's more, those teachers who do use Scratch still have to do so within the structures and constraints of their classroom environments. They may generate worthwhile learning experiences within these constraints, but they probably won't align perfectly with the constructionist's teaching and learning ideals.[20]

The curse of the familiar may be a far cry from the promise of transformation that many new technologies offer (or more specifically, their creators and funders).[21] And maybe that's okay. Reich proposes a middle path that's both more realistic than instantaneous, wholesale transformation and more optimistic than the status quo.

Reich suggests the value of introducing new technologies to make incremental changes to processes of teaching and learning. In other words, *tinker* rather than *transform*.[22]

A tinkerer's mindset might look something like this: At first, new technologies would be used to make existing practices more efficient (kind of like the computerized reading and math quizzes in my fourth-grade classroom). Over time, they'd spur conversations among teachers about shifts in teaching practices that—if combined with systems-level change and support (a crucial ingredient)—could eventually lead to meaningful changes to children's experiences of learning in school.

For incremental change to be successful, it requires that technology designers understand school contexts and communicate and collaborate with teachers and administrators over the long term.[23] (To their credit, the Scratch team has done a lot of work over the years to do just that, with positive results.) The tinkerer's approach also requires a willingness on the part of teachers, administrators, and policymakers (like local school boards) to try out new ways of doing things in the classroom, which is no easy mandate due to the inflexible structure of most school systems.

UNEQUAL ACCESS TO EDTECH INNOVATION

The curse of the familiar is more likely in some schools than in others. Better resourced schools, typically serving mostly affluent, mostly white students, are usually the ones to benefit from innovative uses of technology. This was the case before the pandemic, and the discrepancy only became more apparent after many schools across the United States moved online in March 2020.

Justin Reich refers to this unfortunate reality as the *edtech Matthew effect*, a biblical reference that evokes the idea that the rich get richer and the poor get poorer when new technologies are introduced.[24]

There are two digital divides that help explain how the edtech Matthew effect works.[25] The first is about access: specifically, what kind of access children have to the internet and computing devices that technology-mediated learning requires. Among the biggest disparities in technology access is between children living in low-income versus high-income households.[26] The children in low-income households are less likely than their more affluent counterparts to have broadband internet access and a home computer, making it difficult to impossible for them to do things like conduct research online, type school reports, communicate remotely with teachers and classmates, and log on to online school.

The good news is that, by 2021, more low-income families in the United States had access to broadband internet and a home computer than they had just a few years ago.[27] However, *having* access is only one part of this digital divide. Considerations of *how* children and their families access the internet are also important.

Researcher Vikki Katz uses the term *under-connectivity* to convey the idea that children have varying levels of access to learning technologies and the infrastructures those technologies depend on.[28] So, a child may be able to access the internet through a home computer, but the connection may be too slow, or there may be too many people sharing the computer, or the service may get disconnected due to nonpayment. Similar challenges arise when trying to access the internet through a mobile device (itself a form of under-connectivity due to the narrower range of activities available); families may be cut off after hitting their data plan limits or not paying their bill.

These forms of under-connectivity limit what children can do online and with computers. They also help explain why online school was so difficult for so many children during the pandemic, and why the pandemic exacerbated preexisting disparities in children's access to technology-based learning experiences.

The second digital divide is about how children *use* technology.[29] Inside school, it's common to see the exact same technology used very differently in schools serving students from privileged backgrounds compared to schools serving less privileged students.[30] In the former, students tend to use technology in a way that engages higher-order skills like problem-solving and creativity, whereas schools serving low-income students or students from marginalized backgrounds are more likely to use technology for drill and practice and to reinforce basic skills.[31]

Outside of school, the amount of money that affluent families invest in so-called "enrichment" activities for their children (things like coding camps and video production workshops) far exceeds what lower-income families are able to invest.[32] Affluent families are also well positioned to ensure their children get the types of social support (from family members, peers, and adult mentors) that will help them use technology in ways that align with school-based measures of academic success.[33]

This comparison points to the broader social and cultural forces at play,[34] even when barriers related to income and technology access are removed. Justin Reich and Mizuko Ito have identified two forces that are particularly powerful and underlie failed initiatives to use technology to democratize learning opportunities.[35]

The first is institutionalized, unconscious bias. Even when intentions are good, implementation may be undermined by hidden prejudices and assumptions. For instance, teachers working in schools serving low-income students or students of color can hold unconscious assumptions about their students' interests, motivations, and abilities, as well as the manner in which students engage with technology. These biases can shape the way teachers incorporate technology into their classrooms. They can also explain why teachers are more likely to label their students as disruptive slackers when they explore technology in open-ended, creative ways, a perception that contrasts starkly with the manner in which precocious hackers are celebrated by teachers in more affluent schools.[36]

The second cultural-level force is the social distance between developers and end users. Developers of new technologies tend to be white or Asian, male, and highly educated.[37] When they create new technologies, they're more likely to draw on their own experiences as guides for how children learn, what motivates them, and the types of supports they have access to than they are to do the work of understanding children's varied contexts and lived experiences.[38] Odds are, such experiences are pretty far from those of the vast majority of today's technology developers.

These examinations of domesticated technologies and digital divides make clear that one cannot talk about the enterprise of learning with technology without considering the social, cultural, and systems-level forces at play.

Technology is unlikely to make much difference in the way children learn in school without attending simultaneously to teachers' professional development, school curricula, the way school days are structured, and the resources (both material and social) available to students in and outside of school.[39]

With this broader context in mind, let's look at the design of learning technologies, focusing on designs that support interest-driven learning; designs that account for the diversity of skills, abilities, and ways of learning that children bring to their learning experiences; and designs that include the communities that children belong to and participate in. These are by no means the only areas worth pursuing when it comes to designing learning technologies, but they're illustrative of the potential to approach design in a way that promotes self-directed, community-supported learning experiences in middle childhood.

DESIGNING FOR INTEREST-DRIVEN LEARNING

One Saturday a few years ago, my colleague Josh Lawler, a conservation biologist and landscape ecologist at the University of Washington, was trying to meet a grant-writing deadline. His son, then eight, wasn't making it easy. Spotting his phone lying on his desk, Josh gave it to him and challenged him to go outside and take five photos of something in nature. It worked. His son came back after an hour to show off the (many more than five) photos he had taken of interesting elements in his natural surroundings.

This experience gave Josh an idea for an app that encourages kids to go outside, explore, and learn about nature through the photos they take. The app would let children collect and sort their nature-based photos similar to how many children collect and sort stickers and baseball cards. Maybe they could even share their photos with their friends, like the way children trade game or sports cards.

I was fortunate that Josh invited me to work with him to turn his idea into a reality. I can now turn on my phone and see on my screen the icon for the *NatureCollections* app that Josh and I developed with our graduate students.[40]

NatureCollections adopts the somewhat counterintuitive approach of taking the very technology that seems to be distracting children from their natural surroundings and using it to connect them to nature. At its most basic level, the app allows children to take photos of what they see in nature, sort them into different photo collections (e.g., birds, trees, insects, landscapes), and share them with their friends.

There's also a game-like quality to the app: children are encouraged to explore their natural surroundings to complete photo challenges, scavenger hunts, and even challenges sent to them from their friends. They can earn badges for their accomplishments. For instance, the Aspiring Mammalogist badge is awarded for taking their first ten photos of mammals and the Oh My G-ostrich badge is earned on reaching the milestone of thirty bird photos.

The ultimate goal of *NatureCollections* is to bring children closer to nature by getting them interested in exploring their natural surroundings, whether it's a weed pushing through a sidewalk crack or a redwood tree holding court in a national park forest. In the process, children learn about nature, their mental and physical well-being is enhanced, and they're positioned to become good stewards of the natural world.

The path from Josh's original idea and our beta version of *NatureCollections* wasn't a straight one, and intentionally so. Like so many app developers before us, we had what we thought was a cool idea for an app. Unlike most app developers, we had the luxury of a research grant that gave us the time and resources to design our app intentionally to support the kind of active, interest-driven, and inquiry-based learning that we wanted to promote.[41]

We used three strategies to accomplish this goal. First, we talked with teachers and parents about the idea and how it might fit into their existing teaching and parenting practices. We wanted to make sure that we understood the contexts where children were most likely to use the app and how it might complement (or get in the way of) the kind of learning that's already happening there.

Next, we consulted educational research that gave us insight into strategies for supporting active learning that's driven by children's interests.[42] These evidence-based insights led us to develop an interest-centered design framework, a set of design principles that place children's interests and autonomy front and center in the design process.[43]

Our third strategy was to involve children directly in the design of *NatureCollections*, a process that involved several iterations and rounds of field testing to evaluate how the app was used by different children in different settings.[44] For the initial design of the app, we partnered with my colleague Jason Yip, who directs KidsTeam UW, a group of children between the ages of seven and eleven who work alongside University of Washington researchers as equal design partners. Trained in participatory design methods,[45] this impressive group of children helped us generate ideas for features, such as the scavenger hunts, and identify usability issues, such as text that was too complex for younger children still learning to read.

The experience of designing an app collaboratively with children is eye-opening. My first and perhaps most profound lesson was that children will use technology in ways you had never anticipated . . . and this can be a very good thing, both for the tech developer and for children.

In our first design session with KidsTeam UW, we gave each child a phone and invited them to take pictures of their natural surroundings (in the form of a campus garden) for twenty minutes. What do you suppose was the first thing they did with their phones? That's right—they took a bunch of selfies and pictures of each other.

When I saw this, I felt the sort of panic I experienced as a new elementary school teacher when my students' behavior started to get out of my control. Why weren't they following our prompt? Did this mean they would go "off script" with the actual app? Yes, it did.

When we gave a working prototype to another group of children, they also took selfies and photos of each other, classifying these photos as "mammals" and putting them into the corresponding photo collection.

In both cases, however, something interesting happened after about five minutes of taking selfie and friend photos. The children began turning their attention to their natural surroundings and quickly became absorbed in the central activity of photographing, classifying, and sorting nature photos.

Rather than changing the design of the app to somehow "force" children to take photos exclusively of nature, we decided to embrace this unanticipated use of *NatureCollections*. After all, the children were doing exactly what our interest-centered design framework called for: following what interested them and making the activity their own. Our research suggests that the positive results we've seen in our evaluations of *NatureCollections* stem from its open-ended design that allows children to explore nature with their friends and family in ways that feel meaningful to them.[46]

Before my personal experiences designing an app with and for children, I believed intellectually that the best technologies were those that put youth in the driver's seat of their technology-based experiences—in other words, designs that allowed for self-directed digital experiences.[47] Since working on *NatureCollections* and other participatory design-based projects with youth, my appreciation for this point has only deepened, as well as the recognition that all too many of the technologies designed for children fall short in this regard.

DESIGNING FOR DIVERSE WAYS OF LEARNING

As a graduate student, I was advised by two developmental psychologists, Howard Gardner and the late Kurt Fischer, whose work has illuminated the variety of ways that children think, learn, and develop.[48] Howard and Kurt's mentorship, combined with my firsthand observations as an elementary school teacher, have impressed upon me that variation is the rule, not the exception, when it comes to the way children learn. Fortunately, today's learning technologies, if designed intentionally, are good at handling individual variation.

The concept of universal design is a useful way to think about how learning technologies can and should be designed to accommodate the many different ways children learn. Universal design comes originally from the realm of architecture and product design, but in the 1990s, researcher David Rose and his colleagues applied it to the design of learning experiences.[49] Their influential universal design for learning framework underscores the value of designing for individual differences right from the start when creating learning environments, school curricula, educational technologies, and so on.

Fundamental to universal design for learning is the recognition that no two brains are exactly alike or engage in the process of learning in precisely the same way.[50] The brain has a complicated structure, and it's influenced both by genetic factors and by people's experiences in their environments. There are similarities across individuals, to be sure, but we each harness the different parts of our brain in slightly different ways to accomplish particular tasks and engage in different forms of thinking. It's also the case that some people use their brains in more distinct ways than others.

It therefore makes little sense to adopt a "one size fits all" approach to teaching new concepts and skills, which, unfortunately, is what most American schools do. Instead, effective learning experiences are those that recognize and work with the diversity of individual brains and their distinct ways of learning.[51]

Recalling universal design's roots in architecture, Rose has used the example of a universally designed building to highlight some of its core tenets. Buildings that are designed universally can be accessed by anyone, regardless of their distinct profile of abilities. Take ramps as one example.[52]

Ramps are used by people in wheelchairs, caregivers pushing strollers, workers using dollies to deliver boxes, and those who just want to walk up a ramp instead of using the stairs.

The essential idea of universal design is that if you design for those people at the margins, you'll be more likely to deliver a satisfying experience for everyone. This is a very different mindset from the way most school curricula and assessments are designed: with the "average" learner in mind (who, by the way, doesn't exist).[53]

I first learned about universal design for learning when I was a student in Rose's class twenty years ago, way back when Amazon was still "just" an online bookstore, Mark Zuckerberg had not yet enrolled at Harvard, and Steve Jobs was six years away from revealing the first iPhone. Thus, the conversations we had in class about technology and its promise were mostly focused on Web 1.0 instead of the social web (Web 2.0). Even in this more static, less participatory context, however, we still had rich conversations about the ways digital and networked technologies could support learners at the margins.

Literacy instruction is a good case in point. Reading is a complex process that involves a lot of different parts of the brain working in a distributed way. This complexity means that we all learn to read in slightly different ways. We also have different motivations for reading and learning to read. It follows, then, that teaching reading should be personalized for individual learners' particular blends of strengths, challenges, and motivations. This is especially true for learners with specific reading challenges, such as dyslexia or dysgraphia.

Rose and his colleague Bridget Dalton described how digital technologies (still mostly the Web 1.0 kind) had the potential to support a wider range of readers than standard print books because of the specific ways they aligned with the principles of universal design for learning.[54]

The most obvious distinction between print and digital text is that the digital kind allows for customization and flexibility. If you've ever read an e-book, you know that you can easily change the size, font, and color of the text that's displayed. Even more significantly, digital text lets you separate content from the way it's displayed. In other words, it's possible to display digital content in modalities other than text.

I found this feature helpful when I was first learning German during my sabbatical in Berlin. I would listen to an audiobook as I followed along with the text on my phone, the dual modalities helping me map the sound of words to their textual representation. This ability to represent content in multiple ways is a core tenet of universal design for learning.

In addition, thanks to markup languages like HTML, which let you link to and view content across networked platforms, reading doesn't have to be a linear activity. This may suit some readers whose brains process and represent information in more of a web-like than a linear way.

And last, the interactive nature of many digital technologies means that learners can receive just-in-time feedback to support their learning, something we considered in chapter 4 when discussing the affordances of video games.[55]

Rose and Dalton didn't explore other, more emerging technologies such as augmented or virtual reality systems that provide immersive interactions with ideas and information, intelligent tutors that adapt in real-time to the performance of individual learners, or networked platforms whose communities of participants offer peer-guided learning experiences. But that just means the possibilities they laid out have grown even larger with the introduction of these newer technologies.

There are a lot of good models out there of schools that have successfully incorporated universal design for learning principles into their curricula and teaching practices to better address students at the margins.[56] What's less clear is what it would be like to incorporate this approach directly into the design of learning technologies.

The work of design researcher Laura Benton offers insight in this regard. Benton's work designing learning technologies for children with disabilities illustrates how individual differences can be placed front and center in the design process, with positive results. In contrast to a "medical model" approach, where problems are identified in the individual and it becomes the designer's job to "fix" them through technological solutions, Benton instead highlights the distinct skills of children with disabilities, treating them as strengths that can inform and even guide the process of designing new technologies for these children.[57]

To help guide this work, Benton and her colleagues developed an approach to participatory design involving neurodiverse children. The approach helps designers to recognize and leverage the specific strengths of neurodiverse children while at the same time accounting for and working with difficulties they may encounter during the design process.[58]

For example, she recommends structuring the environment in a way that foregrounds children's abilities and provides supports to increase their understanding of the design activities. Also important is identifying and bringing in children's individual interests and motivations so that they experience the design work as personally meaningful.

Benton and her colleagues used their approach, called Diversity for Design, to engage a group of dyslexic children in the design of a learning tool intended to help them improve their reading and writing skills. The researchers developed activities that were multisensory in an effort to target dyslexic children's unique strengths.

For instance, Lego-based tasks gave children a way to engage kinesthetically in the design process. Recognizing the visual-spatial strengths of many dyslexic learners, the researchers provided visual recaps of the previous session, a visual schedule of upcoming design activities (which included a dyslexia-friendly font), and a visual design template for children to document their ideas.

Children were also encouraged to share their ideas in a variety of forms, such as drawing, speaking, and acting out concepts using materials as props. To enhance children's engagement and motivation, design workshops were themed according to children's particular interests and hobbies.

Although Benton's Diversity for Design approach doesn't mention anything about universal design for learning, it aligns well with its core principles: represent information in multiple forms; allow children to demonstrate their understanding in different ways; and tap into and incorporate children's existing interests and passions. But Benton goes a step further by demonstrating the value of building these principles directly into the design process itself, not just the product. The logic here is that a design process that embraces differences in the way children learn is likely to result in a learning technology that does the same.

DESIGNING WITH AND FOR COMMUNITY

As the two digital divides make clear, there's considerable inequity when it comes to children's opportunities to learn with technology. Access to learning technologies, the infrastructures undergirding them, and the social support needed to use them is unevenly distributed in U.S. society (and many other societies) due to systemic inequities tied to class, race, and ability, among others.[59] Children in families with specific social, cultural, and economic resources are better positioned to engage with digital technologies in ways that set them up for future educational and career success.[60]

Design alone can't solve these complex and persistent challenges. But it should be part of the solution.

Today's learning technologies are, by and large, designed to support and reinforce dominant cultural ideas about what counts as learning, both inside and outside of school, and how it should be measured and rewarded. What's more, learning technologies are typically designed by people who've succeeded within this dominant paradigm.[61]

The perspectives and experiences of children and families who are marginalized from this view of learning are largely missing from the design process. This reality mirrors a larger pattern of marginalization among children whose cultural practices, languages, and ways of knowing don't align with the cultural practices, languages, and ways of knowing they encounter in school.[62]

The work of researcher Alexander Cho and colleagues illustrates how marginalized communities can be centered in the design process to create technologies that leverage the social and cultural resources that already exist in these communities instead of imposing external, top-down solutions.[63] Motivated by the widening gap between wealthy and low-income children's access to out-of-school learning programs, Cho and colleagues developed a technology that connects low-income Latinx parents with low-cost, out-of-school opportunities for their children.[64]

The researchers could have done what a lot of tech developers do: identify a problem that needs solving, and then draw on their own expertise and experiences to design a solution. Instead, they began their design process by talking to low-income Latinx parents living in southern California, many of whom were first- and second-generation immigrants with roots tracing to Mexico.

The researchers learned a lot through these conversations. They learned about parents' strong social ties with family and friends, including the "mom networks"—mothers who were suspicious of the school bureaucracy and proactive about seeking out opportunities for their children on their own. They also learned about the challenges that parents routinely faced: long work commutes, caring for aging parents, inconsistent or nonexistent internet services at home, and aging laptop computers.

The researchers decided to create a system that functioned as a mom network. Leveraging parents' reliance on mobile phones for internet access and their preference for SMS communication, they developed a bilingual SMS system that delivered timely, well-curated learning opportunities located in close proximity to the families' homes. After they signed up, parents received two to three messages a week alerting them to learning opportunities in their area.

One of the team members, a first-generation college student, came up with the system's name: *Comadre*. The researchers explained: "This roughly translates in Spanish to 'Godmother' but also colloquially has the polite meaning of 'the other friendly mom that you know from your extended networks, with whom you share much in common.'"[65]

The *Comadre* project illustrates the power of including community voices in the design process, focusing on their existing strengths, and using these strengths to produce technologies that augment a community's ability to support children's learning experiences.

TAKING STOCK WITH THE THREE *D*'S

What's going on *developmentally*: Middle childhood is an industrious phase when children are constantly learning new skills and acquiring new knowledge about how the world works. As they leave early childhood's realm of open-ended play and unbridled exploration, children engage increasingly with more structured learning experiences that are focused on mastery rather than discovery.[66] School is a central context for these experiences, but by no means the only one. Children learn new skills with their families, in their neighborhoods, and while participating in extracurricular activities.

Thanks to their flexibility and customization, today's learning technologies have great potential to support how children learn best: through experiences that are interest-driven and inquiry-based,[67] that account for children's diverse ways of learning,[68] and that recognize and build on the skills found in children's homes and communities.[69] As this chapter has shown, however, this potential so far has been largely unrealized.

Going *deeper*: Looking past the potential, we're confronted with the reality that new technologies typically get domesticated by schools before they have any chance to transform them.[70] The *curse of the familiar* explains how schools tend to use new technologies to replicate old ways of doing things instead of rethinking how teaching and learning happen.[71] This pattern is even more common in under-resourced schools serving children from low-income families.[72]

As the pandemic made clear, many of the same inequities that pervade schools, families, and neighborhoods are replicated, and often magnified, in the technological realm. It's pretty difficult to participate in online school without stable internet access, a reliable computer, or a quiet place to study. Beyond access, there are class-based differences in the way children's technology use is supported and recognized inside and outside of school. These differences are tied to the social, cultural, and economic resources that position affluent families to connect their children's technology use to future academic and career pursuits.[73]

***Design* considerations**: Instead of wholesale transformation, tinkering may prove a more effective approach to designing and introducing new technologies into existing learning environments.[74] A tinkering approach recognizes and works with—instead of trying to blow apart—the longstanding practices, structures, and constraints that shape schools. It creates space for educators to reflect on new possibilities without uprooting their existing practices. Importantly, a tinkering approach requires that designers spend time in the environments they're designing for, talking to and learning from the educators, families, children, and members of the broader communities who ultimately will use their technologies. This community-oriented approach to design is more likely to lead to community-supported learning experiences for children.

Three additional design strategies can result in self-directed, community-supported learning technologies. The approach used to design the *NatureCollections* app illustrated how to design for interest-driven learning. Before diving into the development of the app, our team took time to understand the contexts where it was most likely to be used; identify what researchers already know about supporting interest-driven learning; and involve children directly as design partners. Instead of trying to control and direct children's interactions with the prototype, researchers leaned into the unexpected ways they used it, recognizing that children's greater ownership over their interactions was consistent with our goal of creating a self-directed digital experience.

Self-directed digital experiences won't look the same for all children, as the discussion of universal design for learning made clear. The great variety of skills, motivations, and ways of learning that children bring to their experiences calls for a variety of entry points into learning activities. Design processes that foreground this variation from the beginning, such as Laura Benton's Diversity for Design approach, are more likely to produce learning technologies that resonate with diverse learners.

In addition to individual variation, design should foreground variation in children's communities. Currently, learning technologies are mostly used to reinforce the social, cultural, and economic privilege of affluent families. But as we saw with the *Comadre* project,[75] designers can help buck this trend by centering communities that have traditionally been marginalized from education systems and technology design. Instead of drawing on their own frame of reference, designers can shape their designs around the strengths, values, practices, and challenges of these communities.

As we leave middle childhood, family dynamics start to change. Parents continue to play an important role in supporting their children's technology use, but peers increasingly take center stage. As we'll see in chapter 6, this transition brings with it a number of fraught dynamics within families and peer groups alike, but it also introduces new opportunities for self-directed, community-supported digital experiences.

6

TWEENS: A TIME OF TRANSITIONS AND TENSIONS

The developmental period from childhood to adolescence is often fraught. Referred to colloquially as the "tween" years, early adolescence—roughly spanning age ten to fourteen—is truly a betwixt and be*tween* period of development.

This chapter examines how networked technologies add layers of complexity to the evolving relationship between parents and their tween children. It also explores technology's central role in the way tweens conduct their friendships and manage their newly expanding and increasingly intertwined social worlds.

Until this point, we've been dealing with children who are young enough that their parents are, for the most part, setting rules and managing their children's time, including when it comes to technology use. What happens when children start to own their own devices, discover applications unknown to their parents, and expect greater autonomy in their technology use?

"I REMEMBER SCHOOL DANCES A LOT DIFFERENTLY"

The middle school dance represents a familiar rite of passage for many tweens in North America. I'll use one father's description of his eleven-year-old daughter's middle school dance as an entry point to the themes in this chapter.

When we interviewed him in 2018, this father told us:

She had a school dance a month ago, or so. They had a glow dance after school from 5:00 to 7:00pm, or something like that. We [the parent volunteers] spent a lotta time breaking open glow sticks and creating awesome shirts and stuff. And then when she got done, I was like, "How was your dance?" And she's like, "Well"— and the only thing she could express about her time at the dance was how they'd take pictures, and then they would all take turns using different filters and apps to create different images of the— it's like, "You didn't dance or talk?" It seems like they just played on their phone. They took a picture of themselves having fun and then they spent 15, 20 minutes creating different images of that one moment in time. They had fun, but that was their dance instead of—I remember school dances a lot differently.[1]

"Boys on one side, girls on the other," replied a mother in the same focus group.[2]

This vignette illustrates some of today's dynamics involving parents, tweens, and technology, as well as peer groups and technology. Let's start with parents.

Dad is still very much involved in his daughter's social life, volunteering to prepare decorations for the dance and aware of when the event starts and ends. Although he wasn't actually at the dance, other parent chaperones were present. At the same time, a middle school dance is clearly a peer-oriented affair, one of several initial steps by tweens towards a peer-centered—and away from a family-centered—social world.[3]

It goes without saying that this can be a difficult transition for both parents and children to navigate. Tweens are becoming independent in some areas faster than in others.

Their ideas about *which* areas and *how fast* their independence should progress don't always align with their parents' perspectives.[4] Moreover, race, culture, socioeconomic status, and gender give rise to considerable variation across families in what this transition looks like.[5]

The concept of *individuation* illustrates the ideal outcome of a renegotiated parent-child relationship during this time. Individuation involves finding a balance between separating from one's parents and remaining connected to them.[6]

On the one hand, tweens need to figure out who they are apart from their parents, and that requires some degree of separation. They start to spend more time with peers, notice symbols, trends, and memes in the broader culture, and begin to adopt some of what they're seeing as aspects of their own identity.

On the other hand, separation from one's parents is by no means total. While they're often loathe to show it, tweens still depend on their parents for the basics, such as shelter, food, and clothing, as well as their emotional needs, such as companionship, advice, and emotional support. Home is still home base for most tweens. These dual forces explain why it's not uncommon for a tween to walk ten steps behind their parents in public only to snuggle up with them on the sofa at night.

So, part of what we're seeing in the description of the middle school dance is a father who's coming to terms with a changing relationship with and understanding of his daughter. What's relatively new is the inclusion of powerful, networked smartphones, which gives rise to new behaviors that befuddle the parents who "remember school dances a lot differently."

SMARTPHONES: DIGITAL BLANKIE, OR THE KEY TO ULTIMATE FREEDOM?

Technology is now a flashpoint for negotiating the delicate balance between separation and connection during early adolescence.[7] One of the biggest flashpoints is how parents navigate their tweens' smartphone ownership and use.

Many parents struggle over deciding when to give their child a phone, feeling pressure not just from their child but also from the norms in their child's peer group, their own social sphere, and society more broadly. In the United States, these norms place the age of initial smartphone ownership somewhere between the ages of ten and twelve.[8]

Parents and their children might agree that it's time for a tween to own a phone, but their ideas of what phone ownership means can vary considerably. Our research team talked to a group of eighth-grade students in Seattle who explained to us that their parents initially gave them a smartphone to monitor their safety as they moved between school and home, or between their home and a friend's house.[9]

For parents, the phone is a way to give their children some autonomy in their physical movements while keeping close track of those movements.[10] In this way, the phone has been characterized as a "transitional object" for children entering adolescence.[11]

We typically think of transitional objects as things like blankies and teddy bears, used by small children who are getting used to sleeping in their own bedroom, away from their parents. It's the same idea for tweens, only now the transition involves independent movement outside of the house (and the transitional object may provide more comfort to parents than to their tween children).

For tweens, the phone represents much more than a safety precaution. Yes, the phone provides a way to check in with their parents, something the tweens in our research didn't seem to mind, a small price to pay for increased freedom of independent communication and decision-making.[12]

While many parents approach the phone from a standpoint of safety and control,[13] their tween children see it as a gateway to independence. These distinct views of what smartphone ownership represents heighten an already tense period of child development—one that represents the struggle to strike a satisfactory balance between independence and connection in changing parent-child relationships.

It's to be expected that tweens resist their parents' phone-related restrictions, from rules about when, where, and for how long they can use their phone to parental controls that track their physical location and limit the apps they can use.[14] Many tweens feel that these seemingly arbitrary restrictions don't account for the varied ways they use their phones, many of which they consider critical to their increasingly meaningful social worlds.[15] Some tweens see such restrictions as a signal from their parents that they don't trust them.[16] Others believe their parents' restrictions are hypocritical when they see their parents using their own phones as much, if not more, than they do.[17]

It's also to be expected that parents want to protect their children from exposure to cyberbullying, predators, and harmful online content (all of which are real, though often over-hyped by the news media) as well as the potential for phone or internet addiction (about which there's considerable scholarly debate).[18] There's a generalized concern accepted almost as a truism that screens—whether TV, computer, laptop, tablet, or smartphone—are just plain bad and should be limited in use as much as possible.[19]

Many parents also feel insecure about their relative lack of tech sophistication compared to their children. They're unnerved that they can't see (or understand) what their children are doing on their phones; but whatever they're doing, it has the effect of tuning out parents.[20] This sense of being ostracized from their child's experiences by technologies they don't understand likely contributes to parents' tendency to set uniform restrictions as opposed to more nuanced guidelines around their children's phone use.[21]

As tempting as a safety-and-control approach might be, it risks cutting off valuable opportunities for tweens to develop independence and a relationship of trust with their parents. If handled carefully, parents' involvement in their tweens' smartphone use—and technology use more broadly—can become a meaningful component of tweens' community-supported digital experiences.[22]

That's easier said than done, of course, but researchers have found that many children actually *do* want guidance from their parents when it comes to their technology use.[23] They recognize the potentially negative impact on their well-being, and they want help using technology more responsibly.[24]

However, because of where they are developmentally, many tweens are likely to be more receptive to a mediation approach based on trust and respect rather than one of unilateral restrictions and surveillance.[25] Unfortunately, most technical solutions available to parents (like parental controls and online safety apps) favor restrictions and surveillance over open communication and trust building.[26]

Also, a tween's particular social and cultural context and individual characteristics will impact how parents involve them in decisions about their phone use, and what sorts of rules follow from these conversations.

Researcher Lynn Schofield Clark found that the low income and less educated families in her research were more likely to navigate their children's digital lives with an "ethic of respectful connectedness" that emphasized using technology in ways that honor parents (for instance, by following their restrictive technology rules) and reinforce family and cultural ties.[27] In contrast, an "ethic of expressive empowerment" was more common among higher income and more educated families. These families sought empowering technology experiences for their children focused on learning and self-development.[28]

A more restrictive approach may make sense when parents or their children or both lack the digital skills (e.g., critical information literacy, communication and content-creation skills) to navigate online risks successfully, or when children are at increased vulnerability to specific online risks such as cyberbullying.[29] Although restrictions may be preferable under these types of circumstances, they could also end up reinforcing existing inequalities in a young person's digital experiences.[30] This is because youth who enjoy access to the social, cultural, and economic resources to use technology in developmentally supportive ways will keep on doing so, while children who are excluded from these resources may be further sidelined by the restrictions placed on them.

This is tricky territory for parents to navigate. Researchers Sonia Livingstone and Alicia Blum-Ross observe that there's a significant burden of responsibility being placed on parents when it comes to managing their children's digital lives.[31] Society tells them to prepare their children for a digital future at the same time as it cautions them to limit their children's screen time. Without a model from their own childhood to draw on, parents are often left feeling ill equipped to figure out the best path forward.

Livingstone and Blum-Ross believe that parents shouldn't have to figure this out on their own. After all, community support extends beyond the family and includes societal institutions such as schools and government bodies. Unfortunately, the rise of an individualistic ethos over the last several decades has meant that the family unit, rather than societal institutions, bears the burden of figuring out how best to support children's technology use.[32]

REVISITING THE MIDDLE SCHOOL DANCE

Had we heard about the middle school dance from the daughter mentioned earlier, research suggests she would not have characterized what she and her friends were doing at the school dance as "just" playing with their phones.[33] Rather, her description would have revealed the multilayered, charged social dynamics surrounding the pictures that were taken and shared that evening. Who posed together? Who was tagged in the post, and what was the caption? Who liked the post? Who commented, and how quickly? What were their reactions?

And there's the rub. Smartphones and social media have given rise to a double layer of interwoven social subtleties: one layer in the physical space of the dance (or whatever social gathering it might be), and one in the networked space of social media. The fact that the second layer transcends time and physical space makes the stakes that much higher because they're more persistent and potentially far-reaching.

Tweens need to figure out this duality quickly. The price for failing to do so can be high. One wrong move during early adolescence may mean you find yourself on the outside of the in-group—for a day, a week, or possibly through the rest of middle school and beyond. This is serious business: defining who's in and who's out has never been so important to one's sense of self (and self-worth).[34]

While mainstream media tends to reinforce and inflate the negatives related to young people's use of social media,[35] there are positives. Networked technologies allow tweens to coordinate plans with their friends, strengthen peer-group bonds through sharing photos, jokes, and memes, and deepen friendships through intimate self-disclosures.[36]

But it would be naïve not to acknowledge the considerable stress that accompanies tweens' (and teens') networked communications. Digital stress comes in several forms, from fear of missing out (FOMO) to connection overload.[37] Within the context of the middle school dance, a tween who wasn't at the dance might experience FOMO when images of their friends start showing up on their Instagram feed. These are public declarations of peer group affiliation, and this tween is missing out.

As for the tweens who are at the dance, they might be anxious about the responses they're getting to their photos, or whether they're making it into a sufficient number of their friends' photos. As posting, tagging, liking, and commenting persist beyond the dance, some tweens might start to feel a sense of connection overload when their phone pings with notifications throughout the night, causing tension between the desire (and need) for sleep and the desire (and pressure) to participate in a shared peer group experience.[38]

An added layer of stress might emerge if a friend communicates feelings of despair about something that happened at the dance; the tween on the receiving end might feel they need to be on call and available to support their struggling friend, even if it means a disrupted night of sleep.[39]

Compare this fraught set of social dynamics to the father's comment that his daughter and her friends "just played on their phone" all night.[40] The dissonance between the two perspectives reflects the gap between what adults think tweens (and teens) are doing with their phones and what those tweens are actually experiencing[41]—a symbol of the digital disconnect that the generations find themselves trying to bridge.

ADOLESCENT DEVELOPMENT MEETS TECHNOLOGY DESIGN

The charged nature of tweens' social media experiences starts to make a lot of sense when we consider where tweens are developmentally alongside the design of the technologies they're using.

"Who am I?" and "Who are my friends?" become focal questions during the transition from childhood to adolescence—regardless of the presence of technology. Thanks to their developing skills in abstract thinking and perspective taking,[42] tweens answer these questions in more complex ways than they would have just a few years earlier.

For instance, instead of—or in addition to—defining themselves based on the things they can do, as children typically do, tweens increasingly point to the qualities they possess, like being outgoing, hard-working, or funny.[43] The same is true of friendships. Compared to when they were young children, tweens define their friendships and peer group affiliations less in terms of engaging in shared activities and more in terms of shared values, trust, and loyalty.[44] Notably, these qualities tend to be more difficult to negotiate than deciding whose house to go to or what game to play.

The new characteristics of tweens' friendships can inspire considerable stress and anxiety in tweens. During adolescence, the parts of the brain related to emotions are developing faster than those related to self-regulation and decision-making, resulting in heightened emotional responses to daily events—especially social ones—that we adults might take more in stride.[45]

With all these changes in how they see themselves as individuals and in relation to others, it's little wonder that tweens experience more daily fluctuations in self-esteem than younger children and older adolescents do.[46] Add the design features of social media platforms to these developmental patterns and we start to see why digital stress is common among tweens (and teens).

Every like and comment that a tween receives on their post represents a public, permanent, and quantifiable sign of their friendships and peer affiliations.[47] Publicness, permanence, and quantifiability are affordances of platforms like TikTok and Instagram that distinguish them from offline contexts of peer interaction. At a time when friendships and peer group memberships feel so consequential, the ability to quantify them online publicly and permanently can cause considerable anxiety among tweens.

In their book exploring the complexities of teens' networked lives, my colleagues Emily Weinstein and Carrie James distinguish between *public displays* and *inner circles*.[48] The former belong to the realm of posting and reacting to public content on social media. Public displays can be stressful because of the potential for a tween to be publicly excluded from a peer group or found wanting in some marker of social status. Inner circles, by contrast, are less public, but communicating with friends through a private group chat on Discord or Snapchat can still be stressful.

Again, design matters. If you've ever used WhatsApp or iMessage, you know about the *read receipt* feature, which shows whether a person has read your message or not. You may even have experienced the anxiety of waiting for a reply from someone after seeing a read receipt. Weinstein and James found that being left "on read" (message was read but not yet responded to) can make a teen feel extremely anxious about the status of their friendship.[49] Due to their heightened emotional reactivity and the weight they attach to friendships and social status, a teen's anxiety in this situation is likely to be more intense than yours or mine.

Read receipts are anxiety provoking in part because of what they can't tell us. We know that the recipient has seen our message, but we don't know why they haven't responded. (Our anxiety only increases if their status shows them as being online.) This kind of cue absence is common to many features of networked platforms, both public and private.[50] For instance, when a tween sees that a friend is typing a message but then the typing symbol suddenly stops before a message has been sent, does this mean the friend is annoyed? Has their phone run out of battery? Or maybe they've been called to the dinner table, and they're fretting too, about leaving their friend waiting?

The social media platforms currently popular among tweens share many of the same kinds of features, including some form of liking, tagging, commenting on, and sharing posts, as well as public user profiles and scrollable feeds. But there are some differences and they can give rise to specific dynamics across platforms. For instance, Snapchat's messages disappear after a period of time, making them less permanent than posts on platforms like Instagram or TikTok. This greater ephemerality can make "snaps" feel less weighty and consequential (though it's possible for a recipient to take a screenshot before a snap disappears).

Snapchat also has Snap scores (the total "snaps" a person has ever sent and received), Snap maps (showing the physical location of one's friends), and Snapstreaks (tracking the consecutive days of communication between two friends). Each one of these features can generate anxieties and peer-related tensions among tweens, for instance, if their Snap score is lower than their friends' scores; if a Snap map shows

their friends are hanging out without them; or if a friend
suddenly breaks an ongoing Snapstreak.[51]

FROM DIGITAL STRESS TO OVERT AGGRESSION

Clearly, networked technologies complicate and intensify
the way tweens negotiate their friendships, peer group affiliations, and social status. Things like being left on read or
receiving a delayed comment on one's post can lead to mis-
communication and unintended conflict between friends.
When it comes to *intentional* conflict, networked technologies can have similarly complicating and intensifying effects.

When I entered graduate school in 2005, adults were
beginning to notice that young people could be pretty mean
to each other online. But very few people were using the
word *cyberbullying* to refer to this online meanness. The term
is now part of our common vernacular and has become the
focus of a lot of research, news stories, education interventions, and parent worry.

News stories tend to report on the most extreme cases
of cyberbullying— so severe that the bullied young person
drops out of school, moves to a new neighborhood, or even
takes their own life. Unfortunately, these are the stories that
often come to mind when we read that about one in five
American tweens (aged nine to twelve) has been exposed to
cyberbullying as a target, a witness, or an aggressor.[52]

Thankfully, the incidence of suicide as a result of cyberbullying is relatively rare and there are usually other significant stressors that have contributed to a teen's distress.[53]
Still, cyberbullying is associated with poorer mental health
outcomes like depression, anxiety, and suicidal ideation—all

of which have increased markedly among tweens and teens in recent years (see chapter 7)—and it warrants our attention and concern.[54]

Cyberbullying is, ultimately, bullying, which is commonly defined by four characteristics: it's *repeated* over time, it's *willful*, it causes someone *harm*, and it involves a *power imbalance* between the bully and the victim.[55] Digital technologies transform bullying, introducing new dynamics and new variations on harmful behaviors.[56]

WHY DO KIDS (CYBER)BULLY EACH OTHER?

Very often, the bullying that tweens experience online is happening to them offline, too,[57] and this bullying is bound up in the many different social, cultural, economic, and historical influences that affect tweens' daily lives.[58]

There's also a strong developmental component to bullying behavior. The changes in peer relationships and self-understanding described earlier can give rise to some pretty heady peer dynamics during early adolescence. Many of these dynamics revolve around *cliques*, perhaps the most consequential peer unit of early adolescence next to best-friendships.[59]

The members of a clique signal their connection to each other through the clothes they wear, the way they speak, and these days, the emojis they use and the group chats they belong to.[60] As in generations past, not all cliques are created equal; the most enviable ones are at the top of the *popularity hierarchy*,[61] while the majority fall somewhere on the lower rungs. The tweens and cliques at the top of the popularity hierarchy are typically the ones whose appearance, behavior, and skills align most closely with the values and ideals of the surrounding social and cultural context.[62]

Tweens use their membership in a clique to help them define their emerging sense of identity.[63] This is why it's so incredibly important to them to define who's in and who's out of a particular group. After all, any sort of ambiguity in definition threatens the very definition of one's *self*.

This is also why bullying often happens within cliques—and why most victims of cyberbullying know the person who's bullying them.[64] If you're in a clique and your behavior flouts group norms, you're threatening the identity of the clique and its members. To get you back in line (or to banish you from the clique for good), you may find yourself the object of bullying behavior.

Bullying in early adolescence is often tied to social status in a mutually reinforcing way.[65] The higher up you are in the popularity hierarchy, the more power you have over those who are less popular, setting up the power imbalance that's foundational to bullying. Popular kids are also more likely to enjoy support for their bullying behavior from the members of their clique, as well as from peers who aspire to be members of (or at least accepted by) the clique. There's evidence, too, that the act of bullying itself results in increased social status for the bully, thus setting up a reinforcing cycle between social status and bullying.[66]

Who gets to be popular and who gets bullied depends a lot on the values and structures that define the social and cultural contexts surrounding young people. For instance, tweens who present a gender-typical identity (e.g., biologically male and identifying as male) are more likely to be popular, while those who are less gender typical are more likely to be teased.[67]

The dynamics between bullying and social status also play out online. Tweens who are popular offline will more than likely be popular online, too. In fact, popular tweens and teens use their online activities to brandish and augment their popularity, attracting likes and favorable comments on their Instagram posts, creating widely viewed TikTok videos, and amassing impressively long Snapstreaks. And if they're bullies offline, they're probably going to be bullies online, too.[68]

BUT CYBERBULLYING IS DIFFERENT

For all the parallels and interweaving between traditional bullying and cyberbullying, there are important differences between the two.

Consider one of the standard features of bullying: *repetition*. There's no final bell online signaling the end of the day, as there is at school. Thanks to always-connected mobile devices, bullies can torment their victims round the clock and across multiple online platforms.[69] They can also strike at any time of the day or night, from any location, putting their victims on constant alert.[70]

With features like tagging, commenting, liking, and reposting, just one mean act can be repeated and amplified without much effort from the aggressor. Consider a tween who screenshots a private message containing sensitive information shared by a former friend who's since fallen out of grace. With a click or two, the tween can broadcast the message to a wide group of people, who themselves can increase its visibility and permanence by commenting on, tagging, and reposting it. This is very different from offline contexts, where the bully typically has to put in more effort to sustain their bullying behavior. Even then, their reach is likely to be far less widespread than what they can accomplish online.

Sometimes, a single mean act can turn into a repetitive bullying experience whether the aggressor intended it to or not.[71] For instance, consider the possibility that the tween from the preceding example shares the screenshot to a group chat containing just three or four friends, not intending it to spread any further. But then, one of the recipients decides to post it more publicly, without considering the damage it could do.

In this scenario, there's a good chance real harm could be done, and it could end up reverberating for quite a while as the screenshot is viewed and spread on social media. And yet, the first tween didn't engage in *repetitive* behavior (one of the criteria for bullying), and the second tween didn't intend any *harm* (another criterion for bullying). Are these tweens bullies? As this example illustrates, the boundaries between who is and isn't a bully, as well as what counts and doesn't count as bullying behavior, are blurred online.[72]

Another complicating factor associated with cyberbullying is the absence of common social cues, especially eye contact, which can embolden would-be bullies.[73] Many tweens and teens have told me over the years that it's just easier to be mean when you don't have to look someone in the eye.[74] It's also easier to misinterpret the intended meaning of a post without social cues like facial expressions and tone of voice, further increasing the likelihood of harm, even if none was intended.

Sometimes, online meanness takes forms that would be familiar to anyone who's experienced adolescent peer aggression, such as sending a hateful text message (the digital version of a handwritten note stuffed in a locker) or kicking someone out of an online chat group (the digital version of excluding someone from the lunch table). Other times, tweens use the anonymity (or at least, the *feeling* of anonymity) afforded by social media to create inventive forms of bullying. Weinstein and James describe instances of teens creating fake social media accounts to impersonate other teens, posting embarrassing content or otherwise damaging their victims' reputation.[75]

Due to the permanence and publicness of social media, the harm caused by these types of cyberbullying acts can be long-lasting and difficult to escape. In a study of cyberbullying among Swiss tweens, participants identified anonymous bullying and public bullying to be worse than non-anonymous or private bullying, lending support to the idea that the cue absence and publicness of social media intensify the experience of bullying and being bullied.[76]

The *power imbalances* associated with traditional bullying can also be complicated online. In many cases, power dynamics online mirror power dynamics offline. This is why victims of traditional bullying, like LGBTQ+ youth and youth with disabilities, are also more likely to be victims of cyberbullying.[77] But there are also cases where marginalized youth use the anonymity, availability, and publicness of networked technologies to turn the tables on their tormentors in an effort to reclaim the power they lack offline.[78]

MANAGING THE STRESS OF DIGITAL LIFE

Tweens' networked communications introduce the potential for considerable stress, and sometimes even torment. Though more research is needed, the stress associated with FOMO, connection overload, and approval anxiety appears to increase the likelihood that teens will experience negative mental health outcomes.[79] Girls, teens low in offline popularity, and teens who experience peer victimization at school may be at particular risk.[80]

Research on cyberbullying shows a clearer connection to mental health outcomes such as anxiety and depression.[81] Cyberbullying also places teens at increased risk of suicidal ideation and suicide attempts, especially when experienced alongside traditional bullying.[82]

Despite the potential toll on their mental health, many tweens understandably don't see opting out of online participation as a viable strategy—the social costs are simply too high.[83] In lieu of opting out, then, what can be done to make tweens' social interactions less stressful?

Throughout this book, I've shown how the best digital experiences for young people are self-directed and community supported. When it comes to managing the stress of digital life, these two qualities prove instructive.

Digital stress appears to be wrapped up in a feeling of lacking control—over the number of likes and types of comments your post will elicit; when, how many, and what kinds of notifications you receive; if and when a friend in need will reach out for help or a bully will send a nasty message.[84] Feeling out of control is incompatible with feeling self-directed.

Impressively, many teens are coming up with their own strategies to take back some control over their digital lives, such as unfollowing or muting accounts that make them feel stressed, turning off notifications, and putting their phones in silent mode or in another room while they're sleeping or studying.[85] Sometimes, these are individually driven strategies, but sometimes they're developed with friends.

Friends working together to change peer group norms strikes me as particularly promising because it's a community-supported approach to relaxing the imperative to be always available and active online. The social support that friends provide each other can also help mitigate the negative effects of cyberbullying.[86]

Adults can provide community support by talking about their own struggles and strategies for managing digital stress, and by showing tweens how to do things like turn off notifications or put their phone in a do-not-disturb mode.[87] Adults can help tweens to reframe their social media interactions,[88] observing that a friend who doesn't respond immediately may simply be unavailable rather than uninterested, or that the stream of attractive images and videos tweens see on their social media feeds were likely produced with considerable effort (and possibly a filter or two). Simply asking tweens about their sources of digital stress and listening with empathy to what they say can also be helpful.[89]

Community support can be found outside of the home, too. For instance, the Youth, Media, & Wellbeing Research Lab at Wellesley College has developed a series of workshops to help middle schoolers reflect on their social media experiences and identify positive approaches to networked engagement.[90] The nonprofit organization Common Sense Media is continually adding new content to its digital citizenship curriculum to support youth of all ages engage in reflection and dialogue about their online participation.[91]

These initiatives point to an increasing recognition that helping youth develop the skills, habits, and strategies to engage safely, positively, and proactively with technology is a better way to support their development than trying (and inevitably failing) to prevent online participation altogether.

There's reason to believe these types of community-based efforts will help. Research evidence suggests that teens who experience some kind of community support, whether from parents, schools, peers, or mental health professionals, are better positioned to manage digital stress and cyberbullying.[92]

These interventions address technology *as it currently is*. But technology doesn't have to be the way it is now. Snap Inc. (the company behind Snapchat) could decide to get rid of Snapstreaks, Snap scores, and Snap maps tomorrow and dream up new features that deemphasize transactional exchanges and mitigate feelings of social obligation and anxiety.

Some social media companies are (slowly, incrementally) starting to address the digital stress they've helped create. For instance, in 2021, Facebook and Instagram introduced a new feature giving users the option to hide other people's likes and views and to hide their own like and view counts from others.[93] The company didn't go so far as to remove like counts altogether; individual users can still see how many likes they receive on their own posts even if others can't. And, as of this writing, users must actively choose to disable like counts post by post instead of setting it as an option that applies to all of their posts. Still, it's a step in the right direction, as well as an important acknowledgment by a major tech company that the design decisions that are initially made to increase activity on a platform can have negative consequences for the health and well-being of individual users.

WHEN ONLINE IS BETTER THAN OFFLINE

Perhaps counterintuitively, tweens' online participation can sometimes help them cope with the challenges they face offline. Tweens with autism are a case in point.

Social interactions can be especially challenging for people with autism—making and sustaining eye contact, interpreting nonverbal cues, inferring and mirroring another person's emotional state.[94] These challenges are likely to take on new significance during early adolescence, when peer interactions become increasingly salient and central to tweens' worlds. Social connection is just as important to autistic tweens' social development and well-being as it is for their non-autistic peers, making their difficulties with interpersonal interactions an important focus of attention and intervention.

Autcraft is a semi-private server that runs a version of *Minecraft* specifically for children with autism.[95] Created by a web developer and father of an autistic son and moderated by adults, many of whom are parents of an autistic child or autistic themselves, Autcraft quickly grew from a few dozen players to several thousand. The description on the homepage of the Autcraft wiki gives some insight into the secret to the server's popularity: "Autcraft is more than just a community for those on the Autistic spectrum. It is also a place where adults and children alike with Autism can play and enjoy the game with others like them without the fear of being bullied or misunderstood. . . . Because of how open and compassionate members of this community are, this gives children and adults the most powerful tool they can wield—the ability to be themselves."[96]

The Autcraft wiki does more than celebrate the positive environment of the Autcraft community; it claims to make participants' lives better by making them happier and helping them speak, read, and make friends.

Researcher Kate Ringland spent more than sixty hours hanging out in the Autcraft community to find out whether Autcraft really has such a powerful impact. She focused on whether the platform could help tweens overcome their interpersonal challenges and experience genuine social connection.

The Autcraft community—and the scope of Ringland's research—is considerably more expansive than the actual server, including a community website, Facebook group page, Twitter account, and video content posted on YouTube and Twitch.[97] By immersing herself in this community, observing how community members interacted with each other and participating in community activities both inside and outside the virtual world, Ringland gained deep insight into how members—many of them tweens with autism—participate in and view their social interactions.

For many tweens with autism, Autcraft is a place where they can share their feelings about not fitting in or being bullied "IRL" (in real life) with a receptive and supportive audience who can relate to their experiences.[98] In this context of shared interests (*Minecraft*) and personal experiences (autism), tweens develop meaningful friendships with other players, as well as a sense of belonging. They're able to practice social skills that can be difficult for autistic people, such as the back-and-forth nature of social reciprocity.

The features and affordances of the Autcraft platform are key to tweens' positive social experiences.[99] Most communication in the virtual world happens through in-game chat, which, compared to in-person communication, is slower paced and text-based. By removing challenges like making and sustaining eye contact and responding instantly to what someone else said, autistic tweens have an easier time expressing their emotions and engaging in reciprocal conversations.

It's common in Autcraft for teams of players to work together to build complex structures in the virtual world. Ringland observed that players often worked together on a team project in parallel, focused on a common task or goal but not communicating directly with each other. This structure removes the intensity of direct one-on-one communication while maintaining a sense of shared focus.

Autcraft and its distributed online community expand the ways players can be social, giving autistic tweens the opportunity to experience social connection and practice the social skills they struggle with in person.

TAKING STOCK WITH THE THREE *D*'S

What's going on *developmentally*: We entered new territory in this chapter with the transition from childhood to adolescence. We saw how, as tweens begin to assert their independence from their parents, they may start to develop different ideas from their parents about appropriate technology use. Ideally, parents find a way to respond that's consistent with the concept of *individuation*, striving for a balance between independence and connection with their tween child.[100] In the context of technology, this would be something between unfettered technology access (total independence) on the one hand, and a top-down, restrictive approach to technology (total dependence) on the other.

We also considered tween development from the perspective of peer relationships, which represent an important context for identity formation and social development. The dynamics involved in figuring out who you are and how you fit into the social world around you can be complicated and stressful during early adolescence. Networked technologies play a big role in this developmental work for many of today's tweens, creating new forms of digital stress such as FOMO, connection overload, and approval anxiety.[101] That's why we should do our very best to resist dismissing what tweens are doing as "just" taking and sharing pictures on their phones. The stakes associated with online social interactions feel every bit as high for them as a job interview might feel to us.

Going *deeper*: Parent-child tensions and how they're negotiated are shaped by a variety of factors within and outside the family: skills and vulnerabilities of individual tweens, as well as their parents; relational dynamics and levels of trust within families; expectations and pressures coming from peers, other parents, and perhaps extended family members. These tensions are further complicated by the design of parental controls and online safety apps, and cultural and societal norms around technology-related risks and appropriate parental mediation strategies.[102] As a result, parent-child tensions vary considerably across families.

Tweens also vary both in their risk of being cyberbullied and how they respond to sources of digital stress. Girls, teens low in offline popularity, and teens who also experience peer victimization at school are more likely to experience negative mental health outcomes related to digital stress.[103] Tweens who are bullied offline, including LGBTQ+ youth and youth with disabilities, are more likely to be bullied online.[104]

Many tweens are developing strategies—sometimes on their own, sometimes with friends—to take back some of the control that digital stress is so good at undermining. Some peer groups are refashioning digital norms in an effort to ease the pressures that come with constant connectivity and public displays of peer group affiliation.[105] Parents and teachers can support these efforts by helping tweens develop strategies (like muting notifications) and reframe their experiences (maybe their friend has a good reason for not responding immediately), and by being present to listen and offer emotional support.[106]

Design **considerations**: The features and affordances of various platforms interact in specific ways with the developmental dynamics at play during early adolescence. The portability and constant connectivity of mobile phones, together with the ceaseless buzzing of social media notifications, can play into the here-and-now focus and emotional reactivity common at this stage of development.

Popularity metrics such as likes, tags, comments, and reposts, found across many social media platforms, as well as features that are more platform-specific, such as Snapstreaks and Snap scores, play directly into the heightened peer dynamics and self-appraisal evident in early adolescence. Such features may be great for the success of the platform, but they risk introducing added stress and anxiety into tweens' developmental work of negotiating peer relationships and forming a satisfying identity.

Design does a lot to create digital stress, so it follows that design can do something to mitigate it. The decision by Facebook and Instagram to give users the option to hide public likes and views is a step in the right direction, but more is needed.[107] How about removing metrics altogether? This would be a bolder move, but one that no doubt cuts into tech companies' imperative to drive user engagement in order to grow their bottom line.[108]

In an ideal world, the devices and platforms that tweens use would be designed right from the beginning with consideration for the shifting parent and peer dynamics that occur during this period of development. Rather than amplifying the anxieties of tweens and the protectionist impulses of parents, as so many tools and platforms currently do, these designs would aim to support positive peer interactions and trusting parent-child relationships.

If only.

As we move further into adolescence in chapter 7, we'll see that teens continue to grapple with digital stress as they explore who they are in online and offline contexts, and design continues to play an influential role.

7

ADOLESCENCE: THE "WHO AM I?" YEARS

There is no time in a child's psychological development that's as marked by both vulnerability and potential as the teenaged years (approximately thirteen to eighteen). Amid the massive neurobiological changes taking place, teens face an increased risk of mental health challenges in the face of stressful life experiences.[1] Unfortunately, rates of depression, anxiety, self-harm, and suicide have been increasing alarmingly in recent years,[2] especially among girls and LGBTQ+ youth, with many pointing a finger at smartphones and social media.[3]

Still, most teens aren't depressed.[4] The vulnerability of adolescence doesn't have to result in diminished well-being. Under the right conditions, teens can and do learn to cope with the challenges they face, using them to develop resilience, experience well-being, and establish a meaningful sense of identity.[5]

This chapter continues the exploration begun in chapter 6 of adolescents' everyday experiences with technology, with the goal of identifying how and when these experiences (and the design features that shape them) magnify adolescent vulnerability and when they support adolescent well-being and identity development. We'll see that teens who bring preexisting vulnerabilities to their online activities struggle to achieve self-directed digital experiences, especially when they lack community support from parents, friends, and the cultural ideologies that shape their digital experiences.

HIGHLIGHT REELS: A DESTRUCTIVE LURE

In her appearance before the UK Parliament's Joint Committee examining online safety, Frances Haugen, the former Facebook employee who publicly leaked internal Facebook documents in 2021, testified that Instagram (owned by Facebook, now called Meta) encourages teens to engage in self-esteem-damaging social comparison and an unhealthy focus on their bodies. "Instagram is about social comparison and about bodies," she said bluntly.[6] Haugen's testimony to governments in the United States, UK, and across Europe caused the already simmering public condemnation of social media's negative influence on teens (especially teen girls) to boil over.

While Facebook's internal research fell short of being a smoking gun,[7] mounting external research supports Haugen's claims. Researchers are finding that teens who compare themselves to the images—especially the idealized ones—that they see in their social media feeds are more likely to feel worse about their bodies and report lower self-esteem and depressive symptoms.[8] These patterns are visible across genders,[9] but girls may be at particular risk for negative effects.[10]

Once again, the interaction between adolescent development and technology design can create a potent mix. In chapter 6, we saw that peers take on increased importance during the transition to adolescence. As the center of teens' social worlds, peers help shape each other's developing sense of identity.[11] Teens figure out who they are in part by comparing themselves to their friends and by seeking positive feedback from them. They use what they see reflected back from their peers to define how they see themselves.

Social media platforms thrive on comparison and feedback seeking. Instagram, in particular, has been portrayed as a "24/7 prom" and as a "princess,"[12] comparisons that emphasize the platform's focus on appearance and performance.

As a profile-based, photo-sharing platform, Instagram has emphasized appearance and performance from its inception in 2010.[13] This emphasis has only grown over the years with the addition of features such as an expanding range of filters (including face filters), Stories (a self-deleting, curated collection of photos and videos), and Highlights (a more permanent collection of themed Story segments). These appearance-oriented features are reinforced by metric-based features such as likes, comments, and view counts. The infinitely scrollable feeds that are algorithmically (rather than chronologically) curated keep users' attention fixed on other people's carefully-crafted personal highlight reels.

These features give rise to specific practices and norms as they interact with existing cultural ideologies and adolescent proclivities. A teen girl interviewed by researcher Beth Bell explained a common teen practice of taking several selfies in order to produce a single 'Insta-worthy' image: "You take fifty photos, delete forty-nine and use one." Many teens (boys as well as girls) use filters to enhance the chosen image, but there's a fine line to navigate. Too much editing and peers might call out a teen for veering too far from their offline appearance.[14]

Teens (and adults) use hashtags like #thinspo, #thinspiration, and #fitspiration to identify, consume, and circulate appearance ideals of thinness and lean, toned bodies.[15] When Instagram banned some of these hashtags, users were quick to come up with alternatives such as #thynspiration and #thinspoooo, showing how participants in the cultures that rise up around a platform's features will find ways to bend these features to their purposes.[16]

Instagram may be the princess and the 24/7 prom, but it's by no means the only social media platform that focuses on appearance. Body-related hashtags promoting thinness and fit bodies can be found on TikTok. And so-called "Snapchat dysmorphia" has patients requesting plastic surgery to make them look more like filtered versions of themselves.[17]

At the same time, not all social media activities focus on idealized self-representations. Teens create their fair share of goofy TikTok videos and take advantage of the ephemerality of snaps and stories to share playful versions of themselves on Snapchat that buck beauty ideals.[18]

Still, there's a lot of idealized imagery on social media, and there's evidence that viewing it can trigger social comparisons and make many teens feel worse about their own bodies.[19] In one experiment, researcher Mariska Kleemans and her colleagues showed teen girls Instagram photos of young women that were either untouched or manipulated with common Instagram effects and filters (eye bags, wrinkles, and impurities were removed, legs and waists were reshaped to be thinner). The teens who saw the edited images reported feeling worse about their bodies at the end of the experiment, and the effect was strongest for teens who already had higher social comparison tendencies.

But it's not just physical appearance that sparks teens to engage in social comparison online. For instance, researchers Melissa Brough, Iona Literat, and Amanda Ikin found that the aspirational nature of many social media posts made some low-income youth feel inadequate, prompting them to try to hide their financial condition in their own posts.[20]

THE CULTURAL DIMENSIONS OF POSTING

Filters and other visual effects may encourage teens to focus on appearance, but they didn't create the beauty ideals against which teens compare themselves. Those ideals are embedded in the broader cultural contexts of teens' lives. As Chloe, a teen interviewed by researchers Sarah Metcalfe and Anna Llewellyn explained: "with social media, you can't put your personality out there so easily, so instead you use your body . . . people are attracted to stereotypically attractive people."[21]

What is considered stereotypically attractive, and by whom, will vary across race, class, and cultures. In Metcalfe and Llewellyn's research in North East England, for example, masculine athleticism was expressed through rugby by boys attending an elite English private school, whereas football (soccer in North America) was the prized sport among boys attending state schools. The boys' Instagram feeds reflected these two class-based ideals.

Researcher S. Craig Watkins and colleagues describe how Black and Latinx teens living on the margins of Austin, Texas, used social media to explore hip hop culture and signal their identification with it. Some teens followed their favorite artists and bands on Twitter and posted lyrics of their favorite songs. Others found creative inspiration on YouTube, which they channeled into their own hip hop music production.[22]

Although the content that teens post on social media is largely directed at and viewed by their peers, some teens "go viral" and gain large followings on sites like TikTok, Instagram, and YouTube. Who gets seen and celebrated beyond their peer group is again shaped by broader cultural ideologies and reinforced by a platform's algorithm.[23] Researcher Melanie Kennedy has observed that the most popular girls on TikTok are white and affluent, while the videos of Black teens get less attention.[24] The combination of TikTok's algorithm and society's race- and class-based ideals of girlhood and beauty, argues Kennedy, "renders some girlhoods hypervisible and others hidden in their shadows."[25]

When Black girls do attract attention online, it's not always welcome. In her analysis of Black teen girls' twerking videos on YouTube, researcher Kyra Gaunt describes the complicated relationship between race and gender that shapes how these videos are received within the predominantly white, patriarchal context of YouTube, a reception that often involves slut-shaming, sexual propositions, and racial slurs left in the videos' comments.[26]

THE CULTURAL DIMENSIONS OF SEXTING

Cultural norms operate in the public posts on Instagram, and in the more private realm of sexting.[27]

Typically referred to as "nudes" by teens, sexting refers to the practice of sending, receiving, or forwarding sexually explicit text or images online.[28] Not all teens sext; the rate seems to be around 12–17 percent, with older, sexually active teens and LGBTQ+ teens most likely to engage in the practice.[29]

Teen sexting is more likely to be consensual than coerced, and it often takes place in the context of new or existing romantic relationships as a way to build intimacy and establish trust.[30] For this reason, sexting can contribute positively to teens' sexual development and experiences of intimacy.

At the same time, the permanency and reproducibility of digital images add a significant layer of complexity that can lead to harm if the relationship ends and one partner (often the boy in a heterosexual relationship) decides to share the images with others. There are also strong societal messages that teens receive about the deviance and danger associated with sexting, which may further complicate the practice and its role in teens' lives.[31]

Just as they do offline and on social media, cultural norms around gendered behavior shape teens' sexting practices. Boys are more likely to ask girls to send them sexually suggestive pictures.[32] When a relationship ends, it's often the boy who decides to share images of his ex with others.[33] Boys are also more likely to "collect" sexts of different girls and show them off to their friends as a display of masculine conquest.[34] These are all ways that boys perform masculine dominance and prowess through their sexting practices.

Compared to boys, girls face a greater moral panic around their sexting behavior,[35] which is consistent with other moral panics around girls' sexuality and sexual behavior.[36] These moral panics often position girls as being more at risk of sexual victimization while simultaneously blaming them for their sexual promiscuity. As such, girls risk greater reputational loss and slut-shaming in the event that sexting images are distributed to unwanted audiences.[37] Teen girls may recognize these cultural pressures, but they have difficulty applying this awareness to their personal experiences of unwanted requests and unsolicited sexts.[38]

PUSHING BACK

Many teens (and adults) are finding ways to push back against the technical features and cultural expectations that pressure them to look, act, and measure themselves in certain ways.

The emergence of *finstagrams*, or fake Instagram accounts, is one example. Unlike a person's public, main Instagram account (or *rinsta*, real account), which may have hundreds of followers from diverse online and offline networks, a finsta is typically locked, pseudonymous, and limited to a much smaller number of close, trusted friends.[39] When only your most trusted friends can see you, there's more freedom to be goofy, annoyed, bored, and unkempt.

Researcher Sijia Xiao and colleagues use the term "intimate reconfigurations" to describe how youth use finstas to create new norms, expectations, and cultures with their close friends that stand in opposition to the prevailing social pressures on the platform.[40] In this way, the ironically named finstagram may actually be more reflective of who teens feel themselves to be than their "real" Instagram account.

Beyond finstas, many teens are pushing back by following #bopo content, body-positive content that challenges mainstream beauty ideals, instead of #fitspo or #thinspo content.[41] They're following the "Instagram vs. reality" trend on Instagram where women post an idealized self-image alongside a more natural depiction.[42] And in 2021, a TikTok trend emerged showing boys rejecting the culture of sharing sexts.[43]

These are all examples of teens attempting to create digital experiences for themselves that are self-directed rather than externally compelled.

When it comes to community support, some governments are attempting to disrupt the cycle of social comparison and body dissatisfaction fueled by social media. In 2021, Norway passed a bill that requires social media influencers and advertisers to add a disclaimer label to edited photos.[44] Other countries, including the UK, are considering similar legislation.[45]

Though these are well-intentioned efforts, research suggests that warning labels aren't effective at diminishing body image concerns and could even increase appearance comparisons.[46] What appears more promising are community-led trends such as body-positive content and "Instagram vs. reality" posts.[47]

EXPLORING MARGINALIZED IDENTITIES ONLINE

So far, I've focused on mainstream social media sites and the mainstream identities that they promote. But an early and enduring (though complicated) feature of the internet is its provision of spaces for people to express more marginalized identities, whether based on race, class, gender, sexuality, migration status, or the intersections of these identities.[48]

For instance, youth who are exploring sexual-minority and gender-minority identities have found online subcultures that center and celebrate these identities, rather than marginalize and stigmatize them, as many mainstream contexts (online and offline) do. These youth represent a small but growing percentage of youth overall—according to a 2021 Gallup poll, about one in five members of Generation Z identify as LGBT.[49]

Chances are, you're connected to at least one such young person. I am.

My sibling, Molly, who had a starring role in my first book, *The App Generation*,[50] came out to me as liking girls more than boys during their senior year of high school and, around the time I started writing this chapter, shared with me that they were using they/them pronouns for now while discovering the expansiveness of their gender identity. Molly agreed to share their experiences with me about the role that networked technologies played in exploring their sexuality as a teen and gender as an emerging adult.

Though Molly and I are siblings, our seventeen-year age difference places us in different generations. As a member of Generation X, I first discovered the internet in high school, didn't get an email account until college, and was still using a flip phone at the age of twenty-five. Born in 1996, Molly is part of Generation Z, often touted as the first generation to come of age not knowing a world without smartphones and social media.

Molly discovered the TV show *South of Nowhere*—an American series that featured teen characters exploring their sexuality—when they were nine. By this time, Molly had the feeling that they were different from the girls in their all-girls' school, but they didn't fully understand how. *South of Nowhere* gave them the conceptual frame to start making sense of how they were feeling. Molly would sneak downstairs to the living room when their parents (my mother and stepfather) thought they were asleep and record episodes to watch the next day after school.

Over the next couple of years, Molly turned to the internet to explore the show beyond its broadcast episodes, which is how they discovered fanfiction (stories written by fans based on beloved TV shows, movies, and books, among other media). Fanfiction did more than help Molly understand what they were feeling; it also helped them feel okay about feeling this way: "The shows that they [fanfiction stories] are based off of were their own form of validation, but the fanfiction took it to another level that made it feel like, 'Oh, all of what I'm feeling is okay.' . . . It just gave me something to aspire to that you can't get on a TV show because it's so censored . . . and so much for a broad audience."

Although I hadn't known before talking to them that fanfiction had played such a pivotal role in Molly's sexual identity exploration, their description felt very familiar to me. My own research into fanfiction has given me an appreciation for the important role that online fanfiction communities can play for youth (and adults) who are exploring non-normative sexual and gender identities.[51] Through fanfiction, LGBTQ+ youth can rewrite popular characters in their own image, an image they don't often see expressed or celebrated.[52]

As Molly recounted their experiences with fanfiction, I thought of Ruby Davis (no relation), a former undergraduate student at the University of Washington who contributed to *Writers in the Secret Garden*, my book about youth fanfiction writers that I coauthored with Cecilia Aragon.[53] Like Molly,

Ruby told Cecilia and me just how critical her fanfiction participation had been for her during adolescence: "When I started writing fanfiction in 2010, at age thirteen, I was a queer, autistic middle schooler who had not yet realized that she was either of these things. I had difficulty with many of the social situations that came naturally to others my age, and I became isolated from my peers at school. Fanfiction communities were a vital social outlet for me. . . . Today, I see fanfiction—and fandom in general—as fundamental to my culture, identity, and community. All of my closest friends both in the physical and virtual worlds are fannish, and fandom has shaped my gender identity, sexual orientation, and political ideologies."

Molly isn't autistic, but, like Ruby, they struggled socially at school. Girls teased them for wearing clothes that came from the boys' section of The Gap, calling them "dish rag." Like Ruby and Molly, many LGBTQ+ youth who feel isolated in one or more of their offline contexts seek and find people online who are expressing and exploring similar identities, asking similar questions, and offering their own support to others.[54]

Fan communities represent one of the many varieties of online communities that provide such support.[55] Another example is the queer reading communities that have emerged on TikTok and that center teens.[56] Connecting with people in these online spaces can help LGBTQ+ youth feel safe, accepted, and part of a broader community.[57]

Although finding acceptance online was vital to Molly's identity development, online acceptance was not a panacea. In fact, the experience of online acceptance and celebration often felt jarring in comparison to Molly's offline experiences: "It was hard because you could go online and get such a sense of validation, and such a sense of "There are people out there like me" but it also made it harder in real life because . . . it just deepens the secret, I found. Not being able to share that with anyone [offline] was pretty lonely. So, while [the internet] definitely helped me feel that I wasn't the devil, it furthered my sense of "I don't belong here," so it was a double-edged sword."

What Molly ultimately desired was the experience of alignment between their online and offline lives and the freedom to express who they knew themselves to be inside. This type of self-integration is an important part of identity development and a foundation for psychological well-being.[58]

During the course of their adolescence, Molly was eventually able to bring their online and offline lives into greater alignment. In the early years of their online identity explorations, Molly assiduously avoided posting anything remotely related to their sexuality on Facebook. In time, however, when they felt more confident in their sexual identity, Facebook and Instagram gave Molly a way to test the waters with offline friends and family members by posting pictures with their girlfriend. They came out on these platforms, not with a post declaring "I'm queer," but instead by posting pictures with their girlfriend that gradually made it clear that they were more than just friends.

Molly's coming out experience is reminiscent of other teens who are exploring marginalized identities online. These teens use specific platform features to control how, when, and to whom they come out. For instance, Snapchat stories can be shared with a smaller group, as can an Instagram Close Friends story.[59]

Paul/a, a nonbinary youth interviewed by researchers Adam Bates, Trish Hobman, and Beth Bell, described how they used the privacy controls on social media to come out gradually and subtly to their family members.[60] At first, Paul/a blocked all content related to gender and sexuality from their family members. Over time, they increased their family's access to such content, using their Facebook posts as an indirect way to come out to their family instead of engaging them in explicit conversation: "if I don't have to come out to them, and they just know, that's so much easier."

During this process of gradual coming out on Facebook, Paul/a posted a trans awareness video that they'd created and allowed their family access to it. They described how they used the video to gauge their family's reaction to their gender identity: "My caption also kind of implied that I was non-binary, though obviously, the video says it explicitly, so I'm gonna post this, and see if anyone comments on it. . . . And I think a couple of like my aunts or something did like it, so I'm like, ok so cool, so they know . . . but erm, my grandparents didn't mention it, but like, I kind of want to start . . . doing that more and I feel like social media is . . . helpful for that, because I'm a bit naff [British slang for unsophisticated] at like talking about serious things face-to-face."

In addition to enabling Paul/a to come out to their family on their own terms, privacy controls also facilitated their process of integrating their online and offline identities. Like Molly, their online identity exploration was less about trying on entirely new identities online and more about exploring various identity expressions that aligned with who they already knew they were.[61]

DESIGN AND MARGINALIZATION

Not all youth with marginalized identities experience safety and acceptance online.[62] Some teens are outed by others without their consent, with negative social and psychological consequences.[63] Other teens find acceptance of their queer identity in fan communities only to experience racism for their nonwhite identity.[64]

Technology didn't create homophobia, racism, or other forms of discrimination. But certain design features and the actions they make possible can and do contribute to the risk that marginalized teens experience on a daily basis.

Researcher Alexander Cho has described the *default publicness* of online spaces that heightens this risk. Default publicness isn't so much about whether a post is made public or private as it is about a design bias that places a premium on connecting one's online and offline identities.[65] Mark Zuckerberg made this design bias explicit when he said in 2010: "The days of you having a different image for your work friends or co-workers and for the other people you know are probably coming to an end pretty quickly. . . . Having two identities for yourself is an example of a lack of integrity."[66]

It's probably safe to assume that Mark Zuckerberg cares less about our moral character than he does about his company's bottom line. Default publicness is part of the business model of platforms like Facebook, Instagram, and Twitter. They make more money when they know more about their users because this allows their advertisers to target users with personalized content. Posting under different names that don't match one's offline name or social networks makes this task more difficult.

Default publicness ignores the fact that, for many people, including queer youth, expressing certain identities can carry real risk. For example, two queer youth of color interviewed by Cho recounted how they'd been disowned by their families after family members had seen unintended content on Facebook (despite their careful use of privacy controls and other workarounds).[67]

Default publicness isn't the standard for all social media sites. Tumblr became popular among queer people—including queer youth—in part because there was no expectation to use one's state-validated name, provide census-aligned demographics, or map connections on the platform to people known offline.[68] Tumblr was also far less likely to be known, let alone used, by grandparents, aunts, and uncles, making it easier for queer youth to experience the anonymity that often eludes them on other social media sites.[69]

Tumblr made other design and governance decisions in its early days that attracted marginalized youth.[70] Tumblr isn't profile-based; instead, users create blogs to which they're free to add whatever information they wish (versus the pre-labeled cells one typically finds on social media platforms). Users can create as many secondary or side blogs as they want to, which can be made private and password protected. Tumblr invites a wider range of content than sites like Instagram through buttons signaling text, photo, quote, link, chat, and audio or video posts. The absence of copyright enforcement, targeted advertising (until 2015), and censoring of sexually explicit content (until 2018) further contributed to a sense of freedom to express a wide range of identities.

Because so many queer people were attracted to the features of Tumblr, there emerged a positive ethos around queer identity expression and discussion on the platform.[71] Molly, whose fanfiction reading has taken place primarily on Tumblr, observed: "It's a great website for people who don't feel they have a space in the [mainstream] media." This ethos extended to queer people of color, who found on Tumblr a safe haven for discussing issues related to the intersections of race, gender, and sexuality.[72]

Tumblr's features stand in stark contrast to other social media platforms like Facebook and Instagram. Consider that Facebook had existed for over ten years before it changed its code from a binary choice of male or female gender to allow for a greater variety of gender expressions.[73]

Unlike the pseudonymity of Tumblr, sites like Facebook and Instagram lean far more toward default publicness.[74] This design bias is evident when a platform requests access to your phone contacts and suggests you connect with them on their platform.[75] It's evident when you're asked to connect your user account to your mobile number, email account, and physical address, among other verifiable forms of identity. It's also evident in the skill you must acquire just to figure out how to switch your privacy settings away from the public sharing of content that's the default for many social media platforms.

All of these design decisions are fundamental to the distinct experiences that marginalized youth have on Tumblr versus Facebook and Instagram.

BEWARE THE ALGORITHMIC RABBIT HOLE

Design also plays a role in shaping the algorithms that keep users on social media platforms considerably longer than they intended. Many teens report diminished well-being after losing an hour (or six) at the hands of such algorithmic rabbit holes.[76] Though a teen may have initially gone to YouTube or TikTok to watch a single video, the algorithms that seem to know them so well kept them watching far longer than they'd originally anticipated.

Consider the experiences of eighteen-year-old Brandon, who had just finished his senior year of high school when I spoke with him in the summer of 2020. Brandon had been interviewed by my research team towards the beginning of the pandemic and had since responded to a series of short surveys about his daily activities, including how he was feeling and the way he was using technology.

Like the other teens we spoke to, technology had been a lifeline for Brandon during the pandemic.[77] He was able to complete his senior year of high school via Zoom, and he even took (and passed) two Advanced Placement (AP) tests on his computer at home. With most sports seasons cancelled, he had sustained his deep interest in professional sports by listening to podcasts, watching ESPN shows and YouTube videos, and scrolling through sports-related feeds on Instagram and Twitter.

With no commute to or from school, less time required for online classes, and the cancellation of regular commitments like ultimate frisbee and afterschool jobs, Brandon had a lot more time to play his favorite video games. He spent around two to four hours on any given day playing games like *Fallout 3* and *NBA 2K*. He found relaxation and entertainment through music and videos on Spotify, Netflix, and YouTube. Brandon's increased technology use during the pandemic mirrors broader trends among teens in the United States. From 2015 to 2019, teens' average media use increased by just 3 percent; from 2019 to 2021, it increased by 17 percent.[78]

Brandon stayed connected to his close friends by chatting with them via SMS, Snapchat, and Instagram. Twitter kept him updated on news related to the pandemic and the Black Lives Matter (BLM) protests. He also used Instagram to learn about the times and locations of BLM protests in his area: When I spoke to him, he had attended four protests with his closest friends (we'll explore social media's role in youth civic engagement in chapter 8).

Needless to say, Brandon was very grateful to have access to technology during a highly unusual time that had cut him off from many aspects of his daily routine. Even as technology kept him busy, entertained, and connected, Brandon nevertheless felt as though he was "sitting idle" a lot of the time. He described himself as less productive than he had been before the pandemic, when there were a lot more demands on his time. "I have more time to do stuff, but it's just more time to do nothing. . . . I don't have anything I'm, like, aiming towards or have to do."

Brandon acknowledged that his access to and use of technology played a role in this feeling: "With all the technology I have there's a lot of time I'm spending doing nothing and causing me to stay up till two o' clock in the morning versus going to bed at a reasonable hour and I could be getting more sleep. I could be maybe going on a run or something versus doing all this stuff, or maybe finding new hobbies. I understand that there are definitely downsides to having all this stuff at my fingertips and just watching random stuff all the time."

Technology was a lifeline, yes, but it was also a way to fill time with "random stuff" (suggested to him by social media algorithms) that left Brandon feeling unproductive and unsatisfied.

We heard similar comments from several teens we interviewed during the first months of the coronavirus pandemic, and we found that these teens were also more likely to report lower levels of well-being.[79] Fifteen-year-old Sophie said: "I kind of wish I wasn't using my phone as much, just doing stupid things. I'll be re-watching old TV shows or playing dumb games, and I don't really know what else to do." Seventeen-year-old Lily reflected: "I kind of wish I wasn't using [technology] as much, but also there's not much else to do."

There's nothing particularly alarming in these descriptions of technology use, and I imagine many of us can relate to the feeling of using technology to fill time and then feeling as though that time has been wasted. My colleagues and I have termed this experience "the thirty-minute ick factor,"[80] when people look up from their devices, typically after about thirty minutes or so, and wonder where the time has gone and what they have to show for it.

At the same time, the lack of intentionality that these quotes reveal is important, because it suggests a stance toward technology defined by a lack of self-direction. Simply put, these teens don't appear to be in the driver's seat of many of their technology experiences, and they've got little community support to help them take back some control. Instead, social media algorithms are calling the shots.

BUT ARE THE KIDS ALL RIGHT?

I've already mentioned the rising rates of depression, anxiety, self-harm, and suicide among teens in recent years,[81] as well as connections between online social comparison and negative mental health outcomes.[82] How worried should we be when it comes to teen well-being and social media, and who, exactly, should we be worried about?

Similar to debates about children's television viewing (chapter 2) and video game playing (chapter 4), it's not hard to find evidence for positive, negative, and neutral effects of social media on adolescent well-being.[83] In the aggregate, and using population level data, the effects of technology on adolescents' mental health and well-being whether positive or negative appear to be pretty small.[84]

But recall my observation in the introduction that this type of data, though useful for identifying general trends, isn't helpful in providing insight into the experiences of individual youth. When it comes to teens and well-being, we might look at the small effects identified in large-scale studies and conclude that technology isn't having such a big impact, good or bad, on teens' well-being. And while that may be true on an aggregate level, it might be overlooking important individual dynamics and variations.

When researchers look more closely at aggregate-level data, such as differences across ages, they start to see some interesting patterns. Researcher Amy Orben and colleagues identified two periods of adolescence when teens' social media use corresponds to lower well-being—the first around puberty (ages eleven to thirteen for girls and ages fourteen to fifteen for boys) and the second around age nineteen.[85] The increased specificity that studies like this provide are useful; for instance, they suggest periods when teens might benefit from delaying their social media use (early adolescence) and ages when teens may need some added community support (late adolescence). Still, such population-level studies don't tell us much about the experiences that *individual* teens are having with social media.

Fortunately, there's a growing appreciation among researchers for the value of focusing on person-specific as well as aggregate-level dynamics involving teens, technology, and well-being.[86] One method that researchers are turning to increasingly is called experience sampling, which involves collecting real-time data from individual teens—in the form of quick surveys sent directly to their phones, or passive collection of data (e.g., heartrate, steps taken) from wearable devices—as they go about their daily lives. One of the benefits of experience sampling is its ability to generate a lot of data for a single person over time, allowing researchers to get specific about how technology use and well-being change and relate to each other over time for individual teens.

For instance, in one study using experience sampling, researchers Ine Beyens, Patti Valkenburg, and their colleagues at Project AWeSome (Adolescents, Wellbeing, and Social media) surveyed a group of teens six times per day for a week to examine connections between individual teens' social media use and their subjective well-being. Forty-two surveys each for sixty-three teens, minus a few missed surveys, produced 2,155 individual assessments—that's a lot of data for a relatively small group of teens!

The researchers found that the connection between social media use and well-being differed from teen to teen.[87] For nearly half of the teens (about 44 percent), there was either no relationship or a very small relationship between passive social media use and well-being[88]; for nearly 10 percent of the teens, there was either a weak or moderate negative relationship; and for the rest (about 46 percent) there were varying levels of positive relationship between social media use and well-being, ranging from weak to strong.

If the researchers had examined their data at the group level only, and if they had not distinguished between *how* teens were using social media (active versus passive), they would have missed important variation between individual teens.[89]

Overall, then, most teens seem to be doing okay, but there are individual teens whose social media use is implicated in negative mental health outcomes. Based on our discussions in this chapter and chapter 6, teens who feel overwhelmed by digital stress, suffer from cyberbullying, engage in social comparison, and experience negative repercussions when expressing marginalized identities are the teens we should be most concerned about. This is especially true if they bring existing mental health challenges to their online activities, lack surrounding community supports, or both.

TAKING STOCK WITH THE THREE *D*'S

What's going on *developmentally*: Adolescence is a time of increased vulnerability thanks to the massive neurobiological changes that heighten teens' emotional reactivity in the face of life challenges, both big and small.[90] Though most teens develop resilience in response to the challenges they experience, rates of depression, anxiety, self-harm, and suicide have been increasing at alarming rates in recent years, especially among teen girls and LGBTQ+ teens.[91]

While we can't draw a direct line from social media to increasing rates of teen mental health challenges, there's ample evidence—including Facebook's own internal research—suggesting that social media are at the very least implicated. Research evidence shows that exposure to idealized images on social media—even for a short period of time—can trigger social comparisons and make many teens feel they don't measure up.[92]

At a time when teens are figuring out who they are in relation to their friends and society more broadly, constant reminders that one doesn't measure up to society's ideals can take a psychological toll. Those teens with marginalized identities face an added challenge due to the fact that the algorithms powering platforms like TikTok and Instagram celebrate and magnify mainstream ideals of beauty and popularity.[93]

Going *deeper*: When looking at aggregate data, researchers have found small relationships between teens' technology use and mental well-being.[94] Sometimes these relationships are positive, sometimes—and it seems more often—they're negative.[95] However, when we look more closely at individual teens—such as with in-situ data collection methods like experience sampling—we see quite a large variation in the valence (positive or negative) and strength of this relationship.[96]

Among those teens at greatest risk of negative outcomes are those who feel overwhelmed by digital stress, experience cyberbullying, engage in social comparison, and experience negative repercussions when expressing marginalized identities. Also implicated in teens' diminished well-being are experiences of getting pulled down the algorithmic rabbit hole, which can leave teens feeling they've wasted their time and displaced other, more meaningful pursuits.[97] All of these experiences are marked by a lack of self-direction, a key ingredient for developmentally supportive digital experiences.

We also went deeper in this chapter by considering teens who express and explore marginalized identities online. The experiences of my sibling, Molly, illustrated how these teens can find community and validation in online communities composed of other people with similar identities and their allies. This can be a boon for these teens' sense of self-worth and process of identity development, but it's not without complications. For example, before Molly came out to their broad network of friends and family, they sometimes found it jarring and even lonely to keep their gender identity siloed in pseudonymous online communities like Tumblr. Other teens may find acceptance for one aspect of their identity, like identifying as LGBTQ+, only to experience discrimination based on another part of their identity, such as their race.[98] These are instances when community support for teens' digital experiences is lacking.

Design considerations: Design and culture interact in complicated ways when it comes to teens' social media experiences. Tech companies didn't create today's mainstream ideals of beauty, just as they didn't create racism, misogyny, homophobia, or transphobia. However, their algorithms—programmed to attract the most attention from the greatest number of people—amplify all of these things. Combine these algorithms with image-focused features such as profiles, filters, and effects, and metric-based features such as likes, comments, and reposting, and you've got the potential for real harm to teens' mental health.

Another source of potential harm is the default publicness of mainstream sites like Instagram, Twitter, and Facebook, which encourage users to tie their online profiles to their offline identities and social networks.[99] This design bias can feel threatening to teens with marginalized identities, who may face negative repercussions if their online and offline worlds collide in unintended ways.[100]

Many teens have found ways to push back against these design features and the pressures they face online. They're searching for #bopo instead of #thinspo content, following Instagram vs. reality posts, and circumventing the default publicness of social media sites by creating *finstas*—locked, pseudonymous, and restricted Instagram accounts—which give them greater freedom to show the less packaged, polished dimensions of their identity.

Although it's encouraging to see teens take control of their technology experiences in this way, the onus shouldn't be on them alone. We know from examples like Tumblr (at least its pre-2018 instantiation)[101] that it's possible for social media companies to take into account more than the size of their advertising revenue when making decisions about the design of their platforms. Default publicness doesn't have to be the default design.

For instance, instead of making attention the ultimate goal, tech companies could shift their focus to include greater emphasis on teen well-being. This shift would require rethinking features such as recommender systems, filters, and metrics including likes and comments.[102] It would also require centering the developmental dimensions of teens in the design process, including teens' focus on identity development and peer acceptance, as well as their increased vulnerability to social comparison, body concerns, and mental health challenges.

When platforms fail to support teen well-being, community pushback has proven to be effective. Tumblr users did this following the 2018 ban on adult content by using social movement tactics like petitioning and boycotting.[103] When TikTok users became aware that the For You Page algorithm made visible certain LGBTQ+ identities (e.g., white LGBTQ+ people) while hiding others (e.g., LGBTQ+ people of color), they protested by reposting or recreating content that had been taken down, engaging with LGBTQ+-specific hashtags, and excessively using the "like" feature to promote hidden content.[104] In chapter 8 we'll look more closely at the variety of ways that young people are using networked technologies to organize and develop their voices as civic actors.

8

THE ONLINE AGENCY OF EMERGING ADULTS

Identity development doesn't end with adolescence. As young people transition into emerging adulthood (roughly ages nineteen to twenty-five), their sense of identity often expands to align with a growing focus on cultural, social, and political issues. For many, the issues that they were introduced to and engaged in during their teen years become increasingly central in their lives during this period of development.

In their late teens and early twenties, many young people have a growing desire to connect their sense of self to issues and concerns beyond themselves. This was true before networked technologies became integral, as they are now, to making these connections. Today's emerging adults are introduced to unparalleled opportunities online to express their voices publicly and connect them to ongoing social conversations.

This chapter explores the ways that young people are using networked technologies to engage in issues they care about. We'll consider how online forms of activism can be either empowering or psychologically stressful for emerging adults depending on whether or not their digital experiences are self-directed and community supported.

A GROWING SENSE OF PURPOSE

The human brain continues to develop in important ways well into the third decade of life.[1] The areas that undergo the most change—like the prefrontal cortex—support the ability to connect one's personal values, desires, and beliefs to people and concerns beyond the self.[2]

The development of a sense of purpose that's larger than the self is an important aspect of healthy personal development in emerging adulthood.[3] Through their involvement in issues like climate change and income inequality, emerging adults embrace a sense of purpose that helps give direction and meaning to their lives.

For instance, civic engagement can promote resilience and well-being among Black and undocumented youth (though, as we'll see later, it can also come with emotional costs such as stress and strained interpersonal relationships).[4] During the pandemic, which had severe negative effects on emerging adults' financial situations and mental health, those U.S. youth who engaged in actions to promote racial justice—regardless of their own race—reported higher levels of well-being.[5]

Today's emerging adults are one of the most purpose-driven generations the world has seen.[6] As they enter the workforce, the issues that these young people must grapple with are vast and, in some cases, existential: disparities in access to quality healthcare, education, voting rights, and safe neighborhoods; laws that prevent undocumented immigrant youth from pursuing higher education; rising income and wealth inequalities; climate change and its unequal impacts across the globe; ongoing discrimination based on gender, sexuality, race, and religion; systemic racism that reproduces and reinforces the unequal treatment of racially marginalized people within society's institutions; and the proliferation of misinformation and disinformation that prevents the kind of informed deliberation needed to address these deeply important issues.

Networked technologies are central to how youth are learning about and engaging in these pressing issues.[7] They have reconfigured what it means to be engaged in our world, introducing new opportunities and also considerable challenges for today's emerging adults.

SMARTER TOOLS, BROADER ENGAGEMENT

About fifteen or so years ago, researchers (and many people in the general public) were bemoaning young people's lack of civic engagement, pointing to decreasing rates of traditional markers of civic participation such as belonging to a union, attending religious services, reading newspapers, and voting.[8]

Other researchers promptly challenged this narrative, pointing to the many young people who were organizing online and acting outside of traditional institutions.[9]

An early example was a student walkout in 2006 that involved nearly forty thousand students across Southern California protesting proposed immigration legislation that would affect undocumented immigrants.[10] The students used the networked tools of the day, including instant messaging, cell phone calls, and MySpace, to get the word out and organize the demonstration. Other student-led demonstrations followed in cities across the country.[11]

These demonstrations turned into the youth-led DREAM movement, named after the Development, Relief and Education for Alien Minors Act (DREAM Act), which, if passed by the U.S. Congress, would provide a pathway to citizenship for undocumented students.

As networked tools have evolved, so too have the practices of "Dreamers." Researchers Liana Gamber-Thompson and Arely Zimmerman describe the thousands of video testimonials that these youth have uploaded to sites like YouTube and Vimeo, sharing personal stories related to their undocumented status. Other actions include sharing political news and opinions with peers on social media and publishing podcasts and blogs about their experiences as undocumented youth.

Digital media practices such as these have enabled Dreamers to build a national movement for immigrant rights.[12] Gamber-Thompson and Zimmerman observe that the ability to leverage digital media for civic purposes holds particular significance for Dreamers, who are barred from many traditional forms of civic participation, such as voting or running for elected office.

Digital tools allow undocumented youth to have their voices heard and connect with others who share similar experiences. Through practices such as posting videos online about coming out as undocumented, Dreamers are asserting their identity publicly and on their own terms, and they're receiving affirmation from others in return.[13] In this way, their digital experiences are both self-directed and community supported.

CULTURAL ENTRY POINTS TO CIVIC ENGAGEMENT

During the course of her research, Arely Zimmerman observed that many of the undocumented youth she spoke to drew on superhero imagery when describing their activism, from X-Men and the Justice League to Spiderman and Superman.[14] On his blog, immigrant rights activist Erick Huerta used Superman comics to explain his experiences as an undocumented youth in the United States. As Huerta explained, Superman was "from another planet . . . and grew up in the United States, just like me."[15]

Youth activists like Huerta use this type of cultural imagery to spark the "civic imagination" of other young people. By connecting fictional worlds like Superman's to real-world concerns like immigration rights,[16] youth can "imagine alternatives to current social, political, or economic institutions or problems."[17]

Media studies scholar Henry Jenkins has written extensively about the civic potential of youth's cultural participation and the central role of digital media in realizing this potential.[18] According to Jenkins and subsequent researchers,[19] digital media have given rise to a *participatory culture* defined by low transaction costs that make it possible for youth to create and distribute their own content to large audiences without having to worry about traditional communication barriers such as geography, time, and institutional gatekeepers. Often, this content involves remixing existing cultural symbols and artifacts, a common practice in fanfiction and fan art.

It's no accident that Tumblr attracts both fans and social justice activists. As discussed in chapter 7, many young people use fanfiction as a vehicle on Tumblr for exploring their marginalized identities.[20] Through writing and circulating fanfiction that reimagines characters to look more like them, fanfiction authors and readers critique their marginalization in mainstream culture and offer a different possibility. This is a form of activism.

Researchers Katrin Tiidenberg, Natalie Ann Hendry, and Crystal Abidin describe how the features and affordances of Tumblr helped create the site's social justice sensibility. For instance, the reblog feature facilitates remixing content by allowing users to repost someone else's post to their own blog and change it in the process (for instance, by shortening or adding to the post). Memes are particularly conducive to this kind of circulation and remixing and are frequently used by young people for socially conscious expression and political dissent across social media platforms, not just Tumblr.[21]

Reblogging on Tumblr—which allows people to join an ongoing conversation, signal their identification with the ideas being shared, and add their own perspective—has proven an effective way to create a shared vocabulary and collective identity around social justice topics like racism, sexism, and transphobia.[22] And the circulation practices (such as sharing/reposting links, memes, and videos) found on other social media platforms like TikTok and Twitter similarly support young people's collective identity formation around social issues.[23]

On Tumblr, youth have found community support from other users, but also from Tumblr Inc.'s corporate commitment to social justice issues.[24] Tumblr Inc. has spearheaded platform-wide campaigns and collaborated with not-for-profit and activist organizations such as Planned Parenthood. In 2020, they launched the #Issues2020 campaign to engage users in the elections taking place across the globe.

The connection between cultural and political participation observed on Tumblr and other social media platforms is particularly significant when placed in the context of youth development. In chapters 6 and 7 we've seen how teens look to their peers and peer cultures as they explore their identities and place in society. When young people use the hashtags #OwnVoices and #DisruptTexts to circulate and celebrate queer young adult (YA) literature on TikTok,[25] we see them connecting their identity work and peer cultures to broader societal concerns.

Such "consequential connections" are beneficial both to individual development and to the health and well-being of our communities.[26] For instance, Gamber-Thompson and Zimmerman observe that "the process of coming out as 'UndocuQueer' [undocumented and queer] is simultaneously about improving the emotional well-being of participants (a 'means of survival') and bringing greater visibility to the undocumented experience (both within immigrant communities and without)."[27]

Connecting to other engaged youth, applying one's digital skills to a civic goal, and observing the real-world effects of expressing one's voice and participating in collective action all provide rich opportunities for youth to experience self-direction and community support in their online activities.

HOW EFFECTIVE IS HASHTAG ACTIVISM?

It might feel good to share cat memes protesting Brexit or Chinese internet censorship,[28] but does it *do* anything? Civic media scholar Ethan Zuckerman observes that engaging around topics that you're personally passionate about may provide great inspiration for becoming engaged online, but it might be less effective when it comes to sustained, collective action.[29]

Zuckerman explains that personally identifying with and adding one's voice to an issue of societal import such as immigration reform, systemic racism, or economic inequality can be an incredibly effective way to bring people together initially and help them set a shared agenda. However, he notes that this ability to bring people together so easily is also one of the weaknesses of participatory media. It can be difficult to *keep* people together, acting in the sort of sustained, coordinated way needed to make institutional change.

Zuckerman refers to a "pointillistic public sphere"[30] that's emerged online: it's easy enough to find and participate in any number of issues, but this variety can lead to a problem of attention as online users move on to the next issue that resonates, leaving prior issues unattended and unresolved. This isn't good news for civic life, whose health depends on people's ability and willingness to engage in public deliberation about important societal issues, including issues that don't necessarily evoke a personal passion.

In short, digital tools and networked technologies hold great potential for supporting emerging adults' issues-related development by making it relatively easy for them to connect their interests and personal identity to broader social issues. However, experience to date indicates there's no guarantee that this potential will be realized.

FROM OPPORTUNITY TO IMPACT

Despite the challenges of the pointillistic public sphere, online engagement can lead to real change, and a lot of this change is being driven by historically marginalized groups and the young people within them.[31] In fact, Black and Latinx youth are more likely than their white counterparts to use social media for civic expression and participation.[32]

To be sure, the civic potential of online platforms isn't restricted to youth of color. Consider the students of Marjory Stoneham Douglas High School in Parkland, Florida, who skillfully used Twitter and the hashtag #NeverAgain to raise widespread awareness of gun violence and help organize the March for Our Lives rally in 2018 that sought to pressure Congress to change U.S. gun laws.[33] Another example is the Fridays for Future school strikes started in 2018 by the young climate change activist Greta Thunberg, which involve youth from a wide variety of cultural and racial backgrounds across the globe.

But there's arguably an added significance to the online activism of youth of color given that social media platforms have helped move their voices from the margins to the very center of today's social and political conversations.

Researcher Deen Freelon and colleagues found that Twitter discussions surrounding the BLM movement helped shape mainstream media coverage about police brutality, which in turn triggered public responses from elected and appointed government officials.[34] Notably, they found that the *commitment* of the BLM activists was key to their effectiveness—more so even than how many people participated on any given day.

The use of hashtags by BLM activists has proven key to sustaining attention online. Hashtags such as #EricGarner, #MichaelBrown, #TrayvonMartin, #PhilandoCastile, #BlackLivesMatter, and #ICantBreathe have been used to link individual killings of Black people by police, helping create an overarching, enduring, and far-reaching narrative about violence against Black people.[35]

From the beginning, youth have been central to the BLM movement. Many readers are likely already familiar with "Black Twitter"—Black users of Twitter who focus on cultural, social, and political issues relevant to Black people.[36] Freelon and his colleagues make the further distinction of *Young* Black Twitter, which they define as Twitter communities that "deal in topics and communication styles that appeal to Black youth: hip-hop music, culturally relevant jokes, fashion, sex and relationship advice, and Black celebrities."[37]

Young Black Twitter is grounded in Black youth culture. Black youth culture—and not politics—is its dominant focus and what keeps youth engaged over time. At the same time, political discussion regularly finds its way into youth's cultural engagement on Twitter and other social media platforms.

For instance, it's common for Black youth to engage with the accounts of hip-hop artists, many of whom use social media to discuss social justice issues.[38] In a study of Black youth (aged thirteen to seventeen) from across the United States, researcher Nkemka Anyiwo and colleagues found that Black youth who engaged with hip-hop artists through social media reported higher levels of critical agency (a belief in one's ability to make change) and activism (behaviors aimed at promoting justice).[39]

When a political issue arises that affects young Black Twitter users directly, such as the killing of unarmed Black youth, they speak out actively and passionately on Twitter.[40] The most active youth on Young Black Twitter have followers numbering in the tens of thousands, so their voices are heard by many people.

A lot of the civic expression on Young Black Twitter comes from Black girls. Researcher Tiera Tanksley observes that young Black women have played a central role in the BLM movement since its inception, particularly through their social media presence, which they use to raise awareness and mobilize people to take action.[41]

For her dissertation research, Tanksley spoke in-depth with seventeen Black girls, aged eighteen to twenty-four (squarely in the period of emerging adulthood), from the United States and Canada, documenting how they used social media (including Twitter, but also other platforms) to engage in resistance and civic participation during their time in college.

Hashtag activism[42] forms a central aspect of the awareness-raising and mobilizing work of Black activist girls. Hashtag activism leverages the indexing system that first emerged on Twitter, which uses hashtags to connect individual expressions and conversations and unite them into a broader, more visible societal discussion that takes place across time and geographical boundaries.[43]

Through the circulation of hashtags like #FastTailedGirls, #BringBackOurGirls, #BlackGirlMagic, and #YouOKSis, Black girls are calling global attention to issues that haven't previously captured the attention of mainstream media. They're also highlighting the challenges associated with navigating the intersection of race and gender in the political sphere.[44]

The hashtags coming from and circulated by Black Twitter are regularly at the top of Twitter's trending topics, a good indication that a lot of people are seeing them.[45] Tanksley observes that Black girls are often at the center of curation and circulation of these hashtags, using the resulting attention to try to change dominant narratives about marginalized people and produce real change.[46]

For instance, young Black women are among the most active participants in Twitter discussions involving #BlackLivesMatter. The widespread attention that the BLM movement has received, in large part due to these active and sustained discussions on Twitter,[47] has no doubt contributed to the movement's success in advocating for the introduction of federal, state, and local legislation around police reform.[48]

THE PERSONAL VALUE OF ONLINE ACTIVISM

The Black girls in Tanksley's research found it empowering to join their voices to a public, active conversation about issues that mattered deeply to them. The fact that the conversation was being led by Black women contributed to their feeling of empowerment and stood in notable contrast to the one-way distribution of information from broadcast media outlets like newspapers and television, which have historically foregrounded the voices of white men.[49]

One of the primary benefits that the girls associated with their social media activism was the visibility afforded by social media platforms. This heightened profile allowed them to define their own counter-narratives to dominant discourses around race and gender. This was a particularly welcome departure from the invisibility that many of the girls experienced offline as they navigated predominantly white college campuses. Another welcome contrast to their university experiences was the sense of community they so readily experienced on Black Twitter.

Less well-known than Black Twitter is Black Tumblr. Here, too, many Black youth experience a sense of empowerment and community as they share their views and mobilize around racial justice.[50]

Researcher Megan Brown got to know the personal story of one such young person in depth.[51] Brown described how nineteen-year-old Hanna—known as Belle on Tumblr—had gained microcelebrity status after posting a social critique of Miley Cyrus's performance at the 2013 Video Music Awards (VMAs).

Hanna's frustration with the way Cyrus, a white pop star, had appropriated the twerking dance movement associated with Black culture resonated with a lot of Black youth on Tumblr,[52] so much so that Hanna's followers increased by more than seven thousand over the course of just one year.

Hanna used her newfound visibility on Tumblr to call attention to the intersection of sexism and racism and call for institutional change. Brown notes Hanna's skill in using the features and conventions on Tumblr to engage in this civic-oriented work. For instance, she started #MelaninMonday, a hashtag she used every Monday for a year to promote the selfies of people of color, with the intent of helping them gain visibility and feel supported in a society that privileges whiteness.

In another example, Hanna used the now-defunct social network service Storify to assemble and organize a Twitter conversation she had had with a well-known singer about Bill Cosby and the sexual assault allegations against him. Hanna posted the exchange on Tumblr (thanks to the site's provision of multimodal posts) so that her followers could follow and respond to the conversation.

On Tumblr, Hanna found the community that eluded her on Facebook, where she had been dismayed by the racist comments of her white high school friends following the acquittal of George Zimmerman, the Florida man who shot and killed unarmed teen Trayvon Martin in 2012. Hanna and her Tumblr followers gave each other emotional support as they spoke out against the racism they experienced on a daily basis and saw in the news. In this way, they nurtured each other's personal development and self-confidence just as much as their developing civic identities.

THE STRESS OF ONLINE ACTIVISM

For all the benefits associated with Hanna's participation on Tumblr, there were challenges. As Hanna's #MelaninMondays gained in popularity, she discovered that another user had started selling branded merchandise related to the hashtag. She never saw a penny of the proceeds, even after confronting the user directly.[53]

In another instance, Hanna discovered that Buzzfeed had used one of her posts in an article, without acknowledgment or consent. It was her followers who linked the article back to her original post so that she received appropriate credit. Unfortunately, this is a familiar trend: users create content for which they aren't compensated, and the platforms that host or otherwise make use of the content enjoy healthy profits. The dynamic shares parallels with labor systems that exploit the unpaid work of women and people of color.[54]

Tanksley's research also uncovered challenges associated with Black girls' social media activism. The girls described the emotional strain associated with regular exposure to graphic images online, particularly videos of Black people being killed by police, as well as the anti-Black rhetoric that typically arises in the wake of such videos.

The girls also spoke about their experiences of direct personal harassment online, which was especially likely to happen when they posted something that was widely circulated. For these girls, their visibility online, while empowering, often came with an emotional cost.[55]

Other researchers have similarly documented the emotional strain of encountering racism, negative stereotypes, and other hurtful content online, which is unfortunately a too-common experience among marginalized youth.[56]

One strategy that the participants in Tanksley's research used to cope with the images of death and anti-Black rhetoric they experienced online was simply to log off and tune out.

This is an understandable response to the emotional exhaustion of witnessing death and defending oneself against hate speech on a daily basis.

However, just a few years after Tanksley's research, logging off doesn't feel like an option for a lot of young people.

Amid a global pandemic, a contentious U.S. election, and mass protests following the murders of George Floyd, Breonna Taylor, and Ahmaud Arbery, young people's cultural, social, and political engagement rose online and offline during 2020.[57] For many, taking a stand on such social issues shifted from a matter of personal preference to a community-enforced imperative.

The youth that researchers Emily Weinstein and Carrie James spoke to during 2020 and 2021 described the pressure they felt from their peer group to speak out online about the issues roiling around them, especially in relation to the BLM movement. Both white youth and youth of color felt pressure to take a stand as their peers monitored who was and wasn't posting. For youth of color, not posting was seen by some of their peers as not caring or even as a betrayal of their race, even if they were highly involved in racial justice work offline. White youth worried that not posting would be seen as implicitly endorsing police brutality and systemic racism.[58]

When they did post, youth felt pressure to get it right.[59] A post seen as too self-centering or superficial could result in accusations of *performative activism*—publicly performing rather than authentically engaging in social and political issues. Pressures around posting were especially complicated for youth living in ideologically diverse communities, where posting in solidarity with the BLM movement might resonate with some followers while offending others.[60] This concern with getting it right, which is also felt by many older adults who want to say and do the right thing, has the unintended consequence of undermining the necessary goal of bringing about sustained social change.

Weinstein and James observe that the stakes are high for youth when it comes to their online civic expressions. Friendships can be severed, while some youth experience online bullying and even physical violence offline. Youth of color experience added risks, such as having their online activities surveilled by law enforcement.[61]

THE DEVELOPMENTAL STING OF ONLINE CONFLICT

What impact do the pressures and challenges associated with online civic expression have on emerging adults' approach to civic participation more generally? Researcher Ellen Middaugh has explored the nature of online political discourse as a context for young people's civic development. Her research addresses head-on a tension associated with participatory media.

On the one hand, as we've discussed, today's digital tools and networked technologies have done a lot to democratize access to and engagement in political conversations, including for youth who are often excluded from institutionalized forms of political and civic engagement. On the other hand, this increased access has also meant more exposure to conflict- and misinformation-filled discussions that bear little resemblance to the deliberative processes that are a hallmark of healthy democracies. There's also the danger of getting caught in algorithmically controlled filter bubbles that reinforce existing beliefs and contribute to ideological polarization.[62]

For anyone who has logged onto Twitter and scrolled through the trending topics, it will come as little surprise that Middaugh and her colleagues found that those young people who are most active in online political discussions— like the Black girls in Tanksley's study—experience the most conflict online.[63] Further, the more participatory the media (i.e., the ability to comment, share, and "like" content), the more conflict these youth experience. Again, this isn't surprising, but it does suggest that young people today are exposed to more political conflict than in previous generations when political information was accessed primarily through broadcast media.

Middaugh and her colleagues raise the concern that participation in highly emotional and conflict-filled political discourse online may undercut the personal and societal benefits associated with participatory media discussed earlier in this chapter.

Researchers have shown how exposure to online conflict and incivility (such as insults, mockery, and name-calling)[64] can cause some people, including young people,[65] to dig into their existing values and beliefs and engage in uncivil behavior themselves.[66] This dynamic undermines public deliberation and contributes to ideological polarization.[67]

DESIGN'S CURRENT AND POTENTIAL IMPACT

Technology isn't neutral in discussions of youth's online civic engagement. Incivility may be unpleasant for some, but it's highly engaging for many.[68] As a result, social media companies have a financial interest in employing algorithms that promote uncivil (but perhaps not extremist) speech online.[69]

Further, platforms that emphasize text (Twitter, Reddit) rather than images and video (Instagram, TikTok, YouTube) may breed more arguments because of the increased visibility of comments, the lack of social cues like facial expressions, and the lack of space to explain the nuances of one's point of view.[70] Coming across a politically-charged tweet while scrolling through a Twitter feed can make it difficult to understand the broader context of the tweet.[71]

Censorship and heavy moderation, such as turning off comments for controversial YouTube videos or removing videos outright, can also introduce barriers to productive discussion online, especially when the motivation behind these decisions is unclear or seen to be excluding the voices of already marginalized people.[72] Even without intentional censorship or moderation, algorithms can replicate cultural biases by magnifying mainstream voices and suppressing marginalized ones.[73]

How might platforms be designed to support good-faith online arguments that empower rather than deplete people? A team of researchers at the University of Washington identified several promising design opportunities. For instance, they proposed a feature that makes it easy to move a contentious discussion seamlessly from a public to a private space, much as people do when offline conversations become heated.[74] Other research demonstrating the relative civility of political discussions on private WhatsApp groups in comparison to the incivility found on Twitter suggests this approach has promise.[75]

The University of Washington researchers also recommend involving users directly in the research and design surrounding platform development, for instance, by giving them a say in algorithmic design and moderation decisions. They also suggest that designers broaden their focus to include not just individual users but rather users engaging in interpersonal interactions—an approach they call *interpersonal design*.

Researchers at Georgia Tech are similarly seeking design-based approaches to supporting online civic engagement. Researcher Andrea Parker and her colleagues observed that social media platforms are currently designed in such a way that makes it difficult to readily see the features of one's network. (Can you name all the people you follow and who follow you on any given platform? What about who *they* follow? Do you have a good sense of the posting patterns of all your followers—how often and what they post?) This opacity makes it challenging for young activists to understand and make strategic use of the social capital within their online social networks.

This challenge led the researchers to explore design solutions that could help young people tap into their online social networks more effectively for the purposes of engaging in strategic collective action. In an initial exploratory study, Parker and her colleagues developed low-fidelity prototype visualization tools that display information and characteristics about a user's (hypothetical) Twitter followers.[76] For instance, one of the tools lists a user's followers along with characteristics of each follower, such as their age, level of activity on social media, number of followers, and their most commonly-used hashtags.

When the researchers showed the tools to a group of youth activists, they resoundingly identified the hashtag feature as being the most useful. Participants felt that seeing commonly-used hashtags would help them understand their followers' interests and mindsets, and based on these insights, give them ideas about how to mobilize them.[77] Although exploratory, this work illustrates how social media platforms and other networked technologies could be designed more purposefully to support young people's civic engagement.

TAKING STOCK WITH THE THREE *D*'S

What's going on *developmentally*: During emerging adulthood, many young people become engaged in social and political issues, using them to develop a sense of purpose. Networked technologies have become integral to this engagement, introducing unparalleled opportunities for emerging adults to express their voices publicly and connect them to ongoing social conversations.[78]

We saw how emerging adults continue to use the features and affordances of social media to circulate cultural symbols like memes and fan-related imagery. These practices help young people tap into their "civic imagination"[79] as they build a common vocabulary and collective identity around the social issues they care about.[80] At its best, online civic expression is self-directed and community supported, marked by feelings of personal empowerment and community recognition and validation.

But there are real challenges associated with emerging adults' online expression, particularly for young people of color and marginalized youth, that can make them feel less than empowered and pressured rather than supported by those around them.[81] Feeling compelled to speak out on certain social issues, or worrying that your friends are policing your posts for substance and authenticity, undercuts the agency afforded by online expression.

Going *deeper*: We explored how Black youth, particularly Black girls, are using platforms like Twitter and Tumblr to speak out against systemic racism, police brutality, and other issues that affect them and their communities.[82] Young Black women have been instrumental in using Twitter to raise the visibility of the BLM movement, skillfully employing hashtags to connect people, events, and instances of violence against Black people and form a lasting movement with real political influence.[83]

Black girls' online participation contributes to their civic development by nurturing feelings of empowerment and a sense of community, but it can also come with challenges.[84] Like other young people, Black girls experience the pressure to signal their social justice commitments online and do so in a way that resonates with their followers, which can be particularly challenging if their followers represent diverse viewpoints.[85] Additional emotional costs come from exposure to violent, racist content and even direct personal harassment.[86]

Design **considerations**: There's a lot to be optimistic about when it comes to technology's role in supporting emerging adults' civic engagement. The fact that anyone with an internet-enabled device can express a viewpoint makes for an extremely low entry bar to civic expression. Young people can bypass traditional gatekeepers such as broadcast media, which is particularly meaningful for marginalized youth whose voices have historically been underrepresented by these gatekeepers.

Platform-created features like reblogging and reposting, and user-generated features like hashtags, facilitate collective identity, discussion, and organizing. Tumblr is one example of how the features, affordances, and cultures that form within a platform can lead to a social justice sensibility that has a powerful influence on young people's civic development.[87]

Technology also presents obstacles to emerging adults' civic engagement. A major challenge is the use of algorithms that magnify sensational—and uncivil—content, which can fuel polarization and dampen public deliberation.[88] Regrettably, this kind of content is far more attention-grabbing than civil discussions, which means social media companies have little financial incentive to alter their algorithms. Algorithms can also highlight certain voices over others, which can further marginalize people and groups already marginalized from mainstream culture.[89]

Design can help address these challenges to generative online discussion, such as by involving users in algorithmic design, focusing on relationships in the design process, and introducing features that help diffuse rather than enflame high-conflict discussions and trolling behaviors (YouTube's decision in 2021 to remove the "dislike" button is an example of one such effort).[90] Unfortunately, design cannot alter the financial incentives of social media companies. As we'll discuss in the final chapter, we need government regulation to help with that.

Another challenge posed by the pointillistic public sphere of online engagement is sustaining young people's attention long enough and deeply enough to bring about desired changes.[91] It's easy enough to post in solidarity of the BLM movement, especially when everyone else is doing it, but what will you do when your friends stop expecting this of you?

Related to sustaining attention is the challenge of leveraging the potential of young people's online social networks to mobilize for real-world change. The social network visualizations created by Andrea Parker and her lab at Georgia Tech are one example of using design to provide real-time, in-situ supports for recognizing and acting on the many opportunities for civic action that networked technologies present.[92]

Although the process of development is a lifelong affair—and technology certainly continues to play an important role in the lives of adults—emerging adulthood is where this book's investigation ends. In the final chapter, I'll bring together the themes explored in these pages and offer a path forward for promoting young people's self-directed, community-supported digital experiences across the stages of child development. Technology design plays an important role, but there are other stakeholders who must also step up.

9

CONCLUSION

Context, technology design, and individual children. These are the three themes I introduced at the beginning of the book, and they are what determines whether digital experiences are self-directed and community supported.

Figure 9.1 brings these components together into a model of developmentally supportive digital experiences. On the left are the three themes. In the best of circumstances, they give rise to self-directed, community-supported digital experiences, which are shown in the center.

On the right are the three dimensions of healthy development—a sense of ownership and initiative, feelings of competence and mastery, and a sense of belonging and connection[1]—that are made possible when technology experiences are self-directed and community supported.

Now that we know what developmentally supportive digital experiences look like, let's consider how those who have an impact on a child's development can make these positive experiences the rule rather than the exception for technology's child.

Factors shaping children's tech experiences	**Qualities** of developmentally supportive tech experiences	**Outcomes** of developmentally supportive tech experiences

9.1   A model of developmentally supportive digital experiences

TECHNOLOGY DESIGNERS

Technology designers and product teams should adopt a child-centered approach to technology design that prioritizes self-directed, community supported digital experiences. Such an approach to design places children in the driver's seat of their actions and encourages interactions with meaningful people in their lives.[2]

More specifically, a child-centered design approach **prioritizes self-paced, flexible** interactions over system-paced, closed-ended ones. It **enables shared experiences** with meaningful people in children's lives, whether that's parents (for younger children) or peers (for older children, teens, and emerging adults).

Designers who adopt a child-centered design approach **consider the range of cognitive and physical abilities** of the children who will use their technologies, drawing on research-based evidence. They also use research evidence to

identify common developmental vulnerabilities of their target users (for instance, social comparison and body image concerns among teens) and consider how design features (such as social media metrics) are likely to interact with these vulnerabilities, recognizing that not all young people share the same level of risk.

A child-centered design approach **provides opportunities for a broad range of youth**, including those who are marginalized, to engage meaningfully in a digital experience. They don't assume a one-size-fits-all solution to technology design. **Involving children and the members of their communities** (parents, teachers, pediatricians) in the design process can help accomplish this goal. Taking a collaborative approach to design increases the likelihood that the resulting technologies will align with the lived experiences, motivations, and sources of support that children of diverse backgrounds bring to their digital experiences. It also helps avoid a situation—too common today—in which technologies cater to those youth whose cultural, social, political, and economic backgrounds align with the developers who made them.

A child-centered design approach **avoids dark patterns and design abuses** such as autoplay, parasocial relationships, and social media metrics. If such features are employed, they're easy to disable. Other distractions, acting as unnecessary bells and whistles, are also avoided. Instead, design abuses and distractions are replaced by prompts to self-reflect and tune into internal cues and decision-making.[3]

For those tech companies whose platforms control children's access to a wide range of digital content (such as app marketplaces and video-on-demand services), a child-centered design approach would **surface high-quality digital content** rather than placing the burden on users (particularly parents) to search for and identify it on their own.[4]

Some of these strategies will be easier to implement than others. For instance, designing for children's cognitive and physical abilities may take effort, but it's probably effort that companies are willing to invest in because when more children can use a technology, more of that technology is likely to be sold. Other strategies, like avoiding design abuses, are not so well aligned with the bottom line. This reality makes it difficult—if not impossible—for designers alone to implement a child-centered design approach.

TECHNOLOGY COMPANIES

For a child-centered design approach to become standard practice in technology design, the corporate structures and incentives that prioritize engagement and attention over self-direction and community support need to change.

In their 2021 book *System Error: Where Big Tech Went Wrong and How We Can Reboot*, Rob Reich, Mehran Sahami, and Jeremy M. Weinstein observe that most tech companies follow a business model that reflects an engineering mindset, emphasizing measurement and optimization. Those things that can be measured easily, such as click-through rates and time on platform, are prioritized, while values such as human flourishing and well-being, which are much harder to measure, much harder to optimize for, are deemphasized.[5]

It doesn't have to be this way. As Justin Rosenstein, a former engineer at Facebook and Google, observed in the 2020 documentary *The Social Dilemma*: "The way that technology works is not a law of physics. It is not set in stone. These are choices that human beings, like me, have been making. And human beings can change those technologies."[6]

It may require substantial government regulation (discussion to follow), but tech companies can change the way they currently operate. Leadership from within companies is crucial, however. As researchers Amanda Lenhart and Kellie Owens observe: "Leadership sets the tone for organizational culture, values, and decision-making."[7] In their interviews with tech industry insiders, Lenhart and Owens found that adolescents are typically an afterthought in the design process, and concerns over users' well-being are often siloed in peripheral teams or distributed across teams that have no real power to make change. These are organizational decisions that can and must be changed.

Lenhart and Owens recommend that tech companies integrate expertise about well-being into all product teams and across all aspects of the design process—including once a product is launched—to help nurture a positive culture around its use. I suggest extending this recommendation to include expertise about child development so that product teams consider the range of abilities, strengths, and vulnerabilities associated with different stages of child development. Regularly consulting outside experts, including researchers and user subgroups, can be used to complement embedded expertise.[8]

Lenhart and Owens also recommend that tech companies hire, retain, and empower a diverse workforce that can support efforts to design for a broad range of youth experiences. All employees, regardless of their background, should be trained in ethics and humanities to develop their ability to consider a range of perspectives and issues.[9]

POLICYMAKERS

The absence of U.S. law governing technology companies has meant there are few countervailing forces—at least in the United States—to check these companies' focus on maximizing shareholder profit. In 2021, the U.S. Congress took steps to change that. The "Protecting Kids Online" series of hearings included testimony from Facebook whistleblower Frances Haugen and leaders of companies including YouTube, Instagram, Snap, and TikTok responding to pointed questions about their platforms' negative effects on children and adolescents.

With any luck, meaningful legislation will be passed in the U.S. by the time this book is published. It's my hope that such legislation will incentivize tech companies to adopt a child-centered approach to design that places children's well-being front and center, reducing the burden on individual users to seek and curate high-quality digital experiences on their own.[10] Government regulation could also require tech companies to become more transparent about how they operate so that we don't have to rely on occasional whistleblowers such as Haugen for (incomplete) glimpses into these companies' inner workings.[11]

In the meantime, tech companies already have started to make changes in response to legislation passed in recent years by the EU and UK governments.[12] For instance, the UK's Age-Appropriate Design Code, which became law in

2020, seeks to prioritize children's well-being on digital platforms by requiring companies to provide children with a high level of default privacy and limit how much personal data they can collect from young users.[13]

In 2021, the year the law took effect, YouTube turned off default autoplay features for children under eighteen and created "take a break" reminders when children have had YouTube open for several hours.[14] Facebook and TikTok made all new accounts created by teens private by default. TikTok said it would adjust its algorithm so that users don't encounter too much of the same content, such as extreme dieting, drugs, and breakups.[15] Google allowed users who are under eighteen to request that images of them be removed from search results.

Though it has been criticized for falling short in some areas and overreaching in others,[16] the UK law—and tech companies' speedy reaction to it—demonstrates the ability of government regulation to influence the way technologies are designed and presented to children.

In another example, universal design for learning was defined in U.S. federal law in 2008 and included in the National Education Technology Plan presented to Congress in 2010.[17] Federal grants became available for school systems to incorporate universal design into their curricula, illustrating how government can incentivize innovations in supporting children's learning and development.

Given the power of government regulation to influence young people's digital experiences, it's essential that proposed laws are carefully scrutinized for potential unintended consequences.[18]

PARENTS/CAREGIVERS

In the early years, when they have control over their child's digital experiences, parents can seek digital content that's self-paced and provides opportunities for them to engage in the experience with their child. If it's a noninteractive experience, like watching TV, parents and caregivers should aim for content that's educational and nonviolent. When possible, parents can watch with their child and talk to them about what's going on in the show. Whether the digital experience is interactive or not, parents should seek activities that align with their child's particular interests and abilities.

Parents should try to avoid design abuses (like parasocial relationships and autoplay) that co-opt their child's attention as well as unnecessary features that distract from the primary task at hand. They should avoid situations where their child's digital experiences are displacing other worthwhile activities, such as rough-and-tumble play, bedtime reading, and sleep. (Ideally, these efforts would be made easier by the proposed changes to government regulation and technology design described above.)

As their child grows older, and parents have less control over their digital experiences, they can look for opportunities to learn about the platforms their child is using and their experiences on them. They can seek conversations that give their child the chance to share their triumphs and struggles and experience empathy and validation in return.

As much as possible, parents should resist the urge to rush to snap judgments or assume that their child's digital savvy equates with digital wisdom. They should avoid setting blanket restrictions on their child's technology use that don't take into account the nuances of varied digital experiences.

Throughout their child's development, parents should try to model the kind of relationship to technology that they'd like to see their child adopt. Parents are bound to stumble, though (I certainly have!), and that's okay. Technoference is real and being a good enough digital parent is . . . good enough.

TEACHERS AND SCHOOL ADMINISTRATORS

Like parents, teachers can also ask questions about their students' social media experiences and listen with empathy to what they say. This approach is likely to work better than giving students a set of edicts about what not to do online.[19] Teachers can help their students develop strategies to mitigate digital stress (like learning to mute notifications) and reframe negative social comparisons (those images are highly edited!). They can talk with their students about the challenges and opportunities of online engagement in political and social issues.[20] Resources like Common Sense Media's digital citizenship curriculum can help teachers to frame and guide these types of conversations.[21]

When it comes to teaching in their subject area/s, teachers should do their best to seek out and incorporate educational technologies that are open-ended, interest-driven, and supportive of students' diverse ways of learning. This is best achieved when teachers know something about their students' motivations, skills, and broader social contexts,[22] and when they keep in mind the tenets of universal design for learning.[23]

Instead of aiming for radical transformation through educational technology, teachers should try adopting a *tinkering* approach, which will allow them to work within the existing practices, structures, and constraints that shape their particular school.[24] Where possible, they should use new technologies as a vehicle to reflect on their current pedagogical practices, gradually shifting them as circumstances allow.

School administrators and policymakers have an important role to play in creating the conditions to support this work by offering professional development experiences, rethinking the structure and routines of the school day, and encouraging teachers to share ideas and collaborate with each other.[25]

ACADEMICS AND RESEARCHERS

Academics can contribute in two primary ways: through their teaching and through their research.

When it comes to teaching, computer science and other technology-oriented programs are starting to address the ethical dimensions of technology design. For example, in 2020, Harvard University introduced Embedded EthiCS, a program that brings together philosophers and computer scientists to train the next generation of leaders to consider the ethical dimensions of their work in the tech industry.[26] The program is serving as a model for other institutions to emulate, including MIT and Stanford University.

Ideally, programs like Harvard's would also include an explicit focus on the ethical dimensions of designing technologies specifically for children, encouraging students to prioritize self-directed, community-supported digital experiences over maximizing user engagement. These programs should introduce students to major concepts from the field of child development and encourage them to consider how their designs could interact with youth's developmental vulnerabilities, for example, and how to engage marginalized youth in meaningful, safe, and affirming ways. The child-centered design approach I laid out earlier in this chapter could be used to encourage such reflections.

It's evident from the many citations in this book that a lot of researchers are working to understand technology's impact on child development. In the case of design researchers, they're also imagining better technology designs. Their insights have informed (and continue to inform) product teams in tech companies, policymakers at all levels of government, educators and school administrators, parents, news media, and the public at large.

A lot of the research on kids and technology takes place within the context of academia, but nonprofit organizations are also doing important work. Child advocacy organizations like Sesame Workshop, Common Sense Media, Fred Rogers Center, World Economic Forum, UNICEF, the United Nations, and the 5Rights Foundation in the UK are contributing research insights, making design recommendations, and influencing policy discussions.[27]

Going forward, a worthwhile area of focus is research that surfaces measurable indicators of child user well-being.[28] This would help address the difficulty of replacing easy to measure metrics like click-through rates and time on platform with harder-to-measure metrics like well-being. Evidence-based well-being indicators could then be incorporated into the algorithms that push content to users. Researchers Jenny Radesky and Alexis Hiniker suggest that cross-disciplinary collaborations, such as between design researchers and child development experts, are needed to lead this work.[29]

To maximize the impact of their work, researchers should do their best to translate their research for nonacademic audiences and disseminate it through nonacademic channels. For instance, motivated by the existing research-practice gap in technology design,[30] my former PhD student, Saba Kawas, designed a toolkit for her dissertation work that gives industry designers and user experience (UX) practitioners access to evidence-based and actionable design recommendations relevant to children's technology design.[31] Using a digital card format, the toolkit allows industry practitioners to search and browse research relevant to their design goals, and it presents the research in a way that can be readily incorporated into the design process.

As for my own work as a researcher, I'll continue to explore the intersection between child development and technology design, using the insights to identify and promote better technology designs for children, adolescents, and emerging adults. The process of writing this book has reinforced for me the value of research in calling attention to the opportunities and challenges associated with young people's digital experiences. It's also underscored the need for more research to help stakeholders make evidence-based decisions when it comes to kids and technology.

ACKNOWLEDGMENTS

I am so grateful to the many people and institutions that supported me, both professionally and personally, during the process of writing this book.

Thank you to my editor at the MIT Press, Susan Buckley, who's supported this work from the very beginning, when I sent her the book prospectus. Susan helped me with key decisions related to everything from individual paragraphs to the book's title. Thank you also to Julia Collins and Kathleen Caruso for their superb editing of the book manuscript.

Many people provided their expert feedback on various sections and iterations of the manuscript, and I am incredibly grateful to all of them. Thank you to the anonymous reviewers, whose early input was instrumental in guiding the revision process. Thank you to the experts and colleagues who read and gave feedback on selected chapters: Linda Charmaraman, Oliver Haimson, Alexis Hiniker, Carrie James, Vikki Katz, Ellen Middaugh, Jenny Radesky, Justin Reich, Petr Slovak, and Emily Weinstein.

A special thanks to Emma May, Jessie Novotny, and Shelby Wong, members of the Graduate Assistant (GA) Crew at the University of Washington Information School, who worked heroically over many months (including holidays and weekends!) to help format the book manuscript. With GA Crew member Andrea Berg, Shelby also worked on the indexing for the book. Thanks also to Julianne Peeling, another member of the GA Crew, who assisted me with background research.

My mentor, Howard Gardner, was a strong presence in my mind throughout the process of writing this book. Howard, thank you for your friendship and mentorship over the years, as well as for teaching me to be a scholar and writer.

I feel so lucky to have family members who not only supported me with love throughout this process but also gave me their time and expertise to make this book what it is. Thank you to all four of my parents, Wendy Davis Johnson, Tom Davis, Gordon Johnson, and Joyce Heinzerling Davis, and Patrick Baudisch, for cheering me on and playing with Oliver so I could focus on writing. Thank you to my sibling, Molly Johnson, for talking to me about the role technology played during their adolescence and emerging adulthood. Thank you to my aunt, Beth Charlton, an expert in children's literacy development, who provided feedback on chapter 3. Her brother and my uncle, Spencer Critchley, helped me frame the overarching narrative of the book. And their sister, Wendy, my amazing mother, pulled me across the finish line with her unwavering love, support, and expert revisions to just about every sentence you've read.

I would also like to acknowledge the institutional support I have received, which has made writing this book possible. I am grateful to the two institutions that supported my work during the planning and writing phases: Hasso Plattner Institut, where I was a visiting research scientist in Germany, and the University of Washington Information

School, where I am a professor. The research on *NatureCollections* that I discussed in chapter 5 was supported by a University of Washington Innovation Award. And, although their support preceded the writing of this book by over a decade, I owe much gratitude to the MacArthur Foundation and the research group at Harvard Project Zero for helping launch me on this research path.

NOTES

CHAPTER 1

1. Alison Gopnik, *The Gardener and the Carpenter: What the New Science of Child Development Tells Us about the Relationship between Parents and Children* (New York: Macmillan, 2016); Jennifer Senior, *All Joy and No Fun: The Paradox of Modern Parenthood* (London: Hachette UK, 2014).

2. Dan Goldhaber, Thomas J. Kane, Andrew McEachin, Emily Morton, Tyler Patterson, and Douglas O. Staiger, "The Consequences of Remote and Hybrid Instruction during the Pandemic," Center for Education Policy Research, Harvard University, 2022, https://cepr.harvard.edu/files/cepr/files/5-4.pdf?m=1651690491.

3. Tarleton Gillespie, "The Relevance of Algorithms," in *Media Technologies: Essays on Communication, Materiality, and Society*, ed. Tarleton Gillespie, Pablo J. Boczkowski, and Kirsten A. Foot (Cambridge, MA: MIT Press, 2014); Tarleton Gillespie, *Custodians of the Internet* (New Haven, CT: Yale University Press, 2018); Safiya Umoja Noble, *Algorithms of Oppression* (New York: New York University Press, 2018); Shoshana Zuboff, *The Age of Surveillance Capitalism: The Fight for a Human Future at the New Frontier of Power* (London: Profile Books, 2019).

4. Barbara Rogoff, *The Cultural Nature of Human Development* (Oxford: Oxford University Press, 2003).

5. Edward L. Deci and Richard M. Ryan, "The 'What' and 'Why' of Goal Pursuits: Human Needs and the Self-Determination of Behavior," *Psychological Inquiry* 11, no. 4 (2000): 227–268; Richard M. Ryan

and Edward L. Deci, "Intrinsic and Extrinsic Motivation from a Self-Determination Theory Perspective: Definitions, Theory, Practices, and Future Directions," *Contemporary Educational Psychology* 61 (2020): 1–11, https://doi.org/10.1016/j.cedpsych.2020.101860.

6. In *The App Generation*, Howard Gardner and I refer to self-directed technology experiences as app-enabling. Howard Gardner and Katie Davis, *The App Generation: How Today's Youth Navigate Identity, Intimacy, and Imagination in a Digital World* (New Haven, CT: Yale University Press, 2013).

7. Todd Rose, *The End of Average: How to Succeed in a World That Values Sameness* (London: Penguin UK, 2016).

8. Kris D. Gutiérrez and Barbara Rogoff, "Cultural Ways of Learning: Individual Traits or Repertoires of Practice," *Educational Researcher* 32, no. 5 (2003): 19–25; Na'ilah Suad Nasir, Carol D. Lee, Roy Pea, and Maxine McKinney de Royston, "Rethinking Learning: What the Interdisciplinary Science Tells Us," *Educational Researcher* 50, no. 8 (2021): 557–565; Rogoff, *The Cultural Nature of Human Development*.

9. Rogoff, *The Cultural Nature of Human Development*, 3–4.

10. Nasir et al., "Rethinking Learning"; Rogoff, *The Cultural Nature of Human Development*.

11. Gillespie, "The Relevance of Algorithms," 167; Tarleton Gillespie, "Algorithms, Clickworkers, and the Befuddled Fury around Facebook Trends," *Culture Digitally*, May 18, 2016, https://culturedigitally.org/2016/05/facebook-trends/; Gillespie, *Custodians of the Internet*; Tarleton Gillespie and Nick Seaver, "Critical Algorithm Studies: A Reading List," *Social Media Collective*, 2016, https://socialmediacollective.org/reading-lists/critical-algorithm-studies/; Ulrike Klinger and Jakob Svensson, "The End of Media Logics? On Algorithms and Agency," *New Media & Society* 20, no. 12 (2018): 4653–4670; Ruha Benjamin, *Race after Technology: Abolitionist Tools for the New Jim Code* (Cambridge, UK, and Medford, MA: Polity Press, 2019); Noble, "Algorithms of Oppression"; Zuboff, *The Age of Surveillance Capitalism*.

12. Gillespie, "The Relevance of Algorithms."

13. Gillespie, *Custodians of the Internet*.

14. Benjamin, *Race after Technology*.

15. Jeremy B. Merrill and Will Oremus, "Five Points for Anger, One for a 'Like': How Facebook's Formula Fostered Rage and Misinformation," *Washington Post*, October 26, 2021, https://www.washington post.com/technology/2021/10/26/facebook-angry-emoji-algorithm/.

16. Gillespie, "Algorithms, Clickworkers."

17. Evans et al., "Explicating Affordances."

18. danah boyd, "Social Network Sites as Networked Publics: Affordances, Dynamics, and Implications," *A Networked Self: Identity, Community, and Culture on Social Network Sites*, ed. Zizi Papacharissi (New York: Routledge, 2010), 47–66; Katrin Tiidenberg, Natalie Ann Hendry, and Crystal Abidin, *Tumblr* (Cambridge, UK, and Medford, MA: Polity Press, 2021).

19. Tama Leaver, Tim Highfield, and Crystal Abidin, *Instagram: Visual Social Media Cultures* (Cambridge, UK, and Medford, MA: Polity Press, 2020); Tiidenberg, Hendry, and Abidin, *Tumblr*.

20. Tiidenberg, Hendry, and Abidin , *Tumblr*.

21. Leaver, Highfield, and Abidin, *Instagram*.

22. Tiidenberg, Hendry, and Abidin, *Tumblr*.

CHAPTER 2

1. Center on the Developing Child, *Building the Brain's "Air Traffic Control" System: How Early Experiences Shape the Development of Executive Function: Working Paper* (Cambridge, MA: Harvard University, 2011), https://developingchild.harvard.edu/wp-content/uploads/2011/05/ How-Early-Experiences-Shape-the-Development-of-Executive-Func tion.pdf.

2. Marc H. Bornstein, "Sensitive Periods in Development: Structural Characteristics and Causal Interpretations," *Psychological Bulletin* 105, no. 2 (1989): 179.

3. Katherine Jonas and Grazyna Kochanska, "An Imbalance of Approach and Effortful Control Predicts Externalizing Problems: Support for Extending the Dual-Systems Model into Early Childhood," *Journal of Abnormal Child Psychology* 46, no. 8 (November 1, 2018): 1573–1583; Walter Mischel, Yuichi Shoda, and Philip K. Peake, "The Nature of Adolescent Competencies Predicted by Preschool Delay

of Gratification," *Journal of Personality and Social Psychology* 54, no. 4 (1988): 687–696; Walter Mischel, Yuichi Shoda, and Monica L. Rodriguez, "Delay of Gratification in Children," *Science* 244, no. 4907 (May 26, 1989): 933–938; Yuichi Shoda, Walter Mischel, and Philip K. Peake, "Predicting Adolescent Cognitive and Self-Regulatory Competencies from Preschool Delay of Gratification: Identifying Diagnostic Conditions," *Developmental Psychology* 26, no. 6 (1990): 978.

4. Stuart I. Hammond, Ulrich Müller, Jeremy I. M. Carpendale, Maximilian B. Bibok, and Dana P. Liebermann-Finestone, "The Effects of Parental Scaffolding on Preschoolers' Executive Function," *Developmental Psychology* 48, no. 1 (2012): 271–281; Kristine Jentoft Kinniburgh, Margaret Blaustein, Joseph Spinazzola, and Bessel A. Van der Kolk, "Attachment, Self-Regulation, and Competency," *Psychiatric Annals* 35, no. 5 (2005): 424–430; Amanda Sheffield Morris, Jennifer S. Silk, Laurence Steinberg, Sonya S. Myers, and Lara Rachel Robinson, "The Role of the Family Context in the Development of Emotion Regulation," *Social Development* 16, no. 2 (2007): 361–388.

5. Victoria Rideout and Michael B. Robb, *The Common Sense Census: Media Use by Kids Age Zero to Eight* (San Francisco: Common Sense Media, 2020), https://www.commonsensemedia.org/sites/default/files/research/report/2020_zero_to_eight_census_final_web.pdf.

6. Angeline S. Lillard, Marissa B. Drell, Eve M. Richey, Katherine Boguszewski, and Eric D. Smith, "Further Examination of the Immediate Impact of Television on Children's Executive Function," *Developmental Psychology* 51, no. 6 (2015): 792.

7. Lillard et al., "Further Examination."

8. Amy I. Nathanson, Fashina Aladé, Molly L. Sharp, Eric E. Rasmussen, and Katheryn Christy, "The Relation between Television Exposure and Executive Function among Preschoolers," *Developmental Psychology* 50, no. 5 (2014): 1497–1506.

9. Lisa Guernsey, *Screen Time: How Electronic Media—From Baby Videos to Educational Software—Affects Your Young Child* (London: Hachette UK, 2012); Sheri Madigan, Brae Anne McArthur, Ciana Anhorn, Rachel Eirich, and Dimitri A. Christakis, "Associations between Screen Use and Child Language Skills: A Systematic Review and Meta-Analysis," *JAMA Pediatrics* 174, no. 7 (2020): 665–675; Sanne W. C. Nikkelen, Patti M. Valkenburg, Mariette Huizinga, and Brad J.

Bushman, "Media Use and ADHD-Related Behaviors in Children and Adolescents: A Meta-Analysis," *Developmental Psychology* 50, no. 9 (2014): 2228–2241.

10. Nikkelen et al., "Media Use and ADHD-Related Behaviors."

11. Nikkelen et al., "Media Use and ADHD-Related Behaviors."

12. Shunyue Cheng, Tadahiko Maeda, Sakakihara Yoichi, Zentaro Yamagata, Kiyotaka Tomiwa, and Japan Children's Study Group, "Early Television Exposure and Children's Behavioral and Social Outcomes at Age 30 Months," *Journal of Epidemiology* 20, suppl. 2 (2010): S482–S489, https://doi.org/10.2188/jea.JE20090179; Dimitri A. Christakis, Frederick J. Zimmerman, David L. DiGiuseppe, and Carolyn A. McCarty, "Early Television Exposure and Subsequent Attentional Problems in Children," *Pediatrics* 113, no. 4 (April 1, 2004): 708–713; Carlin J. Miller, David J. Marks, Scott R. Miller, Olga G. Berwid, Elizabeth C. Kera, Amita Santra, and Jeffrey M. Halperin, "Brief Report: Television Viewing and Risk for Attention Problems in Preschool Children," *Journal of Pediatric Psychology* 32, no. 4 (May 1, 2007): 448–452; Nathanson et al., "Relation between Television"; Frederick J. Zimmerman and Dimitri A. Christakis, "Children's Television Viewing and Cognitive Outcomes: A Longitudinal Analysis of National Data," *Archives of Pediatrics & Adolescent Medicine* 159, no. 7 (July 1, 2005): 619–625; Frederick J. Zimmerman, Dimitri A. Christakis, and Andrew N. Meltzoff, "Associations between Media Viewing and Language Development in Children under Age 2 Years," *Journal of Pediatrics* 151, no. 4 (October 1, 2007): 364–368.

13. A. Nayena Blankson, Marion O'Brien, Esther M. Leerkes, Susan D. Calkins, and Stuart Marcovitch, "Do Hours Spent Viewing Television at Ages 3 and 4 Predict Vocabulary and Executive Functioning at Age 5?," *Merrill-Palmer Quarterly* 61, no. 2 (2015): 264–289; E. Michael Foster and Stephanie Watkins, "The Value of Reanalysis: TV Viewing and Attention Problems," *Child Development* 81, no. 1 (2010): 368–375; Angeline S. Lillard, Hui Li, and Katie Boguszewski, "Television and Children's Executive Function," in *Advances in Child Development and Behavior*, ed. Janette B. Benson, vol. 48 (2015): 219–248, https://doi.org/10.1016/bs.acdb.2014.11.006; Matthew T. McBee, Rebecca J. Brand, and Wallace E. Dixon, "Challenging the Link between Early Childhood Television Exposure and Later Attention Problems: A

Multiverse Approach," *Psychological Science* 32, no. 4 (April 1, 2021): 496–518; Carsten Obel, Tine Brink Henriksen, Søren Dalsgaard, Karen Markussen Linnet, Elisabeth Skajaa, Per Hove Thomsen, and Jørn Olsen, "Does Children's Watching of Television Cause Attention Problems? Retesting the Hypothesis in a Danish Cohort," *Pediatrics* 114, no. 5 (November 1, 2004): 1372–1373; Tara Stevens and Miriam Mulsow, "There Is No Meaningful Relationship between Television Exposure and Symptoms of Attention-Deficit/Hyperactivity Disorder," *Pediatrics* 117, no. 3 (March 1, 2006): 665–672.

14. Amanda L. Thompson, Linda S. Adair, and Margaret E. Bentley, "Maternal Characteristics and Perception of Temperament Associated with Infant TV Exposure," *Pediatrics* 131, no. 2 (February 2013): e390–397; Brandon T. McDaniel and Jenny S. Radesky, "Longitudinal Associations between Early Childhood Externalizing Behavior, Parenting Stress, and Child Media Use," *Cyberpsychology, Behavior, and Social Networking* 23, no. 6 (June 1, 2020): 384–391; Jenny S. Radesky, Elizabeth Peacock-Chambers, Barry Zuckerman, and Michael Silverstein, "Use of Mobile Technology to Calm Upset Children: Associations with Social-Emotional Development," *JAMA Pediatrics* 170, no. 4 (April 1, 2016): 397–399; Jenny S. Radesky, Caroline J. Kistin, Barry Zuckerman, Katie Nitzberg, Jamie Gross, Margot Kaplan-Sanoff, Marilyn Augustyn, and Michael Silverstein, "Patterns of Mobile Device Use by Caregivers and Children During Meals in Fast Food Restaurants," *Pediatrics* 133, no. 4 (April 1, 2014): e843–849.

So far, existing research suggests that giving young children screen media to regulate their distress does not appear to have a lasting negative effect on their ability to self-regulate as they get older; see Dylan P. Cliff, Steven J. Howard, Jenny S. Radesky, Jade McNeill, and Stewart A. Vella, "Early Childhood Media Exposure and Self-Regulation: Bidirectional Longitudinal Associations," *Academic Pediatrics* 18, no. 7 (September 1, 2018): 813–819; Avigail Gordon-Hacker and Noa Gueron-Sela, "Maternal Use of Media to Regulate Child Distress: A Double-Edged Sword? Longitudinal Links to Toddlers' Negative Emotionality," *Cyberpsychology, Behavior, and Social Networking* 23, no. 6 (June 1, 2020): 400–405. More research is needed, however, and best practices in parenting suggest it's more prudent to use a variety of coping strategies rather than rely solely on screen media to calm one's child; see McDaniel and Radesky, "Longitudinal Associations'";

Jenny S. Radesky, "Smartphones and Children: Relationships, Regulation, and Reasoning," *Cyberpsychology, Behavior, and Social Networking* 23, no. 6 (June 1, 2020): 361–362.

15. Arya Ansari and Robert Crosnoe, "Children's Hyperactivity, Television Viewing, and the Potential for Child Effects," *Children and Youth Services Review* 61 (2016): 135–140; Cliff et al., "Early Childhood Media Exposure and Self-Regulation"; Si Ning Goh, Long Hua Teh, Wei Rong Tay, Saradha Anantharaman, Rob M. van Dam, Chuen Seng Tan, Hwee Ling Chua, Pey Gein Wong, and Falk Müller-Riemenschneider, "Sociodemographic, Home Environment and Parental Influences on Total and Device-Specific Screen Viewing in Children Aged 2 Years and Below: An Observational Study," *BMJ Open* 6, no. 1 (2016): e009113; Gordon-Hacker and Gueron-Sela, "Maternal Use of Media to Regulate Child Distress"; Jill A. Hnatiuk, Jo Salmon, Karen J. Campbell, Nicola D. Ridgers, and Kylie D. Hesketh, "Tracking of Maternal Self-Efficacy for Limiting Young Children's Television Viewing and Associations with Children's Television Viewing Time: A Longitudinal Analysis over 15-Months," *BMC Public Health* 15, no. 1 (May 30, 2015): 517; Deborah L. Linebarger, Rachel Barr, Matthew A. Lapierre, and Jessica T. Piotrowski, "Associations between Parenting, Media Use, Cumulative Risk, and Children's Executive Functioning," *Journal of Developmental & Behavioral Pediatrics* 35, no. 6 (August 2014): 367–377; McDaniel and Radesky, "Longitudinal Associations," 384–391; Gabrielle McHarg, Andrew D. Ribner, Rory T. Devine, Claire Hughes, and The NewFAMS Study Team, "Infant Screen Exposure Links to Toddlers' Inhibition, but Not Other EF Constructs: A Propensity Score Study," *Infancy* 25, no. 2 (2020): 205–222; Radesky, "Smartphones and Children"; Masumi Sugawara, Satoko Matsumoto, Hiroto Murohashi, Atsushi Sakai, and Nobuo Isshiki, "Trajectories of Early Television Contact in Japan: Relationship with Preschoolers' Externalizing Problems," *Journal of Children and Media* 9, no. 4 (October 2, 2015): 453–471.

16. Katarzyna Kostyrka-Allchorne, Nicholas R. Cooper, and Andrew Simpson, "The Relationship between Television Exposure and Children's Cognition and Behaviour: A Systematic Review," *Developmental Review* 44 (June 1, 2017): 19–58.

17. John D. Bransford, Ann L. Brown, and Rodney R. Cocking, *How People Learn: Brain, Mind, Experience, and School* (Washington,

DC: National Academy Press, 1999); Suzy Tomopoulos, Benard P. Dreyer, Purnima Valdez, Virginia Flynn, Gilbert Foley, Samantha B. Berkule, and Alan L. Mendelsohn, "Media Content and Externalizing Behaviors in Latino Toddlers," *Ambulatory Pediatrics* 7, no. 3 (May 1, 2007): 232–238; Zimmerman, Christakis, and Meltzoff, "Associations between Media Viewing," 364–368.

18. Lillard, Li, and Boguszewski, "Television and Children's Executive Function"; John P. Murray, "Media Violence: The Effects Are Both Real and Strong," *American Behavioral Scientist* 51, no. 8 (April 1, 2008): 1212–1230.

19. Rachel Barr, Alexis Lauricella, Elizabeth Zack, and Sandra L. Calvert, "Infant and Early Childhood Exposure to Adult-Directed and Child-Directed Television Programming: Relations with Cognitive Skills at Age Four," *Merrill-Palmer Quarterly* 56, no. 1 (2010): 21–48; Dylan B. Jackson, "Does TV Viewing during Toddlerhood Predict Social Difficulties and Conduct Problems?," *Infant and Child Development* 27, no. 4 (2018): e2086.

20. Fast vs. slow pacing: Anderson et al. found no relationship between pacing and behavioral outcomes, whereas Lillard and Peterson found a negative immediate impact of fast-paced television cartoons on four-year-old children's ability to perform executive function tasks; and Geist and Gibson found that fast-paced programming predicted behavioral problems in four- and five-year-olds; see Daniel R. Anderson, Stephen R. Levin, and Elizabeth Pugzles Lorch, "The Effects of TV Program Pacing on the Behavior of Preschool Children," *AV Communication Review* 25, no. 2 (1977): 159–166; Angeline S. Lillard and Jennifer Peterson, "The Immediate Impact of Different Types of Television on Young Children's Executive Function," *Pediatrics* 128, no. 4 (2011): 644–649, https://doi.org/10.1542/peds.2010-1919; Eugene A. Geist and Marty Gibson, "The Effect of Network and Public Television Programs on Four and Five Year Olds' Ability to Attend to Educational Tasks," *Journal of Instructional Psychology* 27, no. 4 (2000): 250. Lillard et al. ("Further Examination") found that once content is taken into account, pacing doesn't have much effect on children's executive function skills. Realistic vs. fantastic content: Lillard et al. ("Further Examination") found that watching unrealistic events negatively predicted children's executive function performance, whereas Kostyrka-Allchorne et al. found the opposite effect; see Katarzyna

Kostyrka-Allchorne, Nicholas R. Cooper, and Andrew Simpson, "Disentangling the Effects of Video Pace and Story Realism on Children's Attention and Response Inhibition," *Cognitive Development* 49 (January 2019): 94–104, https://doi.org/10.1016/j.cogdev.2018.12.003.

21. Drawing on a variety of coping strategies is advisable for all children, not just those with attention and/or behavior problems; see Jenny S. Radesky, Alexandria Schaller, Samantha L. Yeo, Heidi M. Weeks, and Michael B. Robb, *Young Kids and YouTube: How Ads, Toys, and Games Dominate Viewing* (San Francisco: Common Sense Media, 2020), https://www.commonsensemedia.org/sites/default/files/research/report/2020_youngkidsyoutube-report_final-release_forweb_1.pdf; Gordon-Hacker and Gueron-Sela, "Maternal Use of Media to Regulate Child Distress").

22. Bransford, Brown, and Cocking, *How People Learn*; Shalom M. Fisch and Rosemarie T. Truglio, *G Is for Growing: Thirty Years of Research on Children and Sesame Street* (Mahwah, NJ: Lawrence Erlbaum, 2001).

23. Guernsey, *Screen Time*; Monique K. LeBourgeois, Lauren Hale, Anne-Marie Chang, Lameese D. Akacem, Hawley E. Montgomery-Downs, and Orfeu M. Buxton, "Digital Media and Sleep in Childhood and Adolescence," *Pediatrics* 140, suppl. 2 (November 1, 2017): S92–S96; Amy I. Nathanson, "Sleep and Technology in Early Childhood," *Child and Adolescent Psychiatric Clinics* 30, no. 1 (January 1, 2021): 15–26.

24. Sonia Livingstone and Alicia Blum-Ross, *Parenting for a Digital Future: How Hopes and Fears about Technology Shape Children's Lives* (Oxford: Oxford University Press, 2020).

25. Rebecca Cecil-Karb and Andrew Grogan-Kaylor, "Childhood Body Mass Index in Community Context: Neighborhood Safety, Television Viewing, and Growth Trajectories of BMI," *Health & Social Work* 34, no. 3 (2009): 169–177; Ashlesha Datar, Nancy Nicosia, and Victoria Shier, "Parent Perceptions of Neighborhood Safety and Children's Physical Activity, Sedentary Behavior, and Obesity: Evidence from a National Longitudinal Study," *American Journal of Epidemiology* 177, no. 10 (May 15, 2013): 1065–1073; Livingstone and Blum-Ross, *Parenting for a Digital Future*.

26. Rideout and Robb, *The Common Sense Census*.

27. Sabrina L. Connell, Alexis R. Lauricella, and Ellen Wartella, "Parental Co-Use of Media Technology with Their Young Children in the USA," *Journal of Children and Media* 9, no. 1 (2015): 5–21; Reed Stevens and L. Takeuchi, *The New Coviewing: Designing for Learning through Joint Media Engagement* (New York: Joan Ganz Cooney Center, 2011); Gabrielle A. Strouse, Katherine O'Doherty, and Georgene L. Troseth, "Effective Coviewing: Preschoolers' Learning from Video after a Dialogic Questioning Intervention," *Developmental Psychology* 49, no. 12 (2013): 2368–2382.

28. Jenny S. Radesky, Jayna Schumacher, and Barry Zuckerman, "Mobile and Interactive Media Use by Young Children: The Good, the Bad, and the Unknown," *Pediatrics* 135, no. 1 (January 1, 2015): 1–3.

29. Amy I. Nathanson and Ine Beyens, "The Role of Sleep in the Relation between Young Children's Mobile Media Use and Effortful Control," *British Journal of Developmental Psychology* 36, no. 1 (2018): 1–21; Nathanson, "Sleep and Technology in Early Childhood."

30. Radesky et al., *Young Kids and YouTube*; Jenny S. Radesky, Jennifer L. Seyfried, Heidi M. Weeks, Niko Kaciroti, and Alison L. Miller, "Video-Sharing Platform Viewing among Preschool-Aged Children: Differences by Child Characteristics and Contextual Factors., *Cyberpsychology, Behavior, and Social Networking* 25, no. 4 (2002): 230–236.

31. Patrick Van Kessel, Skye Toor, and Aaron Smith, *A Week in the Life of Popular YouTube Channels*, Pew Research Center, July 25, 2019, https://www.pewresearch.org/internet/2019/07/25/a-week-in-the-life-of-popular-youtube-channels/.

32. Mark Savage, "Baby Shark Becomes YouTube's Most-Watched Video of All Time," *BBC News*, November 2, 2020.

33. Radesky et al., *Young Kids and YouTube*. Radesky et al. found that young children (aged three to five years) from lower socioeconomic households spend more time on average watching YouTube on a mobile device than young children from higher socioeconomic households (Radesky et al., "Video-Sharing Platform Viewing among Preschool-Aged Children").

34. Benjamin Burroughs, "YouTube Kids: The App Economy and Mobile Parenting," *Social Media+ Society* 3, no. 2 (2017): 205630511 7707189; Jenny Radesky and Alexis Hiniker, "From Moral Panic to

Systemic Change: Making Child-Centered Design the Default," *International Journal of Child-Computer Interaction* 31, no. C (March 2022), https://doi.org/10.1016/j.ijcci.2021.100351.

35. Tiffany G. Munzer, Alison L. Miller, Yujie Wang, Niko Kaciroti, and J. Radesky, "Tablets, Toddlers, and Tantrums: The Immediate Effects of Tablet Device Play," *Acta Paediatrica* 110, no 1 (2021): 255–256, https://doi.org/10.1111/apa.15509.

36. Alexis Hiniker, Hyewon Suh, Sabina Cao, and Julie A. Kientz, "Screen Time Tantrums: How Families Manage Screen Media Experiences for Toddlers and Preschoolers," *Proceedings of the 2016 CHI Conference on Human Factors in Computing Systems* (May 7, 2016): 648–660, https://doi.org/10.1145/2858036.2858278.

37. Dan Fitton and Janet C. Read, "Creating a Framework to Support the Critical Consideration of Dark Design Aspects in Free-to-Play Apps," *Proceedings of the 18th ACM International Conference on Interaction Design and Children* (June 12, 2019): 407–418, https://doi.org/10.1145/3311927.3323136; Arvind Narayanan, Arunesh Mathur, Marshini Chetty, and Mihir Kshirsagar, "Dark Patterns: Past, Present, and Future: The Evolution of Tricky User Interfaces," *Queue* 18, no. 2 (April 30, 2020): 67–92.

38. Radesky et al., *Young Kids and YouTube*.

39. Rebecca A. Dore, Marcia Shirilla, Emily Hopkins, Molly Collins, Molly Scott, Jacob Schatz, Jessica Lawson-Adams, et al., "Education in the App Store: Using a Mobile Game to Support U.S. Preschoolers' Vocabulary Learning," *Journal of Children and Media* 13, no. 4 (October 2, 2019): 452–471.

40. Burcu Sari, Zsofia K Takacs, and Adriana G Bus, "What Are We Downloading for Our Children? Best-Selling Children's Apps in Four European Countries," *Journal of Early Childhood Literacy* 19, no. 4 (December 1, 2019): 515–532.

41. Brittany Huber, Joanne Tarasuik, Mariana N. Antoniou, Chelsee Garrett, Steven J. Bowe, Jordy Kaufman, and Winburne Babylab Team, "Young Children's Transfer of Learning from a Touchscreen Device," *Computers in Human Behavior* 56 (March 2016): 56–64, https://doi.org/10.1016/j.chb.2015.11.010; Brittany Huber, Megan Yeates, Denny Meyer, Lorraine Fleckhammer, and Jordy Kaufman, "The Effects of Screen Media Content on Young Children's Executive

Functioning," *Journal of Experimental Child Psychology* 170 (June 1, 2018): 72–85; Amanda Lawrence and Daniel Ewon Choe, "Mobile Media and Young Children's Cognitive Skills: A Review," *Academic Pediatrics* 21, no. 6 (August 1, 2021): 996–1000.

42. Hiniker et al., "Let's Play!"

43. Jenny Radesky, Alexis Hiniker, Caroline McLaren, Eliz Akgun, Alexandria Schaller, Heidi M. Weeks, Scott Campbell, and Ashley Gearhardt, "Design Abuses in Children's Apps," under review.

44. Alexis Hiniker, Kiley Sobel, Sungsoo Ray Hong, Hyewon Suh, India Irish, Daniella Kim, and Julie A. Kientz, "Touchscreen Prompts for Preschoolers: Designing Developmentally Appropriate Techniques for Teaching Young Children to Perform Gestures," *Proceedings of the 14th International Conference on Interaction Design and Children* (June 21, 2015): 109–118, https://doi.org/10.1145/2771839.2771851; Hiniker et al., "Hidden Symbols"; Marisa Meyer, Jennifer M. Zosh, Caroline McLaren, Michael Robb, Harlan McCaffery, Roberta Michnick Golinkoff, Kathy Hirsh-Pasek, and Jenny Radesky, "How Educational Are 'Educational' Apps for Young Children? App Store Content Analysis Using the Four Pillars of Learning Framework," *Journal of Children and Media* 15, no. 4 (2021): 526–548; Uthpala Samarakoon, Hakim Usoof, and Thilina Halloluwa, "What They Can and Cannot: A Meta-Analysis of Research on Touch and Multi-Touch Gestures by Two to Seven-Year-Olds," *International Journal of Child-Computer Interaction* 22 (December 1, 2019): 100151; Nikita Soni, Aishat Aloba, Kristen S. Morga, Pamela J. Wisniewski, and Lisa Anthony, "A Framework of Touchscreen Interaction Design Recommendations for Children (TIDRC): Characterizing the Gap between Research Evidence and Design Practice," *Proceedings of the 18th ACM International Conference on Interaction Design and Children* (June 12, 2019): 419–431, https://doi.org/10.1145/3311927.3323149; Lisa Anthony, "Physical Dimensions of Children's Touchscreen Interactions: Lessons from Five Years of Study on the MTAGIC Project," *International Journal of Human-Computer Studies* 128 (2019): 1–16.

45. Adriana G. Bus, Zsofia K. Takacs, and Cornelia A. T. Kegel, "Affordances and Limitations of Electronic Storybooks for Young Children's Emergent Literacy," in "Living in the 'Net' Generation: Multitasking, Learning, and Development," special issue, *Developmental Review 35*

(March 2015): 79–97; Stephanie M. Reich, Joanna C. Yau, and Mark Warschauer, "Tablet-Based eBooks for Young Children: What Does the Research Say?," *Journal of Developmental & Behavioral Pediatrics* 37, no. 7 (September 2016): 585–591.

46. Lawrence and Choe, "Mobile Media and Young Children's Cognitive Skills."

47. Radesky et al., "Design Abuses in Children's Apps."

48. Brandon T. McDaniel, "Parent Distraction with Phones, Reasons for Use, and Impacts on Parenting and Child Outcomes: A Review of the Emerging Research," *Human Behavior and Emerging Technologies* 1, no. 2 (2019): 72–80; Brandon T. McDaniel and Sarah M. Coyne, "'Technoference': The Interference of Technology in Couple Relationships and Implications for Women's Personal and Relational Well-Being," *Psychology of Popular Media Culture* 5, no. 1 (2016): 85–98.

49. Erin Beneteau, Ashley Boone, Yuxing Wu, Julie A. Kientz, Jason Yip, and Alexis Hiniker, "Parenting with Alexa: Exploring the Introduction of Smart Speakers on Family Dynamics," *Proceedings of the 2020 CHI Conference on Human Factors in Computing Systems* (April 23, 2020): 1–13, https://doi.org/10.1145/3313831.3376344; Ying-Yu Chen, Ziyue Li, Daniela Rosner, and Alexis Hiniker, "Understanding Parents' Perspectives on Mealtime Technology," *Proceedings of the ACM on Interactive, Mobile, Wearable and Ubiquitous Technologies* 3, no. 1 (March 29, 2019): 5.1–19, https://doi.org/10.1145/3314392.

50. Gopnik, *The Gardener and the Carpenter*.

51. Suzanne M. Bianchi, John P. Robinson, and Melissa A. Milke, *The Changing Rhythms of American Family Life* (New York: Russell Sage Foundation, 2006); Ariel Kalil, Rebecca Ryan, and Michael Corey, "Diverging Destinies: Maternal Education and the Developmental Gradient in Time with Children," *Demography* 49, no. 4 (August 11, 2012): 1361–1383; Senior, *All Joy and No Fun*.

52. Sharon Hays, *The Cultural Contradictions of Motherhood* (New Haven, CT: Yale University Press, 1996); Senior, *All Joy*; Judith Warner, *Perfect Madness: Motherhood in the Age of Anxiety* (New York: Penguin, 2006).

53. Charlotte Faircloth, "Intensive Parenting and the Expansion of Parenting," in *Parenting Culture Studies*, ed. Ellie Lee, Jennie Bristow,

Charlotte Faircloth, and Jan Macvarish (London: Palgrave Macmillan UK, 2014): 25–50; Hays, *Cultural Contradictions of Motherhood*; Hiniker et al., "Touchscreen Prompts for Preschoolers"; Senior, *All Joy*; Glenda Wall, "Mothers' Experiences with Intensive Parenting and Brain Development Discourse," *Women's Studies International Forum* 33, no. 3 (May 1, 2010): 253–263; Warner, *Perfect Madness*; Ellie Lee, Jennie Bristow, Charlotte Faircloth, and Jan Macvarish, eds., *Parenting Culture Studies* (New York: Springer, 2014); Radesky and Hiniker, "From Moral Panic to Systemic Change."

54. This view of parenting is largely reflective of middle- and upper-class approaches to parenting, what sociologist Annette Lareau has called "concerted cultivation." In contrast, working-class and poor families are more likely to practice "natural growth parenting" in which children are expected to entertain themselves during long stretches of unstructured time. See Annette Lareau, "Invisible Inequality: Social Class and Childrearing in Black Families and White Families," *American Sociological Review* 67, no. 5 (2002): 747–776, https://doi.org/10.2307/3088916; Annette Lareau, *Unequal Childhoods: Class, Race, and Family Life* (Berkeley: University of California Press, 2003).

55. McDaniel, "Parent Distraction with Phones."

56. Russell W. Belk, "Extended Self in a Digital World." *Journal of Consumer Research* 40, no. 3 (October 1, 2013): 477–500.

57. Andrew K. Przybylski, Kou Murayama, Cody R. DeHaan, and Valerie Gladwell, "Motivational, Emotional, and Behavioral Correlates of Fear of Missing Out," *Computers in Human Behavior* 29, no. 4 (July 1, 2013): 1841–1848.

58. Sudip Bhattacharya, Md Abu Bashar, Abhay Srivastava, and Amarjeet Singh, "NOMOPHOBIA: NO MObile PHone PhoBIA," *Journal of Family Medicine and Primary Care* 8, no. 4 (April 2019): 1297–1300.

59. Mitchell K. Bartholomew, Sarah J. Schoppe-Sullivan, Michael Glassman, Claire M. Kamp Dush, and Jason M. Sullivan, "New Parents' Facebook Use at the Transition to Parenthood," *Family Relations* 61, no. 3 (2012): 455–469; Brandon T. McDaniel, Sarah M. Coyne, and Erin K. Holmes, "New Mothers and Media Use: Associations between Blogging, Social Networking, and Maternal Well-Being," *Maternal and Child Health Journal* 16, no. 7 (October 2012): 1509–1517; Jenny

S. Radesky, Caroline Kistin, Staci Eisenberg, Jamie Gross, Gabrielle Block, Barry Zuckerman, and Michael Silverstein, "Parent Perspectives on Their Mobile Technology Use: The Excitement and Exhaustion of Parenting While Connected," *Journal of Developmental & Behavioral Pediatrics* 37, no. 9 (December 2016): 694–701.

60. McDaniel, "Parent Distraction with Phones"; Jonathan A. Tran, Katie S. Yang, Katie Davis, and Alexis Hiniker, "Modeling the Engagement-Disengagement Cycle of Compulsive Phone Use," *Proceedings of the 2019 CHI Conference on Human Factors in Computing Systems* (May 2, 2019): 312:1–14, https://doi.org/10.1145/3290605.3300542.

61. Guernsey, *Screen Time*; Katie Davis, Anja Dinhopl, and Alexis Hiniker, "'Everything's the Phone': Understanding the Phone's Supercharged Role in Parent-Teen Relationships," *Proceedings of the 2019 CHI Conference on Human Factors in Computing Systems* (May 2, 2019): 227:1–14, https://doi.org/10.1145/3290605.3300457.

Not all parents share this stance, at least not to the same extent and not in precisely the same way. Parenting fears around children and technology vary across race, ethnicity, income, educational level, and immigrant status; see Brooke Auxier, Monica Anderson, Andrew Perrin, and Erica Turner, *Parenting Children in the Age of Screens*, Pew Research Center, July 28, 2020, https://www.pewresearch.org/internet/2020/07/28/parenting-children-in-the-age-of-screens/; Livingstone and Blum-Ross, *Parenting for a Digital Future*; Victoria Rideout and Vikki S. Katz, *Opportunity for All? Technology and Learning in Lower-Income Families*, A Report of the Families and Media Project (New York: Joan Ganz Cooney Center, 2016); Rideout and Robb, *The Common Sense Census*. For instance, Black and Hispanic/Latinx parents, as well as lower-income parents, are more likely than white and affluent parents to perceive educational benefits in their young children's screen media use (Rideout and Robb, *The Common Sense Census*). On the other hand, Hispanic parents and parents with relatively higher levels of education are more likely than other parents to express concern about what their children encounter online (Auxier et al., "Parenting Children in the Age of Screens"). When it comes to how parents think about and manage their children's use of screen media—including how they interpret and respond to the research reported in this book—their perceptions, values, and resources matter a great deal.

62. Michael J. Sulik, "Introduction to the Special Section on Executive Functions and Externalizing Symptoms," *Journal of Abnormal Child Psychology* 45, no. 8 (2017): 1473–1475.

63. Brandon T. McDaniel and Jenny S. Radesky, "Technoference: Longitudinal Associations between Parent Technology Use, Parenting Stress, and Child Behavior Problems," *Pediatric Research* 84, no. 2 (August 2018): 210–218; Brandon T. McDaniel and Jenny S. Radesky, "Technoference: Parent Distraction with Technology and Associations with Child Behavior Problems," *Child Development* 89, no. 1 (2018): 100–109; Radesky et al., "Patterns of Mobile Device Use"; Radesky et al., "Parent Perspectives on Their Mobile Technology Use."

64. Kinniburgh et al., "Attachment, Self-Regulation, and Competency"; Morris et al., "Role of the Family."

65. Mary S. Ainsworth, "Infant–Mother Attachment," *American Psychologist* 34, no. 10 (1979): 932; John Bowlby, *Attachment* (New York: Basic Books, 2008); Erik H. Erikson, *Identity and the Life Cycle* (New York: W. W. Norton & Company, 1994); Kinniburgh et al., "Attachment, Self-Regulation, Competency."

66. Hiniker et al., "Hidden Symbols"; Radesky et al., "Patterns of Mobile Device Use"; Jenny Radesky, Alison L. Miller, Katherine L. Rosenblum, Danielle Appugliese, Niko Kaciroti, and Julie C. Lumeng, "Maternal Mobile Device Use During a Structured Parent–Child Interaction Task," *Academic Pediatrics* 15, no. 2 (March 1, 2015): 238–244; Mariek M. P. Vanden Abeele, Monika Abels, and Andrew T. Hendrickson, "Are Parents Less Responsive to Young Children When They Are on Their Phones? A Systematic Naturalistic Observation Study," *Cyberpsychology, Behavior, and Social Networking* 23, no. 6 (June 1, 2020): 363–370; McDaniel, "Parent Distraction with Phones."

Note that focusing on one's phone is different than occasional glances, which do not appear to interfere with a parent's responsiveness to their child (Vanden Abeele, Abels, and Hendrickson, "Are Parents Less Responsive to Young Children?").

67. Alexis Hiniker, Kiley Sobel, Hyewon Suh, Yi-Chen Sung, Charlotte P. Lee, and Julie A. Kientz, "Texting While Parenting: How Adults Use Mobile Phones While Caring for Children at the Playground," *Proceedings of the 33rd Annual ACM Conference on Human Factors in Computing Systems* (April 18, 2015): 727–736; Radesky et al., "Patterns

of Mobile Device Use"; Kostadin Kushlev and Elizabeth W. Dunn, "Smartphones Distract Parents from Cultivating Feelings of Connection When Spending Time with Their Children," *Journal of Social and Personal Relationships* 36, no. 6 (June 1, 2019): 1619–1639.

68. Nalingna Yuan, Heidi M. Weeks, Rosa Ball, Mark W. Newman, Yung-Ju Chang, and Jenny S. Radesky, "How Much Do Parents Actually Use Their Smartphones? Pilot Study Comparing Self-Report to Passive Sensing," *Pediatric Research* 86, no. 4 (October 2019): 416–418.

69. Sarah E. Domoff, Aubrey L. Borgen, and Jenny S. Radesky, "Interactional Theory of Childhood Problematic Media Use," *Human Behavior and Emerging Technologies* 2, no. 4 (2020): 343–353.

70. The idea of the "good enough" digital parent came from a discussion I had with several scholars in October 2018 during an event that brought together researchers focused on youth, technology, and well-being. I have forgotten some of the scholars sitting at the table during this discussion, but I remember Andrew Przybylski (who brought up Donald Winnicott's work on the good enough mother), Carrie James, and Ellen Wartella.

71. W. Winnicott, "The Theory of the Parent-Infant Relationship," *International Journal of Psycho-Analysis* 41 (1960): 585–595.

72. Lawrence and Choe, "Mobile Media and Young Children's Cognitive Skills."

73. Brittany Huber, Joanne Tarasuik, Mariana N. Antoniou, Chelsee Garrett, Steven J. Bowe, and Jordy Kaufman, "Young Children's Transfer of Learning from a Touchscreen Device," *Computers in Human Behavior* 56 (March 2016): 56–64, https://doi.org/10.1016/j .chb.2015.11.010; Brittany Huber, Megan Yeates, Denny Meyer, Lorraine Fleckhammer, and Jordy Kaufman, "The Effects of Screen Media Content on Young Children's Executive Functioning," *Journal of Experimental Child Psychology* 170 (June 2018): 72–85, https:// doi.org/10.1016/j.jecp.2018.01.006; Lawrence and Choe, "Mobile Media and Young Children's Cognitive Skills"; Kiley Sobel, Kate Yen, Yi Cheng, Yeqi Chen, and Alexis Hiniker, "No Touch Pig! Investigating Child-Parent Use of a System for Training Executive Function," *Proceedings of the 18th ACM International Conference on Interaction Design and Children* (June 12, 2019): 339–351, https://doi .org/10.1145/3311927.3323132.

74. Vanden Abeele, Abels, and Hendrickson, "Are Parents Less Responsive to Young Children?"

75. Domoff, Borgen, and Radesky, "Interactional Theory."

76. Even when all these design considerations are taken into account, researchers have identified cultural differences in the way children and their parents take up the same design, reminding us that children's technology use is embedded in broader social, cultural, political, and economic contexts. Kate Yen, Kate, Yeqi Chen, Yi Cheng, Sijin Chen, Ying-Yu Chen, Yiran Ni, and Alexis Hiniker, "Joint Media Engagement between Parents and Preschoolers in the U.S., China, and Taiwan," *Proceedings of the ACM on Human-Computer Interaction* 2, no. CSCW (November 1, 2018): 192.1–19, https://doi .org/10.1145/3274461.

77. For some concrete examples, see Alexis Hiniker, Bongshin Lee, Kiley Sobel, and Eun Kyoung Choe, "Plan & Play: Supporting Intentional Media Use in Early Childhood," *Proceedings of the 2017 Conference on Interaction Design and Children* (June 27, 2017): 85–95, https:// doi.org/10.1145/3078072.3079752; Hiniker et al., "Let's Play!"; and Sobel, "No Touch Pig!"

78. Brandon T. McDaniel, "Passive Sensing of Mobile Media Use in Children and Families: A Brief Commentary on the Promises and Pitfalls," *Pediatric Research* 86, no. 4 (2019): 425–427.

79. Beneteau et al., "Parenting with Alexa."

CHAPTER 3

1. Catherine Elizabeth Snow, *What Counts as Literacy in Early Childhood?* (Hoboken, NJ: Blackwell Publishing Ltd., 2006).

Early literacy experiences also prepare children for later academic success more generally. See Beverly J. Dodici, Dianne C. Draper, and Carla A. Peterson, "Early Parent-Child Interactions and Early Literacy Development," *Topics in Early Childhood Special Education* 23, no. 3 (2003): 124–136; Roberta Michnick Golinkoff, Erika Hoff, Meredith L. Rowe, Catherine S. Tamis-LeMonda, and Kathy Hirsh-Pasek, "Language Matters: Denying the Existence of the 30-Million-Word Gap Has Serious Consequences," *Child Development* 90, no. 3 (May 2019): 985–992; Victoria Purcell-Gates, "Stories, Coupons, and the 'TV

Guide': Relationships between Home Literacy Experiences and Emergent Literacy Knowledge," *Reading Research Quarterly* 31, no. 4 (1996): 406–428; Catherine E. Snow and Diane E. Beals, "Mealtime Talk That Supports Literacy Development," *New Directions for Child and Adolescent Development* 2006, no. 111 (2006): 51–66. This is a similar pattern to what we observed with children's executive function development in the previous chapter. In fact, high-quality early literacy experiences also help children develop their executive function skills (Golinkoff et al., "Language Matters").

2. Bransford, Brown, and Cocking, *How People Learn*; Dodici, Draper, and Peterson, "Early Parent-Child Interactions"; Golinkoff et al., "Language Matters"; Eileen T. Rodriguez and Catherine S. Tamis-LeMonda, "Trajectories of the Home Learning Environment across the First 5 Years: Associations with Children's Vocabulary and Literacy Skills at Prekindergarten," *Child Development* 82, no. 4 (August 2011): 1058–1075; Snow and Beals, "Mealtime Talk."

The home environment and how parents interact with their children in it play a critical role in young children's language acquisition and development; see Erika Hoff, "How Social Contexts Support and Shape Language Development," *Developmental Review* 26, no. 1 (2006): 55–88; Patricia K Kuhl, "Early Language Acquisition: Cracking the Speech Code," *Nature Reviews Neuroscience* 5, no. 11 (November 2004): 831–843; Lillian R. Masek, Brianna T. M. McMillan, Sarah J. Paterson, Catherine S. Tamis-LeMonda, Roberta Michnick Golinkoff, and Kathy Hirsh-Pasek, "Where Language Meets Attention: How Contingent Interactions Promote Learning," *Developmental Review* 60 (2021). My focus in this chapter, however, is literacy development.

3. Adriana G. Bus, Marinus H. van IJzendoorn, and Anthony D. Pellegrini, "Joint Book Reading Makes for Success in Learning to Read: A Meta-Analysis on Intergenerational Transmission of Literacy," *Review of Educational Research* 65, no. 1 (March 1, 1995): 1–21; / Purcell-Gates, "Stories, Coupons, and the 'TV Guide'"; Rodriguez and Tamis-LeMonda, "Trajectories of the Home Learning Environment"; Meredith L. Rowe, "A Longitudinal Investigation of the Role of Quantity and Quality of Child-Directed Speech in Vocabulary Development," *Child Development* 83, no. 5 (September 2012): 1762–1774; Rachel R. Romeo, Julia A. Leonard, Sydney T. Robinson, Martin R. West, Allyson P. Mackey, Meredith L. Rowe, and John D. E. Gabrieli,

"Beyond the 30-Million-Word Gap: Children's Conversational Exposure Is Associated with Language-Related Brain Function," *Psychological Science* 29, no. 5 (May 2018): 700–710; Catherine Elizabeth Snow, "The Development of Definitional Skill," *Journal of Child Language* 17, no. 3 (October 1990): 697–710; Snow and Beals, "Mealtime Talk."

4. Daniel R. Anderson and Tiffany A. Pempek, "Television and Very Young Children," *American Behavioral Scientist* 48, no. 5 (January 1, 2005): 505–522.

Children younger than this age struggle with the symbolic medium of television due to the fact that their interactions with and understanding of the world are primarily physical. Anderson and Pempek. "Television and Very Young Children"; Georgene L. Troseth and Judy S. DeLoache, "The Medium Can Obscure the Message: Young Children's Understanding of Video." *Child Development* 69, no. 4 (1998): 950–965. Young children's limited information-processing abilities also make it challenging for them to interpret the complex, formal features of television; Rachel Barr, "Transfer of Learning between 2D and 3D Sources during Infancy: Informing Theory and Practice," in "Television and Toddlers: The Message, the Medium, and Their Impact on Early Cognitive Development," special issue, *Developmental Review* 30, no. 2, (2010): 128–154; Mary L. Courage and Mark L. Howe, "To Watch or Not to Watch: Infants and Toddlers in a Brave New Electronic World," in "Television and Toddlers: The Message, the Medium, and Their Impact on Early Cognitive Development," special issue, *Developmental Review* 30, no. 2 (2010): 101–115; Kostyrka-Allchorne, Cooper, and Simpson, "Relationship between Television Exposure and Children's Cognition and Behaviour."

5. See Courage and Howe, "To Watch or Not to Watch"; Madigan et al., "Associations between Screen Use and Child Language Skills."

6. D. R. Anderson, A. C. Huston, K. L. Schmitt, D. L. Linebarger, and J. C. Wright, "Early Childhood Television Viewing and Adolescent Behavior: The Recontact Study," *Monographs of the Society for Research in Child Development* 66, no. 1 (2001): i–viii, 1–147; Deborah L. Linebarger and Sarah E. Vaala, "Screen Media and Language Development in Infants and Toddlers: An Ecological Perspective," in "Television and Toddlers: The Message, the Medium, and Their Impact on Early Cognitive Development," special issue, *Developmental Review* 30, no. 2 (2010): 176–202; Deborah L. Linebarger and Dale Walker, "Infants'

and Toddlers' Television Viewing and Language Outcomes," *American Behavioral Scientist* 48, no. 5 (January 1, 2005): 624–645; Madigan et al., "Associations between Screen Use and Child Language Skills."]

A particularly valuable environmental context is co-viewing screen content with an adult caregiver. Adults can help interpret the narrative, label objects, and reinforce vocabulary, much as they do when reading print books with their children. Linebarger, and Vaala, "Screen Media and Language Development in Infants and Toddlers"; Madigan et al., "Associations between Screen Use and Child Language Skills"; Reich, Yau, and Warschauer, "Tablet-Based eBooks for Young Children"; Strouse, O'Doherty, and Troseth, "Effective Coviewing." In fact, there's evidence that boys in particular benefit from co-viewing with an adult (Madigan et al., "Associations between Screen Use and Child Language Skills").

7. For an accessible overview of this research, I recommend Lisa Guernsey's 2012 book *Screen Time: How Electronic Media—From Baby Videos to Educational Software—Affects Your Young Child*. See also Anderson and Pempek, "Television and Very Young Children"; Bransford, Brown, and Cocking, *How People Learn*; Courage and Howe, "To Watch or Not to Watch," 101–115; Shalom M. Fisch and Rosemarie T. Truglio, *"G" Is for Growing: Thirty Years of Research on Children and "Sesame Street"* (Mahwah, NJ: Lawrence Erlbaum Associates, Inc, 2001); Kostyrka-Allchorne, Cooper, and Simpson, "Relationship between Television Exposure and Children's Cognition and Behaviour"; Linebarger, and Vaala, "Screen Media and Language Development in Infants and Toddlers"; Linebarger and Walker, "Infants' and Toddlers' Television Viewing and Language Outcomes"; Sarah Roseberry, Kathy Hirsh-Pasek, Julia Parish-Morris, and Roberta Michnick Golinkoff, "Live Action: Can Young Children Learn Verbs from Video?," *Child Development* 80, no. 5 (2009): 1360–1375; Strouse, O'Doherty, and Troseth, "Effective Coviewing."

8. Dore et al., "Education in the App Store"; Stamatios Papadakis and Michail Kalogiannakis, "Mobile Educational Applications for Children: What Educators and Parents Need to Know," *International Journal of Mobile Learning and Organisation* 11, no. 3 (January 1, 2017): 256–277; Jenny S. Radesky and Dimitri A. Christakis, "Increased Screen Time: Implications for Early Childhood Development and Behavior," *Pediatric Clinics of North America* 63, no. 5 (October 2016):

827–839; Burcu, Takacs, and Bus, "What Are We Downloading for Our Children?"; Sarah Vaala, Anna Ly, and Michael H Levine, *Getting a Read on the App Stores* (New York: Joan Ganz Cooney Center, 2015).

9. Bransford, Brown, and Cocking, *How People Learn*; Kuhl, "Early Language Acquisition"; Patricia K. Kuhl, "Early Language Learning and Literacy: Neuroscience Implications for Education," *Mind, Brain and Education: The Official Journal of the International Mind, Brain, and Education Society* 5, no. 3 (September 2011): 128–142; Purcell-Gates, "Stories, Coupons, and the 'TV Guide'"; Mitchel Resnick, *Lifelong Kindergarten: Cultivating Creativity through Projects, Passion, Peers, and Play* (Cambridge, MA: MIT Press, 2017); Snow, *What Counts as Literacy?*

10. Dore et al., "Education in the App Store"; Papadakis and Kalogiannakis, "Mobile Educational Applications for Children"; Meyer et al., "How Educational Are 'Educational' Apps for Young Children?"; Radesky and Christakis, "Increased Screen Time"; Sari, Takacs, and Bus, "What Are We Downloading for Our Children?"; Vaala, Ly, and Levine, "Getting a Read."

11. Jonathan S. Beier and Susan Carey, "Contingency Is Not Enough: Social Context Guides Third-Party Attributions of Intentional Agency," *Developmental Psychology* 50, no. 3 (2014): 889–902; Mary C. Blehar, Alicia F. Lieberman, and Mary D. Ainsworth, "Early Face-to-Face Interaction and Its Relation to Later Infant-Mother Attachment," *Child Development* 48, no. 1 (1977): 182–194; Golinkoff et al., "Language Matters"; Lauren J. Myers, Rachel B. LeWitt, Renee E. Gallo, and Nicole M. Maselli, "Baby FaceTime: Can Toddlers Learn from Online Video Chat?," *Developmental Science* 20, no. 4 (2017): e12430; Michael Tomasello and Michael J. Farrar, "Joint Attention and Early Language," *Child Development* 57, no. 6 (1986): 1454–1463.

12. Golinkoff et al., "Language Matters"; Purcell-Gates, "Stories, Coupons, and the 'TV Guide.'"

13. Sarah Roseberry, Kathy Hirsh-Pasek, and Roberta M. Golinkoff, "Skype Me! Socially Contingent Interactions Help Toddlers Learn Language," *Child Development* 85, no. 3 (2014): 956–970.

14. Anderson and Pempek, "Television and Very Young Children."

15. Troseth and DeLoache, "The Medium Can Obscure the Message."

16. Troseth et al. found that toddlers did not learn from video chat when they were asked to complete a more complex task than the tasks found in the studies conducted by Roseberry, Hirsh-Pasek, and Golinkoff and Myers et al.; see Georgene L. Troseth, Gabrielle A. Strouse, Brian N. Verdine, and Megan M. Saylor, "Let's Chat: On-Screen Social Responsiveness Is Not Sufficient to Support Toddlers' Word Learning from Video," *Frontiers in Psychology* 9 (2018): 1–10; and Roseberry, Hirsh-Pasek, and Golinkoff, "Skype Me!"; Myers et al., "Baby FaceTime."

17. Sho Tsuji, Anne-Caroline Fiévét, and Alejandrina Cristia, "Toddler Word Learning from Contingent Screens with and without Human Presence," *Infant Behavior & Development* 63 (May 2021): 101553; Myers et al., "Baby FaceTime."

18. Caroline Gaudreau, Yemimah A. King, Rebecca A. Dore, Hannah Puttre, Deborah Nichols, Kathy Hirsh-Pasek, and Roberta Michnick Golinkoff, "Preschoolers Benefit Equally from Video Chat, Pseudo-Contingent Video, and Live Book Reading: Implications for Storytime During the Coronavirus Pandemic and Beyond," *Frontiers in Psychology* 11 (2020): 2158.

19. Further research is needed to investigate just how early in a young child's life video chat can overcome the video deficit effect. It may be that ten-month-old Oliver was still a bit too young to learn any meaningful literacy skills when video chatting with Grandma and Grandpa on our drives home from daycare (Tsuji, Fiévét, and Cristia, "Toddler Word Learning").

20. Madigan et al., "Associations between Screen Use and Child Language Skills"; Lauren J. Myers, Emily Crawford, Claire Murphy, Edoukou Aka-Ezoua, and Christopher Felix, "Eyes in the Room Trump Eyes on the Screen: Effects of a Responsive Co-Viewer on Toddlers' Responses to and Learning from Video Chat," *Journal of Children and Media* 12, no. 3 (July 3, 2018): 275–294; Gabrielle A. Strouse, Georgene L. Troseth, Katherine D. O'Doherty, and Megan M. Saylor, "Co-Viewing Supports Toddlers' Word Learning from Contingent and Noncontingent Video," *Journal of Experimental Child Psychology* 166 (February 2018): 310–326.

21. Elisabeth McClure, Yulia Chentsova-Dutton, Rachel Barr, Steven Holochwost, and W. Parrott, "FaceTime Doesn't Count: Video Chat

as an Exception to Media Restrictions for Infants and Toddlers," *International Journal of Child-Computer Interaction* 6 (March 1, 2016): 1–6.

22. Verena Fuchsberger, Janne Mascha Beuthel, Philippe Bentegeac, and Manfred Tscheligi, "Grandparents and Grandchildren Meeting Online: The Role of Material Things in Remote Settings," *Proceedings of the 2021 CHI Conference on Human Factors in Computing Systems* (May 7, 2021): 478:1–14, https://doi.org/10.1145/3411764.3445191.

23. McClure et al., "FaceTime Doesn't Count."

24. Elisabeth R. McClure, Yulia E. Chentsova-Dutton, Steven J. Holochwost, W. G. Parrott, and Rachel Barr, "Look at That! Video Chat and Joint Visual Attention Development among Babies and Toddlers," *Child Development* 89, no. 1 (January 2018): 27–36.

25. Sean Follmer, Hayes Raffle, Janet Go, Rafael Ballagas, and Hiroshi Ishii, "Video Play: Playful Interactions in Video Conferencing for Long-Distance Families with Young Children," *Proceedings of the 9th International Conference on Interaction Design and Children IDC '10* (June 9, 2010): 49–58, https://doi.org/10.1145/1810543.1810550; Fuchsberger et al., "Grandparents and Grandchildren Meeting Online"; Tejinder K. Judge, Carman Neustaedter, Steve Harrison, and Andrew Blose, "Family Portals: Connecting Families through a Multifamily Media Space," *Proceedings of the SIGCHI Conference on Human Factors in Computing Systems CHI '11* (May 2011): 1205–1214, https://doi.org/10.1145/1978942.1979122; Hayes Raffle, Glenda Revelle, Koichi Mori, Rafael Ballagas, Kyle Buza, Hiroshi Horii, Joseph Kaye, et al., "Hello, Is Grandma There? Let's Read! StoryVisit: Family Video Chat and Connected e-Books," *Proceedings of the SIGCHI Conference on Human Factors in Computing Systems CHI '11* (May 2011): 1195–1204, https://doi.org/10.1145/1978942.1979121; Javier Tibau, Michael Stewart, Steve Harrison, and Deborah Tatar, "FamilySong: Designing to Enable Music for Connection and Culture in Internationally Distributed Families," *Proceedings of the 2019 on Designing Interactive Systems Conference DIS '19* (June 2019): 785–798, https://doi.org/10.1145/3322276.3322279; Svetlana Yarosh, "Supporting Long-Distance Parent-Child Interaction in Divorced Families," *CHI '08 Extended Abstracts on Human Factors in Computing Systems CHI EA '08* (April 2008): 3795–3800, https://doi.org/10.1145/1358628.1358932; Svetlana Yarosh, Kori M. Inkpen, and A. J. Bernheim Brush, "Video

Playdate: Toward Free Play across Distance," *Proceedings of the SIGCHI Conference on Human Factors in Computing Systems CHI '10* (April 10, 2010): 1251–1260, https://doi.org/10.1145/1753326.1753514; Svetlana Yarosh, Anthony Tang, Sanika Mokashi, and Gregory D. Abowd, "'Almost Touching': Parent-Child Remote Communication Using the Sharetable System," *Proceedings of the 2013 Conference on Computer Supported Cooperative Work CSCW '13* (February 23, 2013): 181–192, https://doi.org/10.1145/2441776.2441798.

26. Yarosh et al., "'Almost Touching'."

27. Rideout and Robb, *The Common Sense Census*.

28. Rideout and Robb, *The Common Sense Census*.

29. Garg et al. also note that the research conducted to date has not paid much attention to working with children from diverse backgrounds and identities, including children from lower socioeconomic backgrounds and living outside the Global North; see Radhika Garg, Hua Cui, Spencer Seligson, Bo Zhang, Martin Porcheron, Leigh Clark, Benjamin R. Cowan, and Erin Beneteau, "The Last Decade of HCI Research on Children and Voice-Based Conversational Agents," *CHI Conference on Human Factors in Computing Systems* (April 28, 2022): 1–19, https://doi.org/10.1145/3491102.3502016.

30. Beneteau et al., "Parenting with Alexa."

31. Neelma Bhatti, Timothy L. Stelter, and D. Scott McCrickard, "Conversational User Interfaces as Assistive Interlocutors for Young Children's Bilingual Language Acquisition," *ArXiv:2103.09228 [Cs]* (March 16, 2021); Radhika Garg and Subhasree Sengupta, "He Is Just Like Me: A Study of the Long-Term Use of Smart Speakers by Parents and Children," *Proceedings of the ACM on Interactive, Mobile, Wearable and Ubiquitous Technologies* 4, no. 1 (March 18, 2020): 11.1–24, https://doi.org/10.1145/3381002; Silvia B. Lovato, Anne Marie Piper, and Ellen Ann Wartella, "'Hey Google, Do Unicorns Exist?': Conversational Agents as a Path to Answers to Children's Questions," *Proceedings of the 18th ACM International Conference on Interaction Design and Children IDC '19* (June 12, 2019): 301–313, https://doi.org/10.1145/3311927.3323150; Naja A. Mack, Dekita G. Moon Rembert, Robert Cummings, and Juan E. Gilbert, "Co-Designing an Intelligent Conversational History Tutor with Children," *Proceedings of the 18th ACM International Conference on Interaction*

Design and Children IDC '19 (June 12, 2019): 482–487, https://doi
.org/10.1145/3311927.3325336.

32. Stefania Druga, Randi Williams, Cynthia Breazeal, and Mitchel
Resnick, "'Hey Google Is It OK If I Eat You?': Initial Explorations in
Child-Agent Interaction," *Proceedings of the 2017 Conference on Interaction Design and Children IDC '17* (June 27, 2017): 595–600, https://doi
.org/10.1145/3078072.3084330.

33. Fabio Catania, Micol Spitale, and Franca Garzotto, "Toward the
Introduction of Google Assistant in Therapy for Children with Neurodevelopmental Disorders: An Exploratory Study," *Extended Abstracts
of the 2021 CHI Conference on Human Factors in Computing Systems*
(May 8, 2021): 272:1–7, https://doi.org/10.1145/3411763.3451666.

34. Kimberly A. Brink and Henry M. Wellman, "Robot Teachers
for Children? Young Children Trust Robots Depending on Their
Perceived Accuracy and Agency," *Developmental Psychology* 56, no. 7
(2020): 1268–1277; Sandra L Calvert, "Intelligent Digital Beings as
Children's Imaginary Social Companions," *Journal of Children and
Media* 15, no. 2 (April 3, 2021): 291–296; Druga et al., "'Hey Google
Is It OK If I Eat You?'"; Anna Hoffman, Diana Owen, and Sandra L.
Calvert, "Parent Reports of Children's Parasocial Relationships
with Conversational Agents: Trusted Voices in Children's Lives,"
Human Behavior and Emerging Technologies 3, no. 4 (June 21, 2021):
606–617; Amanda Purington, Jessie G. Taft, Shruti Sannon, Natalya
N. Bazarova, and Samuel Hardman Taylor, "'Alexa Is My New BFF':
Social Roles, User Satisfaction, and Personification of the Amazon
Echo," *Proceedings of the 2017 CHI Conference Extended Abstracts on
Human Factors in Computing Systems CHI EA '17* (May 6, 2017): 2853–
2859, https://doi.org/10.1145/3027063.3053246; Ying Xu and Mark
Warschauer, "What Are You Talking To?: Understanding Children's
Perceptions of Conversational Agents," *Proceedings of the 2020 CHI
Conference on Human Factors in Computing Systems CHI '20* (April 23,
2020): 1–13, https://doi.org/10.1145/3313831.3376416.

35. Lovato, Piper, and Wartella, "'Hey Google, Do Unicorns Exist?'"
    Other research has found similar patterns of questioning; see, for
example, Cansu Oranç and Azzurra Ruggeri, "'Alexa, Let Me Ask You
Something Different': Children's Adaptive Information Search with

Voice Assistants," *Human Behavior and Emerging Technologies* 3, no. 4 (October 2021): 595–605.

36. Erin Beneteau, Olivia K. Richards, Mingrui Zhang, Julie A. Kientz, Jason Yip, and Alexis Hiniker, "Communication Breakdowns Between Families and Alexa," *Proceedings of the 2019 CHI Conference on Human Factors in Computing Systems CHI '19* (May 2, 2019): 243:1– 13, https://doi.org/10.1145/3290605.3300473; Yi Cheng, Kate Yen, Yeqi Chen, Sijin Chen, and Alexis Hiniker, "Why Doesn't It Work? Voice-Driven Interfaces and Young Children's Communication Repair Strategies," *Proceedings of the 17th ACM Conference on Interaction Design and Children IDC '18* (June 2018): 337–348, https://doi .org/10.1145/3202185.3202749; Druga et al., "'Hey Google Is It OK If I Eat You?'"; James Kennedy, Séverin Lemaignan, Caroline Montassier, Pauline Lavalade, Bahar Irfan, Fotios Papadopoulos, Emmanuel Senft, and Tony Belpaeme, "Child Speech Recognition in Human-Robot Interaction: Evaluations and Recommendations," *Proceedings of the 2017 ACM/IEEE International Conference on Human-Robot Interaction HRI '17* (2017): 82–90, https://doi.org/10.1145/2909824.3020229; Silvia Lovato and Anne Marie Piper, "'Siri, Is This You?': Understanding Young Children's Interactions with Voice Input Systems," *Proceedings of the 14th International Conference on Interaction Design and Children IDC '15* (June 2015): 335–338, https://doi.org/10.1145/2771839.2771910; Ivonne Monarca, Franceli L. Cibrian, Angel Mendoza, Gillian Hayes, and Monica Tentor, "Why Doesn't the Conversational Agent Understand Me? A Language Analysis of Children Speech," *Adjunct Proceedings of the 2020 ACM International Joint Conference on Pervasive and Ubiquitous Computing and Proceedings of the 2020 ACM International Symposium on Wearable Computers UbiComp-ISWC '20* (September 2020): 90–93, https://doi.org/10.1145/3410530.3414401; Oranç and Ruggeri, "'Alexa, Let Me Ask You Something Different'"; Jennifer Ureta, Celina Iris Brito, Jilyan Bianca Dy, Kyle-Althea Santos, Winfred Villaluna, and Ethel Ong, "At Home with Alexa: A Tale of Two Conversational Agents," in *Text, Speech, and Dialogue*, ed. Petr Sojka, Ivan Kopeček, Karel Pala, and Aleš Horák (New York: Springer International Publishing, 2020), 495–503.

37. Margery Mayer, "Speech Recognition Works for Kids, and It's about Time," *TechCrunch* (blog), https://social.techcrunch.com/2021/09/07 /speech-recognition-works-for-kids-and-its-about-time/.

38. Cheng et al., "Why Doesn't It Work?"

39. Lovato, Piper, and Wartella, "'Hey Google, Do Unicorns Exist?'"

40. Lovato, Piper, and Wartella, "'Hey Google, Do Unicorns Exist?'"

41. Leroy Ah Ben, "Irish Tech Firm Helps Kids' Voices Be Heard," *CNN* (August 23, 2021), https://www.cnn.com/2021/08/23/tech/ireland-soapbox-labs-voice-technology-children-spc/.

42. Ying Xu and M. Warschauer, "Young Children's Reading and Learning with Conversational Agents," *CHI Extended Abstracts CHI EA '19* (May 2019): 216–228; Ying Xu and Mark Warschauer, "Exploring Young Children's Engagement in Joint Reading with a Conversational Agent," *Proceedings of the Interaction Design and Children Conference IDC '20* (June 2020): 1–8.

43. Ying Xu, Dakuo Wang, Penelope Collins, Hyelim Lee, and Mark Warschauer, "Same Benefits, Different Communication Patterns: Comparing Children's Reading with a Conversational Agent vs. a Human Partner," *Computers & Education* 161 (February 1, 2021): 104059.

44. Ying Xu and Mark Warschauer, "A Content Analysis of Voice-Based Apps on the Market for Early Literacy Development," *Proceedings of the Interaction Design and Children Conference IDC '20* (June 2020): 361–371, https://doi.org/10.1145/3392063.3394418; Ying Xu, Stacy Branham, Xinwei Deng, Penelope Collins, and Mark Warschauer, "Are Current Voice Interfaces Designed to Support Children's Language Development?," *Proceedings of the 2021 CHI Conference on Human Factors in Computing Systems* (May 7, 2021): 633:1–12, https://doi.org/10.1145/3411764.3445271.

45. Zoe M. Flack, Andy P. Field, and Jessica S. Horst, "The Effects of Shared Storybook Reading on Word Learning: A Meta-Analysis," *Developmental Psychology* 54, no. 7 (July 2018): 1334–1346; Suzanne E. Mol, Adriana G. Bus, Maria T. de Jong, and Daisy J. H. Smeets, "Added Value of Dialogic Parent–Child Book Readings: A Meta-Analysis," *Early Education and Development* 19, no. 1 (February 5, 2008): 7–26.

46. Council on Communications and Media, "Media and Young Minds," *Pediatrics* 138, no. 5 (November 1, 2016): 1–6.

47. Anderson and Pempek, "Television and Very Young Children"; Bransford, Brown, and Cocking, *How People Learn*; Courage and Howe, "To Watch or Not to Watch"; Roseberry et al., "Live Action."

48. Seymour Papert, *Mindstorms: Children, Computers, and Powerful Ideas* (New York: Basic Books, Inc., 1980); Jean Piaget, *The Origins of Intelligence in Children* (New York: W. W. Norton & Co, 1952).

49. Heather L. Kirkorian, Koeun Choi, and Tiffany A. Pempek, "Toddlers' Word Learning from Contingent and Noncontingent Video on Touch Screens," *Child Development* 87, no. 2 (2016): 405–413; Silvia B. Lovato and Sandra R. Waxman, "Young Children Learning from Touch Screens: Taking a Wider View," *Frontiers in Psychology* 7 (2016): 1078.

50. Kristine Kwock, Siba Ghrear, Vivian Li, Taeh Haddock, Patrick Coleman, and Susan A. J. Birch, "Children Can Learn New Facts Equally Well from Interactive Media Versus Face to Face Instruction," *Frontiers in Psychology* 7 (2016): 1603.

51. Alexis R. Lauricella, Rachel Barr, and Sandra L. Calvert, "Parent-Child Interactions during Traditional and Computer Storybook Reading for Children's Comprehension: Implications for Electronic Storybook Design," *International Journal of Child-Computer Interaction* 2, no. 1 (2014): 17–25; Carmen López-Escribano, Susana Valverde-Montesino, and Verónica García-Ortega, "The Impact of E-Book Reading on Young Children's Emergent Literacy Skills: An Analytical Review," *International Journal of Environmental Research and Public Health* 18, no. 12 (January 2021): 6510.

52. Kirkorian, Choi, and Pempek, "Toddlers' Word Learning."

53. Bus, Takacs, and Kegel, "Affordances and Limitations of Electronic Storybooks"; Kathy Hirsh-Pasek, Jennifer M. Zosh, Roberta Michnick Golinkoff, James H. Gray, Michael B. Robb, and Jordy Kaufman, "Putting Education in 'Educational' Apps: Lessons from the Science of Learning," *Psychological Science in the Public Interest* 16, no. 1 (May 1, 2015): 3–34; Reich, Yau, and Warschauer, "Tablet-Based eBooks for Young Children."

54. Bus, Takacs, and Kegel, "Affordances and Limitations of Electronic Storybooks."

55. Koeun Choi and Heather L. Kirkorian, "Touch or Watch to Learn? Toddlers' Object Retrieval Using Contingent and Noncontingent Video," *Psychological Science* 27, no. 5 (May 1, 2016): 726–736; Koeun Choi, Heather L. Kirkorian, and Tiffany A. Pempek, "Touchscreens for Whom? Working Memory and Age Moderate the Impact

of Contingency on Toddlers' Transfer from Video," *Frontiers in Psychology* 12 (2021): 307; Colleen Russo-Johnson, Georgene Troseth, Charlotte Duncan, and Almaz Mesghina, "All Tapped Out: Touchscreen Interactivity and Young Children's Word Learning," *Frontiers in Psychology* 8 (April 12, 2017): 578.

56. Radesky et al., "Design Abuses in Children's Apps"; Meyer et al., "How Educational Are 'Educational' Apps for Young Children?"

57. Radesky et al., "Design Abuses in Children's Apps"; Reich, Yau, and Warschauer, "Tablet-Based eBooks for Young Children"; Xu and Warschauer, "What Are You Talking To?"

58. Melissa N. Callaghan and Stephanie M. Reich, "Mobile App Features That Scaffold Pre-School Learning: Verbal Feedback and Leveling Designs," *British Journal of Educational Technology* 52, no. 2 (2021): 785–806; López-Escribano, Valverde-Montesino, and García-Ortega, "The Impact of E-Book Reading"; Ying Xu, Joanna C. Yau, and Stephanie M. Reich, "Press, Swipe and Read: Do Interactive Features Facilitate Engagement and Learning with e-Books?," *Journal of Computer Assisted Learning* 37, no. 1 (2021): 212–225.

59. Choi, Kirkorian, and Pempek, "Touchscreens for Whom?"; Russo-Johnson et al., "All Tapped Out."

60. Reich, Yau, and Warschauer, "Tablet-Based eBooks for Young Children."

61. Russo-Johnson et al., "All Tapped Out"; Samarakoon, Usoof, and Halloluwa, "What They Can and Cannot"; Anthony, "Physical Dimensions of Children's Touchscreen Interactions."

62. Hiniker et al., "Touchscreen Prompts for Preschoolers"; Hiniker et al., "Hidden Symbols."

63. Hirsh-Pasek et al., "Putting Education in 'Educational' Apps"; Meyer et al., "How Educational Are 'Educational' Apps for Young Children?"; Takeuchi and Stevens, "The New Coviewing"; Strouse, O'Doherty, and Troseth, "Effective Coviewing"; Strouse et al., "Co-Viewing Supports Toddlers' Word Learning."

64. Kathleen Hogan and Michael Pressley, *Scaffolding Student Learning: Instructional Approaches & Issues* (Cambridge, MA: Brookline Books, 1997); L. S. Vygotsky, *Mind in Society: The Development of Higher Psychological Processes* (Cambridge, MA: Harvard University Press,

1978); David Wood, Jerome S. Bruner, and Gail Ross, "The Role of Tutoring in Problem Solving," *Journal of Child Psychology and Psychiatry* 17, no. 2 (1976): 89–100.

65. Allan Collins, John Seely Brown, and Susan E. Newman, "Cognitive Apprenticeship: Teaching the Craft of Reading, Writing and Mathematics," *Thinking: The Journal of Philosophy for Children* 8, no. 1 (March 1, 1988): 2–10.

66. However, in a systematic review of published research, Ewin et al. found mixed effects of parent-child joint media engagement on the quality and quantity of parent and child language, with some studies even showing negative effects. The researchers note that some aspects of the media experience, such as device noises, may interfere with parent-child discussion, suggesting the importance of careful design when developing technologies for children; see Carrie A. Ewin, Andrea E. Reupert, Louise A. McLean, and Christopher J. Ewin, "The Impact of Joint Media Engagement on Parent–Child Interactions: A Systematic Review," *Human Behavior and Emerging Technologies* 3, no. 2 (2021): 230–254. See also Hirsh-Pasek et al., "Putting Education in 'Educational' Apps"; Meyer et al., "How Educational Are 'Educational' Apps for Young Children?"; Reich, Yau, and Warschauer, "Tablet-Based eBooks for Young Children"; Strouse et al., "Co-Viewing Supports Toddlers' Word Learning"; and Catherine Walter-Laager, Kathrin Brandenberg, Luzia Tinguely, Jürg Schwarz, Manfred R. Pfiffner, and Barbara Moschner, "Media-Assisted Language Learning for Young Children: Effects of a Word-Learning App on the Vocabulary Acquisition of Two-Year-Olds," *British Journal of Educational Technology* 48, no. 4 (2017): 1062–1072.

67. Jessa Reed, Kathy Hirsh-Pasek, and Roberta Michnick Golinkoff, "Learning on Hold: Cell Phones Sidetrack Parent-Child Interactions," *Developmental Psychology* 53, no. 8 (2017): 1428–1436.

68. Lauren B. Adamson, Roger Bakeman, Deborah F. Deckner, and P. Brooke Nelson, "From Interactions to Conversations: The Development of Joint Engagement during Early Childhood," *Child Development* 85, no. 3 (May 2014): 941–955; Blehar, Lieberman, and Ainsworth, "Early Face-to-Face Interaction"; Gopnik, *The Gardener and the Carpenter*; and Tomasello and Farrar, "Joint Attention and Early Language."

69. In their systematic review and meta-analysis of data from forty-two studies, Madigan et al. ("Associations between Screen Use and Child Language Skills") found that greater quantity of screen use (i.e., hours per day/week) was negatively associated with children's language skills, while better quality of screen use (i.e., educational programs and co-viewing with caregivers) was positively associated with children's language skills.

70. American Psychological Association, "Socioeconomic Status," accessed May 6, 2022, https://www.apa.org/topics/socioeconomic -status.

The magnitude of and explanations for these disparities are debated among scholars. See Golinkoff et al., "Language Matters"; Douglas E. Sperry, Linda L. Sperry, and Peggy J. Miller, "Reexamining the Verbal Environments of Children from Different Socioeconomic Backgrounds," *Child Development* 90, no. 4 (2019): 1303–1318. However, considerable research has accumulated in support of their existence since Hart and Risley first identified the "30-million-word gap" between high- and low-socioeconomic status children back in the mid-1990s. See Betty Hart and Todd R. Risley, *Meaningful Differences in the Everyday Experience of Young American Children* (Baltimore: Paul H Brookes Publishing, 1995).

71. Rideout and Robb, *The Common Sense Census.*

72. Rideout and Robb, *The Common Sense Census.*

73. Emerging research suggests that children living in low socioeconomic households can benefit from targeted ebook interventions; see Carmen López-Escribano, Susana Valverde-Montesino, and Verónica García-Ortega, "The Impact of E-Book Reading on Young Children's Emergent Literacy Skills: An Analytical Review," *International Journal of Environmental Research and Public Health* 18, no. 12 (2021): 6510, https://doi.org/10.3390/ijerph18126510.

74. Anderson and Pempek, "Television and Very Young Children"; Troseth and DeLoache, "The Medium Can Obscure the Message."

75. Courage and Howe, "To Watch or Not to Watch"; Madigan et al., "Screen Use and Child Language Skills."

76. Roseberry, Hirsh-Pasek, and Golinkoff, "Skype Me!"; Tsuji, Fiévét, and Cristia, "Toddler Word Learning."

77. Kirkorian, Choi, and Pempek, "Toddlers' Word Learning"; Lovato and Waxman, "Young Children Learning from Touch Screens."

78. Choi, Kirkorian, and Pempek, "Touchscreens for Whom?"; Russo-Johnson et al., "All Tapped Out."

79. Reich, Yau, and Warschauer, "Tablet-Based eBooks for Young Children."

80. Rideout and Robb, *The Common Sense Census.*

81. Another area worth further investigation is technology's potential role in supporting children who are learning a second language. For instance, work is just beginning on exploring whether conversational agents can help children's bilingual language acquisition. See, e.g., Bhatti, Stelter, and McCrickard, "Conversational User Interfaces."

82. The strategies discussed here align with the four pillars of active, engaged, meaningful, and socially interactive experiences that researcher Kathy Hirsh-Pasek and colleagues claim are needed to support children's learning through interactive technologies. Hirsh-Pasek et al., "Putting Education in 'Educational' Apps."

83. Lawrence and Choe, "Mobile Media and Young Children's Cognitive Skills."

84. Xu and Warschauer, "Content Analysis of Voice-Based Apps"; Xu et al., "Current Voice Interfaces?"; Xu et al., "Same Benefits, Different Communication Patterns."

85. Hirsh-Pasek et al., "Putting Education in 'Educational' Apps"; Meyer et al., "How Educational Are 'Educational' Apps for Young Children?"

86. Reed, Hirsh-Pasek, and Golinkoff, "Learning on Hold."

CHAPTER 4

1. Theodor Seuss Geisel, *The Cat in the Hat* (New York: Random House Books for Young Readers, 1957).

2. Hirsh-Pasek et al., "Putting Education in 'Educational' Apps"; Jeffrey G. Parker, Kenneth H. Rubin, Stephen A. Erath, Julie C. Wojslawowicz, and Allison A. Buskirk, "Peer Relationships, Child Development, and Adjustment: A Developmental Psychopathology

Perspective," *Developmental Psychopathology: Theory and Method*, vol. 1, 2nd ed. (Hoboken, NJ: John Wiley & Sons, Inc., 2006), 419–493.

3. Simon Nicholson, "How Not to Cheat Children: The Theory of Loose Parts Play," *Landscape Architecture* 62, no. 1 (1971): 30–34.

4. Gopnik, *The Gardener and the Carpenter*; Parker et al., "Peer Relationships, Child Development, and Adjustment."

5. Parker et al., "Peer Relationships, Child Development, and Adjustment," Jean Piaget, *Play, Dreams and Imitation in Children* (New York: Routledge, 1962).

6. Both the forms of play and its benefits are culturally and historically situated. Suzanne Gaskins, "Children's Play as Cultural Activity," in *SAGE Handbook of Play and Learning in Early Childhood*, ed. Elizabeth Brooker, Mindy Blaise, and Susan Edwards (Thousand Oaks, CA: SAGE, 2014); Wendy L. Haight, Xiao-lei Wang, Heidi Han-tih Fung, Kimberley Williams, and Judith Mintz, "Universal, Developmental, and Variable Aspects of Young Children's Play: A Cross-Cultural Comparison of Pretending at Home," *Child Development* 70, no. 6 (1999): 1477–1488. My characterization of play in this chapter is largely informed by twentieth century and twenty-first century Western scholars.

7. Peter Gray, "Play as Preparation for Learning and Life," *American Journal of Play* 5, no. 3 (2013): 271–292.

8. Gopnik, *The Gardener and the Carpenter*.

9. Gopnik, *The Gardener and the Carpenter*.

10. Gopnik, *The Gardener and the Carpenter*, 172.

11. Gopnik, *The Gardener and the Carpenter*; Gray, "Play as Preparation for Learning and Life."

12. Gopnik, *The Gardener and the Carpenter*; Parker et al., "Peer Relationships, Child Development, and Adjustment"; Piaget, *Play, Dreams and Imitation in Children*.

13. William Damon, *The Moral Child: Nurturing Children's Natural Moral Growth* (New York: The Free Press, 1988); Gopnik, *The Gardener and the Carpenter*; Gray, "Play as Preparation for Learning and Life"; Steven Horwitz, "Cooperation Over Coercion: The Importance of Unsupervised Childhood Play for Democracy and Liberalism," June 22, 2015, https://dx.doi.org/10.2139/ssrn.2621848.

14. Daphna Buchsbaum, Sophie Bridgers, Deena Skolnick Weisberg, and Alison Gopnik, "The Power of Possibility: Causal Learning, Counterfactual Reasoning, and Pretend Play," *Philosophical Transactions of the Royal Society B: Biological Sciences* 367, no. 1599 (August 5, 2012): 2202–2212; Gopnik, *The Gardener and the Carpenter.*

15. Marjorie Taylor, *Imaginary Companions and the Children Who Create Them* (Oxford: Oxford University Press, 1999).

16. Alexandra Lange, *The Design of Childhood: How the Material World Shapes Independent Kids* (New York: Bloomsbury Publishing, 2018).

17. Nicholson, "How Not to Cheat Children."

18. Gray, "Play as Preparation for Learning and Life."

19. Lorraine E. Maxwell, Mari R. Mitchell, and Gary W. Evans, "Effects of Play Equipment and Loose Parts on Preschool Children's Outdoor Play Behavior: An Observational Study and Design Intervention," *Children, Youth and Environments* 18, no. 2 (2008): 36–63.

20. Maxwell, Mitchell, and Evans, "Effects of Play Equipment and Loose Parts."

21. Gray, "Play as Preparation for Learning and Life."

22. Elizabeth Bonawitz, Patrick Shafto, Hyowon Gweon, Noah D. Goodman, Elizabeth Spelke, and Laura Schulz, "The Double-Edged Sword of Pedagogy: Instruction Limits Spontaneous Exploration and Discovery," in "Probabilistic Models of Cognitive Development," ed. Fei Xu and Thomas L. Griffiths, special issue, *Cognition,* 120, no. 3 (September 1, 2011): 322–330; However, researchers have also found learning value in adult-guided play, especially in the context of specific learning objectives (Hirsh-Pasek et al., "Putting Education in 'Educational' Apps").

23. Hiniker et al., "Let's Play!"

24. Radesky et al., "Design Abuses in Children's Apps."

25. Pablo E. Torres, Philip I. N. Ulrich, Veronica Cucuiat, Mutlu Cukurova, María Clara Fercovic De la Presa, Rose Luckin, Amanda Carr, et al., "A Systematic Review of Physical–Digital Play Technology and Developmentally Relevant Child Behaviour," *International Journal of Child-Computer Interaction* 30 (December 1, 2021): 100323.

26. Jon Back, Caspar Heeffer, Susan Paget, Andreas Rau, Eva Lotta Sallnäs Pysander, and Annika Waern, "Designing for Children's Outdoor Play," *Proceedings of the 2016 ACM Conference on Designing Interactive Systems DIS'16* (June 4–8, 2016): 28–38, https://doi.org/10.1145/2901790.2901875.

27. At the same time, the researchers observed: "raw nature is much more adaptable than raw interactivity, even when the installations are designed to offer open-ended play." Back et al., "Designing for Children's Outdoor Play."

28. LouAnne Boyd, "Designing Sensory-Inclusive Virtual Play Spaces for Children," *Proceedings of the 18th ACM International Conference on Interaction Design and Children IDC'19* (June 12, 2019): 446–451, https://doi.org/10.1145/3311927.3325315; Mihaela Dragomir, Andrew Manches, Sue Fletcher-Watson, and Helen Pain, "Facilitating Pretend Play in Autistic Children: Results from an Augmented Reality App Evaluation," *Proceedings of the 20th International ACM SIGACCESS Conference on Computers and Accessibility ASSETS'18* (October 8, 2018): 407–409, https://doi.org/10.1145/3234695.3241020; Gill Althia Francis, William Farr, Silvana Mareva, and Jenny Louise Gibson, "Do Tangible User Interfaces Promote Social Behaviour during Free Play? A Comparison of Autistic and Typically-Developing Children Playing with Passive and Digital Construction Toys," *Research in Autism Spectrum Disorders* 58 (February 1, 2019): 68–82; Euan Freeman and Stephen Brewster, "Using Sound to Help Visually Impaired Children Play Independently," *Proceedings of the 2016 CHI Conference Extended Abstracts on Human Factors in Computing Systems CHI EA '16* (May 7, 2016): 1670–1676, https://doi.org/10.1145/2851581.2892534; Antonella Nonnis and Nick Bryan-Kinns, "Mazi: A Tangible Toy for Collaborative Play between Children with Autism," *Proceedings of the 18th ACM International Conference on Interaction Design and Children IDC'19* (June 12, 2019): 672–675, https://doi.org/10.1145/3311927.3325340; Kiley Sobel, Katie O'Leary, and Julie A. Kientz, "Maximizing Children's Opportunities with Inclusive Play: Considerations for Interactive Technology Design," *Proceedings of the 14th International Conference on Interaction Design and Children IDC'15* (June 21, 2015): 39–48, https://doi.org/10.1145/2771839.2771844; Amani Indunil Soysa and Abdullah Al Mahmud, "Interactive Pretend Play (IPPy) Toys for Children

with ASD," *Proceedings of the 31st Australian Conference on Human-Computer-Interaction OZCHI'19* (January 10, 2020): 285–289, https://doi.org/10.1145/3369457.3369480.

29. Dragomir et al., "Facilitating Pretend Play in Autistic Children," 407–409; Nonnis and Bryan-Kinns, "Mazi"; Soysa and Mahmud, "Interactive Pretend Play (IPPy) Toys."

30. Meryl Alper, Juan Pablo Hourcade, and Shuli Gilutz, "Adding Reinforced Corners: Designing Interactive Technologies for Children with Disabilities," *Interactions* 19, no. 6 (November 1, 2012): 72–75; Sobel, O'Leary, and Kientz, "Maximizing Children's Opportunities with Inclusive Play."

31. Sobel, O'Leary, and Kientz, "Maximizing Children's Opportunities with Inclusive Play."

32. Gardner and Davis, *The App Generation*; Jaron Lanier, *You Are Not a Gadget: A Manifesto* (New York: Alfred A. Knopf, 2010).

33. Lanier, *You Are Not a Gadget*.

34. This silo effect could change if Mark Zuckerberg's vision of the metaverse takes hold, making interoperability across platforms a seamless experience.

35. Torres et al., "A Systematic Review."

36. Petr Slovák, Nikki Theofanopoulou, Alessia Cecchet, Peter Cottrell, Ferran Altarriba Bertran, Ella Dagan, Julian Childs, and Katherine Isbister, "I Just Let Him Cry . . . : Designing Socio-Technical Interventions in Families to Prevent Mental Health Disorders," *Proceedings of the ACM on Human-Computer Interaction* 2, no. CSCW (November 1, 2018): 160:1–34, https://doi.org/10.1145/3274429; Nikki Theofanopoulou, Katherine Isbister, Julian Edbrooke-Childs, and Petr Slovák, "A Smart Toy Intervention to Promote Emotion Regulation in Middle Childhood: Feasibility Study," *JMIR Mental Health* 6, no. 8 (August 5, 2019): e14029.

37. A smart toy is an interactive toy whose on-board electronics enable it to respond to children as they play with it.

38. Gopnik, *The Gardener and the Carpenter*.

39. Shane W. Bench and Heather C. Lench, "On the Function of Boredom," *Behavioral Sciences* 3, no. 3 (September 2013): 459–472.

40. Jonathan Haidt and Greg Lukianoff, *The Coddling of the American Mind: How Good Intentions and Bad Ideas Are Setting up a Generation for Failure* (New York City: Penguin Press, 2018).

41. Sonia Livingstone and Alicia Blum-Ross, *Parenting for a Digital Future: How Hopes and Fears about Technology Shape Children's Lives* (New York: Oxford University Press, 2020).

42. Parker et al., "Peer Relationships, Child Development, and Adjustment."

43. Parker et al., "Peer Relationships, Child Development, and Adjustment."

44. There are also differences across income levels, with children in lower-income households spending more time playing video games each day than children in higher-income households; see Victoria Rideout, Alanna Peebles, Supreet Mann, and Michael Robb, *Common Sense Census: Media Use by Tweens and Teens, 2021* (San Francisco, CA: Common Sense, 2022).

45. Katie Davis, Julian A. Boss, and Perry Meas, "Playing in the Virtual Sandbox: Students' Collaborative Practices in Minecraft," *International Journal of Game-Based Learning (IJGBL)* 8, no. 3 (July 1, 2018): 56–76; Michael Dezuanni, *Peer Pedagogies on Digital Platforms: Learning with Minecraft Let's Play Videos* (Cambridge, MA: MIT Press, 2020).

46. Simon Goodson and Kirstie J. Turner, "Effects of Violent Video Games: 50 Years on, Where Are We Now?," *Cyberpsychology, Behavior, and Social Networking* 24, no. 1 (January 1, 2021): 3–4; Mike Snider, "Do Violent Video Games Really Drive People to Commit Mass Shootings?," *USA Today* (August 5, 2019).

47. Daphne Bavelier, C. Shawn Green, Doug Hyun Han, Perry F. Renshaw, Michael M. Merzenich, and Douglas A. Gentile, "Brains on Video Games," *Nature Reviews Neuroscience* 12, no. 12 (December 2011): 763.

48. Craig A. Anderson, Akiko Shibuya, Nobuko Ihori, Edward L. Swing, Brad J. Bushman, Akira Sakamoto, Hannah R. Rothstein, and Muniba Saleem, "Violent Video Game Effects on Aggression, Empathy, and Prosocial Behavior in Eastern and Western Countries: A Meta-analytic Review," *Psychological Bulletin* 136, no. 2 (2010): 151.

49. Christopher J. Ferguson, "Do Angry Birds Make for Angry Children? A Meta-Analysis of Video Game Influences on Children's and

Adolescents' Aggression, Mental Health, Prosocial Behavior, and Academic Performance," *Perspectives on Psychological Science* 10, no. 5 (September 1, 2015): 646–666; Christopher J. Ferguson, "Violent Video Games, Sexist Video Games, and the Law: Why Can't We Find Effects?," *Annual Review of Law and Social Science* 14, no. 1 (2018): 411–426.

50. Evans et al., "Explicating Affordances."

51. Isabela Granic, Adam Lobel, and Rutger C. M. E. Engels, "The Benefits of Playing Video Games," *American Psychologist* 69, no. 1 (January 2014): 67.

52. Geoffrey R. Loftus and Elizabeth F. Loftus, *Mind at Play: The Psychology of Video Games* (New York: Basic Books, 1983).

53. There are notable exceptions in games that deliberately provide little and/or ambiguous feedback to players in an effort to disorient them.

54. Mihaly Csikszentmihalyi, *Finding Flow* (New York: Basic Books, 1997); Loftus and Loftus, *Mind at Play*.

55. This "sweet spot" of challenge has a formal name: the zone of proximal development, named by Lev Vygotsky, the influential Russian developmental psychologist; see L. S. Vygotsky, *Mind in Society: The Development of Higher Psychological Processes* (Cambridge, MA: Harvard University Press, 1980); James V. Wertsch, *Vygotsky and the Social Formation of Mind* (Cambridge, MA: Harvard University Press, 1988). The zone of proximal development is connected to another of Vygotsky's ideas: scaffolding, where children are given support—from more experienced people or from objects like books, computers, and video games—to perform tasks that are beyond what they can accomplish on their own. The range of activities that a child can accomplish with scaffolding is the zone of proximal development, or ZPD. It's in the ZPD where development takes place. Children extend themselves beyond what they can do on their own, eventually they find they are able to accomplish the previously difficult activities without support, and they're ready for the next challenge.

56. Granic, Lobel, and Engels, "Benefits of Playing Video Games"; Jan L. Plass, Bruce D. Homer, and Charles K. Kinzer, "Foundations of Game-Based Learning," *Educational Psychologist* 50, no. 4 (October 2, 2015): 258–283.

57. Daniel M. Shafer and Corey P. Carbonara, "Examining Enjoyment of Casual Videogames," *Games for Health Journal* 4, no. 6 (2015): 452–459.

58. Stephen J. Aguilar, Caitlin Holman, and Barry J. Fishman, "Game-Inspired Design: Empirical Evidence in Support of Gameful Learning Environments," *Games and Culture* 13, no. 1 (2018): 44–70.

59. World Health Organization, "Addictive Behaviours: Gaming Disorder," 2018, https://www.who.int/news-room/questions-and-answers/item/addictive-behaviours-gaming-disorder.

60. Espen Aarseth, Anthony M. Bean, Huub Boonen, Michelle Colder Carras, Mark Coulson, Dimitri Das, Jory Deleuze, et al., "Scholars' Open Debate Paper on the World Health Organization ICD-11 Gaming Disorder Proposal," *Journal of Behavioral Addictions* 6, no. 3 (September 1, 2017): 267–270; Antonius J. van Rooij, Christopher J. Ferguson, Michelle Colder Carras, Daniel Kardefelt-Winther, Jing Shi, Espen Aarseth, Anthony M. Bean, et al., "A Weak Scientific Basis for Gaming Disorder: Let Us Err on the Side of Caution," *Journal of Behavioral Addictions* 7, no. 1 (March 1, 2018): 1–9.

61. Chao-Ying Chen, I-Hua Chen, Amir H. Pakpour, Chung-Ying Lin, and Mark D. Griffiths, "Internet-Related Behaviors and Psychological Distress Among Schoolchildren during the COVID-19 School Hiatus," *Cyberpsychology, Behavior, and Social Networking* 24, no. 10 (October 1, 2021): 654–663.

62. LeBourgeois et al., "Digital Media and Sleep in Childhood and Adolescence."

63. Sarah M. Coyne and Laura Stockdale, "Growing Up with Grand Theft Auto: A 10-Year Study of Longitudinal Growth of Violent Video Game Play in Adolescents," *Cyberpsychology, Behavior, and Social Networking* 24, no. 1 (January 1, 2021): 11–16.

64. Davis, Boss, and Meas, "Playing in the Virtual Sandbox."

65. Connected Camps, "About Us," *Connected Camps: Learning Together Online*, 2021, https://connectedcamps.com/about.

66. Kiley Sobel, "Families and Pokémon GO," *Parenting for a Digital Future* (2017).

67. Kiley Sobel, Arpita Bhattacharya, Alexis Hiniker, Jin Ha Lee, Julie A. Kientz, and Jason C. Yip, "It Wasn't Really about the Pokémon:

Parents' Perspectives on a Location-Based Mobile Game," *Proceedings of the 2017 CHI Conference on Human Factors in Computing Systems* (May 2, 2017): 1483–1496, https://doi.org/10.1145/3025453.3025761.

68. Adrienne L. Massanari, "Gamergate," *The International Encyclopedia of Gender, Media, and Communication,* (July 8, 2020): 1–5, https://doi.org/10.1002/9781119429128.iegmc014.

69. Anderson et al., "Violent Video Game Effects."

70. Teresa Lynch, Jessica E. Tompkins, Irene I. van Driel, and Niki Fritz, "Sexy, Strong, and Secondary: A Content Analysis of Female Characters in Video Games across 31 Years," *Journal of Communication* 66, no. 4 (August 1, 2016): 564–584; Gabriela T. Richard, and Kishonna L. Gray, "Gendered Play, Racialized Reality: Black Cyberfeminism, Inclusive Communities of Practice, and the Intersections of Learning, Socialization, and Resilience in Online Gaming," *Frontiers: A Journal of Women Studies* 39, no. 1 (2018): 112–148; Kishonna L. Gray, *Intersectional Tech: Black Users in Digital Gaming* (Baton Rouge, LA: LSU Press, 2020).

71. Alison Gopnik, Andrew N. Meltzoff, and Patricia K. Kuhl, *The Scientist in the Crib: Minds, Brains, and How Children Learn* (New York: William Morrow & Co, 1999); Gopnik, *The Gardener and the Carpenter.*

72. Gray, "Play as Preparation for Learning and Life."

73. Lanier, *You Are Not a Gadget.*

74. Torres et al., "A Systematic Review."

75. Sobel, O'Leary, and Kientz, "Maximizing Children's Opportunities with Inclusive Play."

CHAPTER 5

1. Gopnik, *The Gardener and the Carpenter*, 180.

2. Gopnik, *The Gardener and the Carpenter.*

3. John Santrock, *Child Development*, 14th ed. (Boston: McGraw-Hill, 2013).

4. Erik H. Erikson, *Childhood and Society*, 1st ed. (New York: W. W. Norton & Company, 1950).

5. Piaget, *Origins of Intelligence in Children.*

6. Gopnik, *The Gardener and the Carpenter*.

7. Flávio S. Azevedo, "The Tailored Practice of Hobbies and Its Implication for the Design of Interest-Driven Learning Environments," *Journal of the Learning Sciences* 22, no. 3 (2013): 462–510; Flávio S. Azevedo, "An Inquiry into the Structure of Situational Interests," *Science Education* 102, no. 1 (January 2018): 108–127; John D. Bransford, Ann L. Brown, and Rodney R. Cocking, *How People Learn: Brain, Mind, Experience, and School: Expanded Edition*, vol. 11 (Washington, DC: The National Academies Press, 2000); Linda Darling-Hammond, Lisa Flook, Channa Cook-Harvey, Brigid Barron, and David Osher, "Implications for Educational Practice of the Science of Learning and Development," *Applied Developmental Science* 24, no. 2 (April 2020): 97–140.

8. Katie Davis, Joanna Christodoulou, Scott Seider, and Howard E. Gardner, "The Theory of Multiple Intelligences," in *Cambridge Handbook of Intelligence*, ed. R. J. Sternberg and S. B. Kaufman (New York: Cambridge University Press, 2011), 485–503; Howard E. Gardner, *The Unschooled Mind: How Children Think and How Schools Should Teach*, 2nd ed. (New York: Basic Books, 2011); David H. Rose and Anne Meyer, *Teaching Every Student in the Digital Age: Universal Design for Learning* (Alexandria, VA: Association for Supervision and Curriculum Development, 2002).

9. Gutiérrez and Rogoff, "Cultural Ways of Learning"; Carol D. Lee, "The Centrality of Culture to the Scientific Study of Learning and Development: How an Ecological Framework in Educational Research Facilitates Civic Responsibility," *Educational Researcher* 37, no. 5 (2008): 267–279; Carol D. Lee, Margaret B. Spencer, and Vinay Harpalani, "'Every Shut Eye Ain't Sleep': Studying How People Live Culturally," *Educational Researcher* 32, no. 5 (June 2003): 6–13; Luis C. Moll and Norma Gonzalez, "Engaging Life: A Funds of Knowledge Approach to Multicultural Education," in *Handbook of Research on Multicultural Education*, 2nd ed., ed. J. Banks and C. McGee Banks, 699–715 (New York: Jossey-Bass, 2004); Na'ilah Suad Nasir, Ann S. Rosebery, Beth Warren, and Carol D. Lee, "Learning as a Cultural Process: Achieving Equity through Diversity," in *The Cambridge Handbook of the Learning Sciences*, ed. R. K. Sawyer, 2nd ed. (Cambridge, UK: Cambridge University Press, 2006), 489–504; Vicki S. Katz, *Kids in the Middle: How Children of Immigrants Negotiate Community Interactions for Their Families* (New Brunswick, NJ: Rutgers University Press, 2014).

10. The hosts are Chris Dede (Harvard Graduate School of Education), Curt Bonk (Indiana University), Punya Mishra (Arizona State University), Shuangye Chen (East China Normal University), Yong Zhao (University of Kansas), and Scott McLeod (University of Colorado, Denver).

11. Cecelia Aragon and Katie Davis, *Writers in the Secret Garden: Fanfiction, Youth, and New Forms of Mentoring* (Cambridge, MA: MIT Press, 2019).

12. Justin Reich, "Ed Tech's Failure during the Pandemic, and What Comes After," *Phi Delta Kappan*, February 22, 2021; Justin Reich, "The Paradox of Pandemic Education: We Changed Everything to Be Mostly the Same. Can Connected Learning Offer a New Way Forward?," *Connected Learning Alliance* (blog), April 19, 2021, https:// clalliance.org/blog/the-paradox-of-pandemic-education-we-changed -everything-to-be-mostly-the-same-can-connected-learning-offer-a -new-way-forward/.

13. Christopher Hoadley and Suraj Uttamchandani, "Current and Future Issues in Learning, Technology, and Education Research," White Paper for the Spencer Foundation, Chicago, September 2021; Vikki Katz and Victoria Rideout, "Learning at Home While Under-Connected: Lower-Income Families during the COVID-19 Pandemic," *New America*, June 2021, https://www.newamerica.org/education -policy/reports/learning-at-home-while-underconnected/; Sarah Mervosh, "The Pandemic Hurt These Students the Most," *New York Times*, July 28, 2021, https://www.nytimes.com/2021/07/28/us/covid-schools -at-home-learning-study.html; Justin Reich and Jal Mehta, "Healing, Community, and Humanity: How Students and Teachers Want to Reinvent Schools Post-COVID," *EdArXiv* (2021), https://doi .org/10.35542/osf.io/nd52b; Goldhaber et al., "The Consequences of Remote and Hybrid Instruction during the Pandemic."

14. Morgan G. Ames, "Charismatic Technology," *Proceedings of The Fifth Decennial Aarhus Conference on Critical Alternatives* (August 17, 2015): 109–120, https://doi.org/10.7146/aahcc.v1i1.21199; Larry Cuban, *Teachers and Machines: The Classroom Use of Technology Since 1920* (New York: Teachers College Press, 1986); Larry Cuban, "The Technology Puzzle," *Education Week*, August 4, 1999, sec. Ed-Tech Policy; Larry Cuban, *Oversold and Underused: Computers in the*

Classroom (Cambridge, MA: Harvard University Press, 2001); Justin Reich, *Failure to Disrupt: Why Technology Alone Can't Transform Education* (Cambridge, MA: Harvard University Press, 2020); Christo Sims, *Disruptive Fixation*, (Princeton, NJ: Princeton University Press, 2017).

15. David Cohen and Jal Mehta, "Why Reform Sometimes Succeeds: Understanding the Conditions That Produce Reforms That Last," *American Educational Research Journal* 54, no. 4 (August 1, 2017): 644–690; Reich, *Failure to Disrupt*.

16. Reich, *Failure to Disrupt*, 236. Reich first used the concept of schools domesticating new technologies in an essay he cowrote with Mizuko Ito; see Justin Reich and Mizuko Ito, "From Good Intentions to Real Outcomes: Three Myths about Education Technology and Equity," *Education Week*, October 30, 2017, sec. Education. This concept has also been described (using different words) by education historian Larry Cuban; see Cuban, *Teachers and Machines*.

17. Reich, *Failure to Disrupt*.

18. Reich, *Failure to Disrupt*.

19. Papert, *Mindstorms*.

20. Reich, *Failure to Disrupt*.

21. Ames, "Charismatic Technology"; Reich, *Failure to Disrupt*; Sims, *Disruptive Fixation*.

22. Ames, "Charismatic Technology"; Reich, *Failure to Disrupt*.

23. Hoadley and Uttamchandani, "Current and Future Issues"; Reich, *Failure to Disrupt*.

24. Reich, *Failure to Disrupt*.

25. Paul Attewell, "Comment: The First and Second Digital Divides," *Sociology of Education* 74, no. 3 (2001): 252–259.

26. Mega Subramaniam, Ligaya Scaff, Saba Kawas, Kelly M. Hoffman, and Katie Davis, "Using Technology to Support Equity and Inclusion in Youth Library Programming: Current Practices and Future Opportunities," *Library Quarterly* 88, no. 4 (October 1, 2018): 315–331. There is also a large difference in internet access between children living in rural versus urban and suburban areas; see Common Sense Media, "Teaching through the Digital Divide | Common

Sense Media," accessed 2021, https://www.commonsensemedia.org
/digital-divide-stories.

27. Katz and Rideout, "Learning at Home"; Rideout and Katz,
"Opportunity for All?"

28. Vikki Katz, "What It Means to Be 'Under-Connected' in Lower-
Income Families," *Journal of Children and Media* 11, no. 2 (2017):
241–244.

29. Attewell, "Comment."

30. Reich and Ito, "From Good Intentions to Real Outcomes." I use
privilege here to refer to the disproportionate allotment of societal
benefits (e.g., quality education) in the United States across socioeconomic, racial, and ethnic categories.

31. Attewell, "Comment"; Matthew H. Rafalow, "Disciplining Play:
Digital Youth Culture as Capital at School," *American Journal of Sociol-
ogy* 123, no. 5 (March 2018): 1416–1452; Matthew H. Rafalow, *Digital
Divisions: How Schools Create Inequality in the Tech Era* (Chicago: Uni-
versity of Chicago Press, 2020); Reich and Ito, "From Good Intentions
to Real Outcomes"; Justin Reich, Richard Murnane, and John Willett,
"The State of Wiki Usage in U.S. K–12 Schools: Leveraging Web 2.0
Data Warehouses to Assess Quality and Equity in Online Learning
Environments," *Educational Researcher* 41, no. 1 (January 1, 2012):
7–15.

People who are marginalized or minoritized experience exclusion
from positions of institutional power and authority; see Mizuko Ito,
Richard Arum, Dalton Conley, K. Gutiérrez, B. Kirshner, S. Livingstone, V. Michalchik, et al., *The Connected Learning Research Network:
Reflections on a Decade of Engaged Scholarship* (Irvine, CA: Connected
Learning Alliance, 2020), https://clalliance.org/wp-content/uploads
/2020/02/CLRN_Report.pdf.

32. Meryl Alper, *Giving Voice: Mobile Communication, Disability, and
Inequality* (Cambridge, MA: MIT Press, 2017); Ito et al., *The Connected
Learning Research Network*; Annette Lareau, *Home Advantage: Social
Class and Parental Intervention in Elementary Education*, (Lanham, MD:
Rowman & Littlefield Publishers, 2000).

33. Joseph B. Giacquinta, Jo Anne Bauer, and Jane E. Levin, *Beyond
Technology's Promise: An Examination of Children's Educational Computing at Home* (New York: Cambridge University Press, 1993); Ito et al.,

The Connected Learning Research Network; Henry Jenkins, with Ravi Purushotma, Margaret Weigel, Katie Clinton, and Alice J. Robison, *Confronting the Challenges of Participatory Culture: Media Education for the 21st Century*, The John D. and Catherine T. MacArthur Foundation Reports on Digital Media and Learning (Cambridge, MA: MIT Press, 2009).

34. Alper, *Giving Voice*; Katz, *Kids in the Middle*.

35. Reich and Ito, "From Good Intentions to Real Outcomes."

36. Rafalow, "Disciplining Play"; Rafalow, *Digital Divisions*.

37. Gillespie, *Custodians of the Internet*.

38. Ames, "Charismatic Technology"; Morgan G. Ames, *The Charisma Machine: The Life, Death, and Legacy of One Laptop per Child* (Cambridge, MA: MIT Press, 2019).

39. Reich, *Failure to Disrupt*.

40. The coding work was done by the company LeapFrog.

41. Azevedo, "The Tailored Practice"; Azevedo, "An Inquiry"; Bransford, Brown, and Cocking, *How People Learn*; Darling-Hammond et al., "Implications for Educational Practice"; Hirsh-Pasek et al., "Putting Education in 'Educational' Apps."

42. Azevedo, "The Tailored Practice"; Azevedo, "An Inquiry"; Suzanne Hidi and K. Ann Renninger, "The Four-Phase Model of Interest Development," *Educational Psychologist* 41, no. 2 (2006): 111–127; K. Ann Renninger, Suzanne Hidi, and Andreas Krapp, eds., *The Role of Interest in Learning and Development*, 1st ed. (New York: Psychology Press, 1992).

43. Saba Kawas, Sarah K. Chase, Jason Yip, Joshua J. Lawler, and Katie Davis, "Sparking Interest: A Design Framework for Mobile Technologies to Promote Children's Interest in Nature," *International Journal of Child-Computer Interaction* 20 (June 2019): 24–34.

44. Saba Kawas, Nicole Kuhn, Mina Tari, Alexis Hiniker, and Katie Davis, "'Otter This World': Can a Mobile Application Promote Children's Connectedness to Nature?," in *IDC '20: Interaction Design and Children*, Virtual Conference (2020): 444–457; Saba Kawas, Jordan Sherry-Wagner, Nicole Kuhn, Sarah Chase, Brittany Bentley, Joshua Lawler, and Katie Davis, "NatureCollections: Can a Mobile Application Trigger Children's Interest in Nature?," in *Proceedings of the 12th*

International Conference on Computer Supported Education (Prague: SCITEPRESS Science and Technology Publications, 2020): 579–592; Saba Kawas, Nicole S. Kuhn, Kyle Sorstokke, Emily E. Bascom, Alexis Hiniker, and Katie Davis, "When Screen Time Is Not Screen Time: Tensions and Needs between Tweens and Their Parents During Nature-Based Exploration," *Proceedings of the 2021 CHI Conference on Human Factors in Computing Systems* (May 7, 2021): 1–14, https://doi .org/10.1145/3411764.3445142.

45. Erling Björgvinsson, Pelle Ehn, and Per-Anders Hillgren, "Participatory Design and 'Democratizing Innovation,'" *Proceedings of the 11th Biennial Participatory Design Conference* (November 29, 2010): 41–50, https://doi.org/10.1145/1900441.1900448; Allison Druin, "Cooperative Inquiry: Developing New Technologies for Children with Children," *Proceedings of the SIGCHI Conference on Human Factors in Computing Systems CHI '99* (May 1, 1999): 592–599, https://doi .org/10.1145/302979.303166; Allison Druin, "The Role of Children in the Design of New Technology," *Behaviour & Information Technology* 21, no. 1 (2002): 1–25; Christiane Floyd, Wolf-Michael Mehl, Fanny-Michaela Reisin, Gerhard Schmidt, and Gregor Wolf, "Out of Scandinavia: Alternative Approaches to Software Design and System Development," *Human-Computer Interaction* 4, no. 4 (1989): 253–350; Ole Sejer Iversen, Anne Marie Kanstrup, and Marianne Graves Petersen, "A Visit to the 'New Utopia': Revitalizing Democracy, Emancipation and Quality in Co-operative Design," *Proceedings of the Third Nordic Conference on Human-Computer Interaction* (October 23, 2004): 171–179, https://doi.org/10.1145/1028014.1028040.

46. Kawas et al., "'Otter This World'"; Kawas et al., "NatureCollections"; Kawas et al., "When Screen Time Is Not Screen Time."

47. Gardner and Davis, *The App Generation*.

48. Kurt W. Fischer and Thomas Bidell, "Dynamic Development of Psychological Structures in Action and Thought," in *Handbook of Child Psychology: Theoretical Models of Human Development* 1 (January 1998): 467–561; Kurt W. Fischer and Thomas Bidell, "Dynamic Development of Action and Thought," in *Handbook of Child Psychology*, vol. 1, 6th ed., ed. W. Damon and R. M. Lerner (New York: Wiley, 2006): 313–399; Howard E. Gardner, *Multiple Intelligences: The Theory in Practice*, 1st ed. (New York: Basic Books, 1993).

49. Katie Bacon, "All Along," *Ed*, Harvard Ed. Magazine (Winter 2014), https://www.gse.harvard.edu/news/ed/14/01/all-along.

50. David Rose, "Universal Design for Learning," *Journal of Special Education Technology* 15, no. 2 (March 1, 2000): 56–60.

51. Gardner, *Multiple Intelligences*; Gardner, *The Unschooled Mind*; Hoadley and Uttamchandani, "Current and Future Issues," 14. Researchers Christopher Hoadley and Suraj Uttamchandani have identified an important tension between personalization and standardization when it comes to learning technologies. They observe that the edtech field often focuses on personalized learning experiences in the service of producing standardized learning outcomes. They note: "These moves bound, rather than expand, the kinds of learning that can take place."

52. CAST, "About Universal Design for Learning," accessed November 30, 2021, https://www.cast.org/impact/universal-design-for-learning-udl.

53. Rose, *The End of Average*.

54. David Rose and Bridget Dalton, "Learning to Read in the Digital Age," *Mind, Brain, and Education* 3, no. 2 (2009): 74–83.

55. Granic, Lobel, and Engels, "Benefits of Playing Video Games."

56. Bacon, "All Along."

57. Laura Benton and Hilary Johnson, "Widening Participation in Technology Design: A Review of the Involvement of Children with Special Educational Needs and Disabilities," *International Journal of Child-Computer Interaction* 3–4 (2015): 23–40.

58. Laura Benton, Asimina Vasalou, Rilla Khaled, Hilary Johnson, and Daniel Gooch, "Diversity for Design: A Framework for Involving Neurodiverse Children in the Technology Design Process," *Proceedings of the SIGCHI Conference on Human Factors in Computing Systems CHI '14* (April 26, 2014): 3747–3756, https://doi.org/10.1145/2556288.2557244.

59. Alper, *Giving Voice*; Ito et al., *The Connected Learning Research Network*.

60. Ito et al., *The Connected Learning Research Network*.

61. Ames, "Charismatic Technology"; Ames, *The Charisma Machine*.

62. Gutiérrez and Rogoff, "Cultural Ways of Learning"; Lareau, "Home Advantage"; Luis C. Moll, Cathy Amanti, Deborah Neff, and Norma Gonzalez, "Funds of Knowledge for Teaching: Using a Qualitative Approach to Connect Homes and Classrooms," *Theory into Practice* 31, no. 2 (1992): 132–141; Nasir et al., "Learning as a Cultural Process"; Nasir et al., "Rethinking Learning"; Rogoff, *The Cultural Nature of Human Development*.

63. Alexander Cho, Roxana G. Herrera, Luis Chaidez, and Adilene Uriostegui, "The 'Comadre' Project: An Asset-Based Design Approach to Connecting Low-Income Latinx Families to Out-of-School Learning Opportunities," *Proceedings of the 2019 CHI Conference on Human Factors in Computing Systems* (May 2, 2019): 1–14, https://doi.org /10.1145/3290605.3300837.

64. While not a learning technology per se, its function is to connect children with meaningful learning opportunities.

65. Cho et al., "The 'Comadre' Project," 7.

66. Gopnik, *The Gardener and the Carpenter*.

67. Azevedo, "The Tailored Practice"; Azevedo, "An Inquiry"; Bransford, Brown, and Cocking, *How People Learn*; Darling-Hammond et al., "Implications for Educational Practice."

68. Davis et al., "The Theory of Multiple Intelligences"; Gardner, *The Unschooled Mind*; Rose and Meyer, *Teaching Every Student*.

69. Gutiérrez and Rogoff, "Cultural Ways of Learning"; Lee, "The Centrality of Culture"; Lee, Spencer, and Harpalani, "'Every Shut Eye Ain't Sleep'"; Moll and Gonzalez, "Engaging Life"; Nasir et al., "Learning as a Cultural Process."

70. Reich, *Failure to Disrupt*; Reich and Ito, "From Good Intentions to Real Outcomes."

71. Reich, *Failure to Disrupt*; Sims, *Disruptive Fixation*.

72. Reich and Ito, "From Good Intentions to Real Outcomes."

73. Alper, *Giving Voice*; Giacquinta, Bauer, and Levin, *Beyond Technology's Promise*; Ito et al., *The Connected Learning Research Network*; Rafalow, "Disciplining Play"; Rafalow, *Digital Divisions*.

74. Ames, "Charismatic Technology"; Reich, *Failure to Disrupt*.

75. Cho et al., "The 'Comadre' Project."

CHAPTER 6

1. Davis, Dinhopl, and Hiniker, "'Everything's the Phone,'" 8.

2. Davis, Dinhopl, and Hiniker, "'Everything's the Phone,'" 8.

3. Parker et al., "Peer Relationships, Child Development, and Adjustment." Not all tweens seek distance from their parents; there are cultural differences in the way parents and their tween children relate to each other (Vikki Katz, personal communication, August 9, 2021).

4. Jacquelynne S. Eccles, Christy Miller Buchanan, Constance Flanagan, Andrew Fuligni, Carol Midgley, and Doris Yee, "Control versus Autonomy during Early Adolescence," *Journal of Social Issues* 47, no. 4 (1991): 53–68; Judith Smetana, Hugh F. Crean, and Nicole Campione-Barr, "Adolescents' and Parents' Changing Conceptions of Parental Authority," *New Directions for Child and Adolescent Development*, no. 108 (Summer 2005): 31–46.

5. Dante Cicchetti and Fred A. Rogosch, "A Developmental Psychopathology Perspective on Adolescence," *Journal of Consulting and Clinical Psychology* 70, no. 1 (2002): 6; Annette Lareau, *Unequal Childhoods: Class, Race, and Family Life* (Berkeley: University of California Press, 2011); Judith Smetana and Susan Chuang, "Middle-Class African American Parents' Conceptions of Parenting in Early Adolescence," *Journal of Research on Adolescence* 11, no. 2 (2001): 177–198; Ming-Te Wang, Nancy E. Hill, and Tara Hofkens, "Parental Involvement and African American and European American Adolescents' Academic, Behavioral, and Emotional Development in Secondary School," *Child Development* 85, no. 6 (2014): 2151–2168.

6. Harold D. Grotevant and Catherine R. Cooper, "Individuation in Family Relationships," *Human Development* 29, no. 2 (1986): 82–100.

7. Kawas et al., "When Screen Time Isn't Screen Time"; Ada S. Kim and Katie Davis, "Tweens' Perspectives on Their Parents' Media-Related Attitudes and Rules: An Exploratory Study in the US," *Journal of Children and Media* 11, no. 3 (2017): 358–366; Livingstone and Blum-Ross, *Parenting for a Digital Future*; Ellen Selkie, "Smartphone Ownership as a Developmental Milestone," *Journal of Adolescent Health* 64, no. 4 (2019): 419–420.

8. Rideout et al., *Common Sense Census*. The parent-led campaign "Wait Until 8th" seeks to increase the age when children first get a phone.

9. Kim and Davis, "Tweens' Perspectives." Other research has found that this motivation for initial phone ownership is particularly salient for children living in rural areas, who often have longer distances to travel; see Megan A. Moreno, Bradley R. Kerr, Marina Jenkins, Esther Lam, and Faisal S. Malik, "Perspectives on Smartphone Ownership and Use by Early Adolescents," *Journal of Adolescent Health* 64, no. 4 (April 1, 2019): 437–442.

10. Toke Haunstrup Christensen, "'Connected Presence' in Distributed Family Life," *New Media & Society* 11, no. 3 (May 1, 2009): 433–451; Emily Weinstein and Katie Davis, "Connecting 'round the Clock: Mobile Phones and Adolescents' Experiences of Intimacy,"in *Encyclopedia of Mobile Phone Behavior*, ed. Zheng Yan (Hershey, PA: IGI Global, 2015), 937–946.

11. Kawas et al., "When Screen Time Isn't Screen Time"; Rivka Ribak, "Remote Control, Umbilical Cord and Beyond: The Mobile Phone as a Transitional Object," *British Journal of Developmental Psychology* 27, no. 1 (2009): 183–196.

12. Kim and Davis, "Tweens' Perspectives."

13. Parents' desire to protect and control their children in the context of today's "risk society" isn't limited to technology use; Livingstone and Blum-Ross, *Parenting for a Digital Future*.

14. C. Blair Burnette, Melissa A. Kwitowski, and Suzanne E. Mazzeo, "'I Don't Need People to Tell Me I'm Pretty on Social Media': A Qualitative Study of Social Media and Body Image in Early Adolescent Girls," *Body Image* 23 (December 1, 2017): 114–125; Davis, Dinhopl, and Hiniker, "'Everything's the Phone'"; Arup Kumar Ghosh, Karla Badillo-Urquiola, Mary Beth Rosson, Heng Xu, John M. Carroll, and Pamela J. Wisniewski, "A Matter of Control or Safety?: Examining Parental Use of Technical Monitoring Apps on Teens' Mobile Devices," *Proceedings of the 2018 CHI Conference on Human Factors in Computing Systems* (April 19, 2018): 1–14, https://doi .org/10.1145/3173574.3173768; Arup Kumar Ghosh, Karla Badillo-Urquiola, Shion Guha, Joseph J. LaViola Jr, and Pamela J. Wisniewski, "Safety vs. Surveillance: What Children Have to Say about Mobile

Apps for Parental Control," *Proceedings of the 2018 CHI Conference on Human Factors in Computing Systems* (April 19, 2018): 124:1–14, https://doi.org/10.1145/3173574.3173698; Kim and Davis, "Tweens' Perspectives."

15. Kim and Davis, "Tweens' Perspectives"; Emily Weinstein and Carrie James, *Behind Their Screens: What Teens Are Facing (and Adults Are Missing)* (Cambridge, MA: MIT Press, 2022).

16. Ghosh et al., "A Matter of Control or Safety?"

17. Davis, Dinhopl, and Hiniker, "'Everything's the Phone.'"

18. Tran et al., "Modeling the Engagement-Disengagement Cycle."

19. Elizabeth K. Englander, *25 Myths About Bullying and Cyberbullying* (New York: John Wiley & Sons, 2020); Simone Lanette, Phoebe K. Chua, Gillian Hayes, and Melissa Mazmanian, "How Much Is 'Too Much'? The Role of a Smartphone Addiction Narrative in Individuals' Experience of Use," *Proceedings of the ACM on Human-Computer Interaction* (November 1, 2018): 101:1–22, https://doi.org/10.1145/3274370; Livingstone and Blum-Ross, *Parenting for a Digital Future.*

20. Livingstone and Blum-Ross, *Parenting for a Digital Future*; Davis, Dinhopl, and Hiniker, "'Everything's the Phone.'"

21. Lindsay Blackwell, Emma Gardiner, and Sarita Schoenebeck, "Managing Expectations: Technology Tensions among Parents and Teens," *Proceedings of the 19th ACM Conference on Computer-Supported Cooperative Work & Social Computing* (February 27, 2016): 1390–1401, https://doi.org/10.1145/2818048.2819928; Sarah E. Domoff, Jenny S. Radesky, Kristen Harrison, Hurley Riley, Julie C. Lumeng, and Alison L. Miller, "A Naturalistic Study of Child and Family Screen Media and Mobile Device Use," *Journal of Child and Family Studies* 28, no. 2 (February 1, 2019): 401–410; Alexis R. Lauricella, Drew P. Cingel, Leanne Beaudoin-Ryan, Michael B. Robb, M. Saphir, and Ellen A. Wartella, "The Common Sense Census: Plugged-in Parents of Tweens and Teens" (San Francisco: Common Sense Media, 2016); Melissa Mazmanian and Simone Lanette, "'Okay, One More Episode': An Ethnography of Parenting in the Digital Age," *Proceedings of the 2017 ACM Conference on Computer Supported Cooperative Work and Social Computing* (February 25, 2017): 2273–2286, https://doi.org/10.1145/2998181.2998218; Pamela Wisniewski, Arup Kumar Ghosh, Heng Xu, Mary Beth Rosson, and John M. Carroll, "Parental

Control vs. Teen Self-Regulation: Is There a Middle Ground for Mobile Online Safety?," *Proceedings of the 2017 ACM Conference on Computer Supported Cooperative Work and Social Computing* (February 25, 2017): 51–69, https://doi.org/10.1145/2998181.2998352.

22. Because tweens and teens are more likely to access the internet through their phone than any other device, there's a lot of overlap between teens' phone use and other kinds of interactive technology use (e.g., video games and social media); David Smahel, Hana Machackova, Giovanna Mascheroni, Lenka Dedkova, Elisabeth Staksrud, Kjartan Olafsson, Sonia Livingstone, and Uwe Hasebrink, "EU Kids Online 2020: Survey Results from 19 Countries," EU Kids Online, 2020, https://doi.org/10.21953/lse.47fdeqj01ofo.

23. Alexis Hiniker, Sarita Y. Schoenebeck, and Julie A. Kientz, "Not at the Dinner Table: Parents' and Children's Perspectives on Family Technology Rules," *Proceedings of the 19th ACM Conference on Computer-Supported Cooperative Work & Social Computing* (February 27, 2016): 1376–1389, https://doi.org/10.1145/2818048.2819940.

24. Hiniker, Schoenebeck, and Kientz, "Not at the Dinner Table"; Lanette et al., "How Much Is 'Too Much?'"; Weinstein and James, *Behind Their Screens*.

25. Hiniker, Schoenebeck, and Kientz, "Not at the Dinner Table."

26. Wisniewski et al., "Parental Control vs. Teen Self-Regulation."

27. Lynn Schofield Clark, *The Parent App: Understanding Families in the Digital Age* (New York: Oxford University Press, 2013).

28. Livingstone and Blum-Ross, *Parenting for a Digital Future*, critique this dichotomy, arguing that the London families in their research didn't fall into such neat categories. For instance, there were plenty of low-income parents who were very much focused on using technology to support their children's learning.

29. Sonia Livingstone, Kjartan Ólafsson, Ellen J. Helsper, Francisco Lupiáñez-Villanueva, Giuseppe A. Veltri, and Frans Folkvord, "Maximizing Opportunities and Minimizing Risks for Children Online: The Role of Digital Skills in Emerging Strategies of Parental Mediation," *Journal of Communication* 67, no. 1 (February 1, 2017): 82–105.

For instance, parents may be justifiably concerned about homophobic cyberbullying of their queer children; see Michelle F. Wright and Sebastian Wachs, "The Buffering Effect of Perceived Parental Social Support in the Longitudinal Relationship Between Homophobic Cyberbullying and LGBTQIA Adolescents' Health Outcomes," *Journal of Early Adolescence* (December 11, 2021): 1–23. Or their concern may focus on racialized digital surveillance by law enforcement of their children of color; see Desmond Upton Patton, Douglas-Wade Brunton, Andrea Dixon, Reuben Jonathan Miller, Patrick Leonard, and Rose Hackman, "Stop and Frisk Online: Theorizing Everyday Racism in Digital Policing in the Use of Social Media for Identification of Criminal Conduct and Associations," *Social Media + Society* 3, no. 3 (2017): 2056305117733344. See also Weinstein and James, *Behind Their Screens*.

30. Mizuko Ito, Candice Odgers, Stephen Schueller, Jennifer Cabrera, Evan Conaway, Remy Cross, and Maya Hernandez, *Social Media and Youth Wellbeing: What We Know and Where We Could Go* (Irvine, CA: Connected Learning Alliance, 2020), https://clalliance.org/wp-content/uploads/2020/06/Social-Media-and-Youth-Wellbeing-Report.pdf; Reich and Ito, "From Good Intentions to Real Outcomes."

31. Livingstone and Blum-Ross, *Parenting for a Digital Future*.

32. Livingstone and Blum-Ross, *Parenting for a Digital Future*; Radesky and Hiniker, "From Moral Panic to Systemic Change."

33. danah boyd, *It's Complicated: The Social Lives of Networked Teens*, (New Haven, CT: Yale University Press, 2014); Jacqueline Nesi, Sophia Choukas-Bradley, and Mitchell J. Prinstein, "Transformation of Adolescent Peer Relations in the Social Media Context: Part 1—A Theoretical Framework and Application to Dyadic Peer Relationships," *Clinical Child and Family Psychology Review* 21, no. 3 (September 1, 2018): 267–294 [hereafter, Nesi, Choukas-Bradley, and Prinstein, "Transformation 2018a"]; Weinstein and James, *Behind Their Screens*.

34. Helen Cowie, *From Birth to Sixteen: Children's Health, Social, Emotional and Linguistic Development*, 2nd ed. (London: Routledge, 2019).

35. Englander, *25 Myths About Bullying*; Lanette et al., "How Much Is 'Too Much?'"; Megan A. Moreno, Aubrey D. Gower, Heather Brittain, and Tracy Vaillancourt, "Applying Natural Language Processing to Evaluate News Media Coverage of Bullying and Cyberbullying," *Prevention Science* 20, no. 8 (2019): 1274–1283; Jan Ole Størup and Andreas Lieberoth, "What's the Problem with 'Screen Time'? A

Content Analysis of Dominant Voices and Worries in Three Years of National Print Media," *Convergence*, January 18, 2022, https://doi.org/10.1177/13548565211065299.

36. Katie Davis, "Friendship 2.0: Adolescents' Experiences of Belonging and Self-Disclosure Online," *Journal of Adolescence* 35, no. 6 (2012): 1527–1536; M. Shankleman, L. Hammond, and F. W. Jones, "Adolescent Social Media Use and Well-Being: A Systematic Review and Thematic Meta-Synthesis," *Adolescent Research Review* 6 (April 2021): 471–492, https://doi.org/10.1007/s40894-021-00154-5; Weinstein and James, *Behind Their Screens*.

37. Ric G. Steele, Jeffrey A. Hall, and Jennifer L. Christofferson, "Conceptualizing Digital Stress in Adolescents and Young Adults: Toward the Development of an Empirically Based Model," *Clinical Child and Family Psychology Review* 23, no. 1 (March 1, 2020): 15–26.

38. Niklas Johannes, Adrian Meier, Leonard Reinecke, Saara Ehlert, Dinda Nuranissa Setiawan, Nicole Walasek, Tobias Dienlin, Moniek Buijzen, and Harm Veling, "The Relationship between Online Vigilance and Affective Well-Being in Everyday Life: Combining Smartphone Logging with Experience Sampling," *Media Psychology* 24, no. 5 (2021): 581–605; Nesi, Choukas-Bradley, and Prinstein, "Transformation 2018a"; Shankleman, Hammond, and Jones, "Adolescent Social Media Use and Well-Being"; Steele, Hall, and Christofferson, "Conceptualizing Digital Stress"; Weinstein and James, *Behind Their Screens*; Jiaxin Yang, Xi Fu, Xiaoli Liao, and Yamin Li, "Association of Problematic Smartphone Use with Poor Sleep Quality, Depression, and Anxiety: A Systematic Review and Meta-Analysis," *Psychiatry Research* (February 2020): 284, https://doi.org/10.1016/j.psychres.2019.112686.

39. Weinstein and James, *Behind Their Screens*; Monique West, Simon Rice, and Dianne Vella-Brodrick, "Exploring the 'Social' in Social Media: Adolescent Relatedness—Thwarted and Supported," *Journal of Adolescent Research* 1, no. 32 (2021): 1–32.

40. Although my description of the tweens' side of the middle school dance is imagined, it's based on considerable empirical evidence accumulated over recent years related to tweens' and teens' social media experience. Nesi, Choukas-Bradley, and Prinstein, "Transformation

2018a"; Steele, Hall, and Christofferson, "Conceptualizing Digital Stress"; Weinstein and James, *Behind Their Screens*.

41. Weinstein and James, *Behind Their Screens*.

42. Robert L. Selman, "The Development of Interpersonal Competence: The Role of Understanding in Conduct," *Developmental Review* 1, no. 4 (December 1, 1981): 401–422.

43. Susan Harter, *The Construction of the Self: Developmental and Sociocultural Foundations*, 2nd ed. (New York: Guilford Publications, 2015).

44. Kenneth H. Rubin, William M. Bukowski, and Jeffrey G. Parker, "Peer Interactions, Relationships, and Groups," in *Handbook of Child Psychology: Social, Emotional, and Personality Development*, vol. 3, 6th ed. (Hoboken, NJ: John Wiley & Sons, Inc., 2006), 571–645.

45. Leah H. Somerville, "The Teenage Brain: Sensitivity to Social Evaluation," *Current Directions in Psychological Science* 22, no. 2 (April 1, 2013): 121–127. According to psychologist Laurence Steinberg, the gap between heightened emotional responses and lagging self-regulation skills in early adolescence may be magnified by the falling age of puberty over the last several decades; Laurence Steinberg, "Cognitive and Affective Development in Adolescence," *Trends in Cognitive Sciences* 9, no. 2 (2005): 69–74. See also Matt Richtel, "'It's Life or Death': The Mental Health Crisis Among U.S. Teens," *New York Times*, April 24, 2022, sec. Health, https://www.nytimes.com/2022/04/23/health/mental-health-crisis-teens.html.

46. Laurence Steinberg and Amanda Sheffield Morris, "Adolescent Development," *Annual Review of Psychology* 52, no. 1 (2001): 83–110.

47. Nesi, Choukas-Bradley, and Prinstein, "Transformation 2018a."

48. Weinstein and James, *Behind Their Screens*.

49. Weinstein and James, *Behind Their Screens*; see also West, Rice, and Vella-Brodrick, "Exploring the 'Social.'"

50. Nesi, Choukas-Bradley, and Prinstein, "Transformation 2018a"; Weinstein and James, *Behind Their Screens*.

51. Weinstein and James, *Behind Their Screens*.

52. Justin W. Patchin and Sameer Hinduja, "Cyberbullying Among Tweens in the United States: Prevalence, Impact, and Helping Behaviors," *Journal of Early Adolescence* 42, no. 3 (March 1, 2022): 414–430.

53. Englander, *25 Myths About Bullying*. Evidence suggests that children and adolescents who experience bullying or cyberbullying are at increased risk of suicidal ideation and suicide attempts; Mitch van Geel, Paul Vedder, and Jenny Tanilon, "Relationship between Peer Victimization, Cyberbullying, and Suicide in Children and Adolescents: A Meta-Analysis," *JAMA Pediatrics* 168, no. 5 (2014): 435–442, https://doi.org/10.1001/jamapediatrics.2013.4143. Suicide is the second leading cause of death among US high-school-aged youth age fourteen to eighteen, and suicide rates in this age group have increased in recent years; Asha Z. Ivey-Stephenson, Zewditu Demissie, Alexander E. Crosby, Deborah M. Stone, Elizabeth Gaylor, Natalie Wilkins, Richard Lowry, and Margaret Brown, "Suicidal Ideation and Behaviors among High School Students—Youth Risk Behavior Survey, United States, 2019," *MMWR Supplements* 69, no. 1 (2020): 47.

54. Samuel E. Ehrenreich, Madeleine J. George, Kaitlyn Burnell, and Marion K. Underwood, "Importance of Digital Communication in Adolescents' Development: Theoretical and Empirical Advancements in the Last Decade," *Journal of Research on Adolescence* 31, no. 4 (2021): 928–943.

55. Dan Olweus, *Bullying: What We Know and What We Can Do* (Hoboken, NJ: Wiley-Blackwell, 1993): 353–365; Dan Olweus, "A Profile of Bullying at School," *Educational Leadership* 60, no. 6 (2003): 12–17.

56. Jacqueline Nesi, Sophia Choukas-Bradley, and Mitchell J. Prinstein, "Transformation of Adolescent Peer Relations in the Social Media Context: Part 2—Application to Peer Group Processes and Future Directions for Research," *Clinical Child and Family Psychology Review* 21, no. 3 (September 1, 2018): 295–319 [hereafter, Nesi, Choukas-Bradley, and Prinstein, "Transformation 2018b"].

57. Katie Davis, Justin Reich, and Carrie James, "The Changing Landscape of Peer Aggression: A Literature Review on Cyberbullying and Interventions," *Journal of Youth Development* 9, no. 1 (March 1, 2014): 129–142; Englander, *25 Myths About Bullying*; Christina Salmivalli, Miia Sainio, and Ernest V. E. Hodges, "Electronic Victimization: Correlates, Antecedents, and Consequences Among Elementary and Middle School Students," *Journal of Clinical Child & Adolescent*

Psychology 42, no. 4 (July 1, 2013): 442–453; Sarah-Jeanne Viau, Anne-Sophie Denault, Ginette Dionne, Mara Brendgen, Marie-Claude Geoffroy, Sylvana Côté, Simon Larose, et al., "Joint Trajectories of Peer Cyber and Traditional Victimization in Adolescence: A Look at Risk Factors," *Journal of Early Adolescence* 40, no. 7 (August 1, 2020): 936–965; Denis Wegge, Heidi Vandebosch, Steven Eggermont, and Sara Pabian, "Popularity through Online Harm: The Longitudinal Associations Between Cyberbullying and Sociometric Status in Early Adolescence," *Journal of Early Adolescence* 36, no. 1 (January 1, 2016): 86–107.

58. Ito et al., *Social Media and Youth Wellbeing*.

59. B. Bradford Brown, "Peer Groups and Peer Cultures," in *At the Threshold: The Developing Adolescent* (Cambridge, MA: Harvard University Press, 1990), 171–196; Parker et al., "Peer Relationships, Child Development, and Adjustment."

60. Weinstein and James, *Behind Their Screens*.

61. Rubin, Bukowski, and Parker, "Peer Interactions, Relationships, and Groups."

62. Cicchetti and Rogosch, "A Developmental Psychopathology Perspective."

63. William M. Bukowski and Lorrie K. Sippola, "Groups, Individuals, and Victimization," in *Peer Harassment in School: The Plight of the Vulnerable and Victimized*, ed. J. Juvonen and S. Graham (New York: The Guilford Press, 2001) 355–377; Parker et al., "Peer Relationships, Child Development, and Adjustment."

64. Englander, *25 Myths About Bullying*.

65. Eddy H. de Bruyn, Antonius H. N. Cillessen, and Inge B. Wissink, "Associations of Peer Acceptance and Perceived Popularity with Bullying and Victimization in Early Adolescence," *Journal of Early Adolescence* 30, no. 4 (August 1, 2010): 543–566; Jaana Juvonen, Sandra Graham, and Mark A. Schuster, "Bullying among Young Adolescents: The Strong, the Weak, and the Troubled," *Pediatrics* 112, no. 6 (2003): 1231–1237; Christina Salmivalli, Arja Huttunen, and Kirsti M. J. Lagerspetz, "Peer Networks and Bullying in Schools," *Scandinavian Journal of Psychology* 38, no. 4 (1997): 305–312; Jelle J. Sijtsema, René Veenstra, Siegwart Lindenberg, and Christina Salmivalli. "Empirical

Test of Bullies' Status Goals: Assessing Direct Goals, Aggression, and Prestige." *Aggressive Behavior* 35, no. 1 (2009): 57–67, https://doi.org /10.1002/ab.20282.

66. Juvonen, Graham, and Schuster, "Bullying among Young Adolescents"; Sijtsema et al., "Empirical Test of Bullies' Status Goals."

67. Jennifer A. Jewell and Christia Spears Brown, "Relations among Gender Typicality, Peer Relations, and Mental Health during Early Adolescence," *Social Development* 23, no. 1 (2014): 137–156.

68. Robin M. Kowalski, Gary W. Giumetti, Amber N. Schroeder, and Micah R. Lattanner, "Bullying in the Digital Age: A Critical Review and Meta-Analysis of Cyberbullying Research among Youth," *Psychological Bulletin* 140, no. 4 (2014): 1073; Wegge et al., "Popularity through Online Harm."

69. Davis, Reich, and James, "The Changing Landscape"; Nesi, Choukas-Bradley, and Prinstein, "Transformation 2018b."

70. Weinstein and James, *Behind Their Screens.*

71. Englander, *25 Myths About Bullying.*

72. Englander, *25 Myths About Bullying.*

73. Noam Lapidot-Lefler and Azy Barak, "Effects of Anonymity, Invisibility, and Lack of Eye-Contact on Toxic Online Disinhibition," *Computers in Human Behavior* 28, no. 2 (2012): 434–443; Weinstein and James, *Behind Their Screens.*

74. Gardner and Davis, *The App Generation.*

75. Weinstein and James, *Behind Their Screens.*

76. Fabio Sticca and Sonja Perren, "Is Cyberbullying Worse than Traditional Bullying? Examining the Differential Roles of Medium, Publicity, and Anonymity for the Perceived Severity of Bullying," *Journal of Youth and Adolescence* 42, no. 5 (2013): 739–750.

77. Davis, Reich, and James, "The Changing Landscape"; Englander, *25 Myths About Bullying*; Shai Fuxman, Shari Kessel Schneider, and Miriam Heyman, "The Ruderman White Paper on Social Media, Cyberbullying, and Mental Health: A Comparison of Adolescents with and without Disabilities," The Ruderman Family Foundation, Boston, 2016; Salmivalli, Sainio, and Hodges, "Electronic Victimization"; Weinstein and James, *Behind Their Screens*; Izabela Zych and

Vicente J. Llorent, "Bias-Based Cyberbullying in Spanish Adolescents and Its Relation to Social and Emotional Competencies and Technology Abuse," *Journal of Early Adolescence* (June 2, 2021): 1–22, https:// doi.org/10.1177/02724316211020365.

78. Ann DeSmet, Maddalena Rodelli, Michel Walrave, Bart Soenens, Greet Cardon, and Ilse De Bourdeaudhuij, "Cyberbullying and Traditional Bullying Involvement among Heterosexual and Non-Heterosexual Adolescents, and Their Associations with Age and Gender," *Computers in Human Behavior* 83 (2018): 254–261; Fuxman, Schneider, and Heyman, "The Ruderman White Paper"; Sameer Hinduja and Justin W Patchin, "Bullying, Cyberbullying, and LGBTQ Students," Cyberbullying Research Center, 2011, accessed May 10, 2022, https://cyberbullying.org/bullying-cyberbullying-sexual-orientation -lgbtq.pdf; Vicente J. Llorent, Rosario Ortega-Ruiz, and Izabela Zych, "Bullying and Cyberbullying in Minorities: Are They More Vulnerable than the Majority Group?," *Frontiers in Psychology* 7 (2016): 1507.

79. Ehrenreich et al., "Importance of Digital Communication"; Jeffrey A. Hall, Ric G. Steele, Jennifer L. Christofferson, and Teodora Mihailova, "Development and Initial Evaluation of a Multidimensional Digital Stress Scale," *Psychological Assessment* 33, no. 3 (2021); Hae Yeon Lee, Jeremy P. Jamieson, Harry T. Reis, Christopher G. Beevers, Robert A. Josephs, Michael C. Mullarkey, Joseph M. O'Brien, and David S. Yeager, "Getting Fewer 'Likes' than Others on Social Media Elicits Emotional Distress among Victimized Adolescents," *Child Development* 91, no. 6 (2020): 2141–2159; Jacqueline Nesi and Mitchell J. Prinstein, "Using Social Media for Social Comparison and Feedback-Seeking: Gender and Popularity Moderate Associations with Depressive Symptoms," *Journal of Abnormal Child Psychology* 43, no. 8 (November 1, 2015): 1427–1438; Steele, Hall, and Christofferson, "Conceptualizing Digital Stress."

80. Lee et al., "Getting Fewer 'Likes'"; Nesi and Prinstein, "Using Social Media for Social Comparison and Feedback-Seeking."

81. Ehrenreich et al., "Importance of Digital Communication"; Englander, *25 Myths About Bullying*; Irene Kwan, Kelly Dickson, Michelle Richardson, Wendy MacDowall, Helen Burchett, Claire Stansfield, Ginny Brunton, Katy Sutcliffe, and James Thomas, "Cyberbullying and Children and Young People's Mental Health: A Systematic Map

of Systematic Reviews." *Cyberpsychology, Behavior, and Social Networking* 23, no. 2 (2020): 72–82, https://doi.org/10.1089/cyber.2019.0370.

82. Sameer Hinduja and Justin W. Patchin, "Connecting Adolescent Suicide to the Severity of Bullying and Cyberbullying," *Journal of School Violence* 18, no. 3 (2019): 333–346.

83. Weinstein and James, *Behind Their Screens*.

84. Weinstein and James, *Behind Their Screens*.

85. Weinstein and James, *Behind Their Screens*.

86. Englander, *25 Myths About Bullying*.

87. Amy Fleming, "Distraction Disaster! Notifications Are Ruining Our Concentration—Here's How to Escape Them," *Guardian*, December 16, 2021, sec. Life and Style.

88. Steele, Hall, and Christofferson, "Conceptualizing Digital Stress."

89. Englander, *25 Myths About Bullying*.

90. Linda Charmaraman and Catherine Grevet Delcourt, "Prototyping for Social Wellbeing with Early Social Media Users: Belonging, Experimentation, and Self-Care," *Proceedings of the 2021 CHI Conference on Human Factors in Computing Systems* (May 7, 2021): 704:1–15, https://doi.org/10.1145/3411764.3445332.

91. Carrie James, Emily Weinstein, and Kelly Mendoza, "Teaching Digital Citizens in Today's World: Research and Insights Behind the Common Sense K–12 Digital Citizenship Curriculum" (San Francisco: Common Sense Media, 2019).

92. Katie Davis and Lucas Koepke, "Risk and Protective Factors Associated with Cyberbullying: Are Relationships or Rules More Protective?," *Learning, Media and Technology* 41, no. 4 (October 1, 2016): 521–545; Englander, *25 Myths About Bullying*; Steele, Hall, and Christofferson, "Conceptualizing Digital Stress"; Wright and Wachs, "The Buffering Effect."

93. Allyson Chiu, "Will Hiding Likes on Instagram and Facebook Improve Users' Mental Health? We Asked Experts," *Washington Post*, May 28, 2021.

94. Marsha Mailick Seltzer, Marty Wyngaarden Krauss, Paul T. Shattuck, Gael Orsmond, April Swe, and Catherine Lord, "The Symptoms of Autism Spectrum Disorders in Adolescence and Adulthood,"

Journal of Autism and Developmental Disorders 33, no. 6 (December 1, 2003): 565–581.

95. Before becoming a member of the server users group, you must first complete an application attesting that you have autism or that you are a friend or family member of someone with autism.

96. AutCraft, "Autcraft—Wiki—Everything You Need to Know about the Autcraft Server," accessed December 19, 2021, https://www.aut craft.com.

97. Kathryn E. Ringland, Christine T. Wolf, Heather Faucett, Lynn Dombrowski, and Gillian R. Hayes, "'Will I Always Be Not Social?': Re-Conceptualizing Sociality in the Context of a Minecraft Community for Autism," *Proceedings of the 2016 CHI Conference on Human Factors in Computing Systems* (May 7, 2016): 1256–1269, https://doi .org/10.1145/2858036.2858038.

98. Ringland et al., "'Will I Always Be Not Social?'"

99. Ringland et al., "'Will I Always Be Not Social?'"

100. Grotevant and Cooper, "Individuation in Family Relationships."

101. Steele, Hall, and Christofferson, "Conceptualizing Digital Stress."

102. Livingstone and Blum-Ross, *Parenting for a Digital Future*.

103. Steele, Hall, and Christofferson, "Conceptualizing Digital Stress"; Nesi and Prinstein, "Using Social Media for Social Comparison and Feedback-Seeking."

104. Englander, *25 Myths About Bullying*; Fuxman, Schneider, and Heyman, "The Ruderman White Paper."

105. Weinstein and James, *Behind Their Screens*.

106. Englander, *25 Myths About Bullying*; Weinstein and James, *Behind Their Screens*.

107. Sophia Choukas-Bradley, "Do Social Media 'Likes' Matter for Teens' Well-Being?," *Psychology Today*, July 6, 2021, https://www .psychologytoday.com/us/blog/psychology-adolescence/202107/do -social-media-likes-matter-teens-well-being.

108. Amanda Lenhart and Kellie Owens, *The Unseen Teen: The Challenges of Building Healthy Tech for Young People*," Data & Society, May 5, 2021, https://datasociety.net/wp-content/uploads/2021/05/The-Un

seen-Teen-.pdf; Radesky and Hiniker, "From Moral Panic to Systemic Change."

CHAPTER 7

1. B. E. Compas, P. G. Orosan, and K. E. Grant, "Adolescent Stress and Coping: Implications for Psychopathology during Adolescence," *Journal of Adolescence* 16, no. 3 (September 1993): 331–349; National Academies of Sciences, Engineering, Medicine, *Promoting Positive Adolescent Health Behaviors and Outcomes: Thriving in the 21st Century* (Washington, DC: National Academies Press, 2020); Steinberg and Morris, "Adolescent Development."

2. A. W. Geiger and Leslie Davis, "A Growing Number of American Teenagers—Particularly Girls—Are Facing Depression," Pew Research Center, July 12, 2019, https://www.pewresearch.org/fact-tank/2019/07/12/a-growing-number-of-american-teenagers-particularly-girls-are-facing-depression/; Derek Thompson, "Why American Teens Are So Sad," *The Atlantic*, April 11, 2022, https://www.theatlantic.com/newsletters/archive/2022/04/american-teens-sadness-depression-anxiety/629524/. Suicide-related rates are growing faster among Black teens than among white teens. Though rates remain higher for white teens, the gap is narrowing; see Richtel, "'It's Life or Death.'"

3. Haidt and Lukianoff, *The Coddling of the American Mind*; Jean M. Twenge, *IGen: Why Today's Super-Connected Kids Are Growing up Less Rebellious, More Tolerant, Less Happy—and Completely Unprepared for Adulthood—and What That Means for the Rest of Us* (New York: Simon and Schuster, 2017). Though the trend in worsening mental health predates it, the pandemic has also had a negative impact on teens' mental well-being; see Matt Richtel, "Surgeon General Warns of Youth Mental Health Crisis," *New York Times*, December 7, 2021, https://www.nytimes.com/2021/12/07/science/pandemic-adolescents-depression-anxiety.html; Katherine Schaeffer, "In CDC Survey, 37% of U.S. High School Students Report Regular Mental Health Struggles during COVID-19," Pew Research Center, April 25, 2022, https://www.pewresearch.org/fact-tank/2022/04/25/in-cdc-survey-37-of-u-s-high-school-students-report-regular-mental-health-struggles-during-covid-19/.

4. Data from the National Institute of Mental Health showed that in 2020, 17 percent of twelve- to seventeen-year-olds reported having at

least one major depressive episode during the past year. NIMH, "Major Depression," National Institute of Mental Health (NIMH), 2020, accessed May 12, 2022, https://www.nimh.nih.gov/health/statistics/major-depression.

5. National Academies of Sciences, Engineering, Medicine, *Promoting Positive Adolescent Health Behaviors and Outcomes*.

6. Shiona McCallum, "Instagram: A Blessing or a Curse?," *BBC News*, November 7, 2021.

7. Anya Kamenetz, "Facebook's Own Data Is Not as Conclusive as You Think about Teens and Mental Health," *NPR*, October 6, 2021, https://www.npr.org/2021/10/06/1043138622/facebook-instagram-teens-mental-health.

8. Kaitlyn Burnell, Madeleine J. George, and Marion K. Underwood, "Browsing Different Instagram Profiles and Associations with Psychological Well-Being," *Frontiers in Human Dynamics* 2 (2020): 6; Grace Holland and Marika Tiggemann, "A Systematic Review of the Impact of the Use of Social Networking Sites on Body Image and Disordered Eating Outcomes," *Body Image* 17 (June 1, 2016): 100–110; Hannah K. Jarman, Siân A. McLean, Amy Slater, Mathew D. Marques, and Susan J. Paxton, "Direct and Indirect Relationships between Social Media Use and Body Satisfaction: A Prospective Study among Adolescent Boys and Girls," *New Media & Society* (2021); Mariska Kleemans, Serena Daalmans, Ilana Carbaat, and Doeschka Anschütz, "Picture Perfect: The Direct Effect of Manipulated Instagram Photos on Body Image in Adolescent Girls," *Media Psychology* 21, no. 1 (2018): 93–110; Nesi and Prinstein, "Using Social Media for Social Comparison and Feedback-Seeking."

9. Jarman et al., "Direct and Indirect Relationships between Social Media Use and Body Satisfaction."

10. Teen girls are considerably more likely to experience body dissatisfaction than boys, regardless of their social media use. Holland and Tiggemann, "A Systematic Review of the Impact of the Use of Social Networking Sites"; Nesi and Prinstein, "Using Social Media for Social Comparison and Feedback-Seeking."

11. Harter, *Construction of the Self*.

12. deray, "Twitter Is Home. Facebook Is Grandma's House. Snapchat Is Your Best Friend's House. Tumblr Is the Lunch Room. Instagram Is 24/7 Prom," Tweet. *@deray*, November 8, 2015, https://twitter.com/deray/status/663393306060021760; Tiidenberg, Hendry, and Abidin, *Tumblr*.

13. Leaver, Highfield, and Abidin, *Instagram*.

14. Beth T. Bell, "'You Take Fifty Photos, Delete Forty Nine and Use One': A Qualitative Study of Adolescent Image-Sharing Practices on Social Media," *International Journal of Child-Computer Interaction* 20 (2019): 64–71.

15. Rachel Cohen, Jasmine Fardouly, Toby Newton-John, and Amy Slater, "#BoPo on Instagram: An Experimental Investigation of the Effects of Viewing Body Positive Content on Young Women's Mood and Body Image," *New Media & Society* 21, no. 7 (July 1, 2019): 1546–1564.

16. Leaver, Highfield, and Abidin, *Instagram*.

17. Susruthi Rajanala, Mayra B. C. Maymone, and Neelam A. Vashi, "Selfies—Living in the Era of Filtered Photographs," *JAMA Facial Plastic Surgery* 20, no. 6 (2018): 443–444.

18. Weinstein and James, *Behind Their Screens*.

19. Rachel Cohen, Toby Newton-John, and Amy Slater, "The Relationship between Facebook and Instagram Appearance-Focused Activities and Body Image Concerns in Young Women," *Body Image* 23 (2017): 183–187; Holland and Tiggemann, "A Systematic Review of the Impact of the Use of Social Networking Sites"; Kleemans et al., "Picture Perfect."

20. Melissa Brough, Ioana Literat, and Amanda Ikin, "'Good Social Media?': Underrepresented Youth Perspectives on the Ethical and Equitable Design of Social Media Platforms," *Social Media + Society* 6, no. 2 (April 1, 2020): 1–11.

21. Sarah Nicola Metcalfe and Anna Llewellyn, "'It's Just the Thing You Do': Physical and Digital Fields, and the Flow of Capital for Young People's Gendered Identity Negotiation," *Journal of Adolescent Research* 35, no. 1 (January 1, 2020): 84–110.

22. S. Craig Watkins, Alexander Cho, Andres Lombana-Bermudez, Vivian Shaw, Jacqueline Ryan Vickery, and Lauren Weinzimmer, *The*

Digital Edge: How Black and Latino Youth Navigate Digital Inequality (New York: New York University Press, 2018).

23. Brough, Literat, and Ikin, "'Good Social Media?'"; Lenhart and Owens, *The Unseen Teen*.

24. Melanie Kennedy, "'If the Rise of the TikTok Dance and e-Girl Aesthetic Has Taught Us Anything, It's That Teenage Girls Rule the Internet Right Now': TikTok Celebrity, Girls and the Coronavirus Crisis," *European Journal of Cultural Studies* 23, no. 6 (December 1, 2020): 1069–1076. Twitter's algorithm has similarly been shown to exhibit racial bias; see Benjamin N. Jacobsen, "Regimes of Recognition on Algorithmic Media," *New Media & Society*, October 26, 2021, https://doi.org/10.1177/14614448211053555.

25. Kennedy, "'If the Rise of the TikTok Dance.'"

26. Kyra D. Gaunt, "YouTube, Twerking & You: Context Collapse and the Handheld Co-Presence of Black Girls and Miley Cyrus," *Journal of Popular Music Studies* 27, no. 3 (2015): 244–273.

27. Kath Albury, "Selfies, Sexts and Sneaky Hats: Young People's Understandings of Gendered Practices of Self-Representation," *International Journal of Communication* 9 (May 15, 2015): 12; Jessica Ringrose, Laura Harvey, Rosalind Gill, and Sonia Livingstone, "Teen Girls, Sexual Double Standards and 'Sexting': Gendered Value in Digital Image Exchange," *Feminist Theory* 14, no. 3 (December 1, 2013): 305–323; Weinstein and James, *Behind Their Screens*; Michael Salter, Thomas Crofts, and Murray Lee, "Beyond Criminalisation and Responsibilisation: Sexting, Gender and Young People," *Current Issues in Criminal Justice* 24, no. 3 (March 1, 2013): 301–316; Katrien Symons, Koen Ponnet, Michel Walrave, and Wannes Heirman, "Sexting Scripts in Adolescent Relationships: Is Sexting Becoming the Norm?," *New Media & Society* 20, no. 10 (October 1, 2018): 3836–3857.

28. Symons et al., "Sexting Scripts in Adolescent Relationships."

29. Research conducted by Thorn, a nonprofit group that develops technology solutions to combat child sexual abuse, found that rates of teen sexting increased over the pandemic, especially among nine- to twelve-year-olds (from 6 percent in 2019 to 14 percent in 2020); see Thorn, *Self-Generated Sexual Abuse Material: Youth Attitudes and Experiences in 2020* (Los Angeles: Thorn, November 2021). See also Bianca Klettke, David J. Hallford, and David J. Mellor, "Sexting

Prevalence and Correlates: A Systematic Literature Review," *Clinical Psychology Review* 34, no. 1 (February 2014): 44–53; Symons et al., "Sexting Scripts in Adolescent Relationships."

30. Symons et al., "Sexting Scripts in Adolescent Relationships."

31. Sander De Ridder, "Sexting as Sexual Stigma: The Paradox of Sexual Self-Representation in Digital Youth Cultures," *European Journal of Cultural Studies* 22, no. 5–6 (October 1, 2019): 563–578.

32. Symons et al., "Sexting Scripts in Adolescent Relationships."

33. De Ridder, "Sexting as Sexual Stigma."

34. Marijke Naezer and Jessica Ringrose, "Adventure, Intimacy, Identity, and Knowledge: Exploring How Social Media Are Shaping and Transforming Youth Sexuality," in *The Cambridge Handbook of Sexual Development: Childhood and Adolescence*, ed. by Jen Gilbert and Sharon Lamb (Cambridge, UK: Cambridge University Press, 2018), 419–438; Ringrose et al., "Teen Girls, Sexual Double Standards and 'Sexting.'"

35. A moral panic is a widespread public concern about some influence having a deleterious effect on the values, norms, and standards of behavior in a society. Moral panics are typically spread by mass media that stoke fear disproportionate to the actual threat, which is often small or nonexistent. See Mia Belle Frothingham, "Folk Devils and Moral Panics (Cohen 1972)," *Simply Psychology*, October 28, 2021, www.simplypsychology.org/folk-devils-and-moral-panics-cohen-1972.html.

36. Salter, Crofts, and Murray Lee, "Beyond Criminalisation and Responsibilisation"; Lenhart and Owens, *The Unseen Teen.*

37. Ringrose et al., "Teen Girls, Sexual Double Standards and 'Sexting.'"

38. Faye Mishna, Elizabeth Milne, Charlene Cook, Andrea Slane, and Jessica Ringrose, "Unsolicited Sexts and Unwanted Requests for Sexts: Reflecting on the Online Sexual Harassment of Youth," *Youth & Society*, November 26, 2021, https://doi.org/10.1177/0044118X211058226.

39. Katie Davis and Emily Weinstein, "Identity Development in the Digital Age: An Eriksonian Perspective," in *Identity, Sexuality, and Relationships among Emerging Adults in the Digital Age* (Hershey, PA: IGI Global, 2017); Sijia Xiao, D. Metaxa, J. Park, K. Karahalios, and Niloufar Salehi, "Random, Messy, Funny, Raw: Finstas as Intimate

Reconfigurations of Social Media," *Proceedings of the 2020 CHI Conference on Human Factors in Computing Systems* (April 23, 2020): 1–13, https://doi.org/10.1145/3313831.3376424.

40. Xiao et al., "Random, Messy, Funny, Raw."

41. Cohen et al., "#BoPo on Instagram."

42. Marika Tiggemann and Isabella Anderberg, "Social Media Is Not Real: The Effect of 'Instagram vs Reality' Images on Women's Social Comparison and Body Image," *New Media & Society* 22, no. 12 (2020): 2183–2199.

43. Weinstein and James, *Behind Their Screens*.

44. Kirsty Grant, "Influencers React to Norway Photo Edit Law: 'Welcome Honesty' or a 'Shortcut'?," *BBC News*, July 6, 2021, sec. Newsbeat, https://www.bbc.com/news/newsbeat-57721080.

45. "MP Proposes Law on Labels for Digitally-Altered Body Images," *BBC News*, September 15, 2020, sec. Leicester, https://www.bbc.com/news/uk-england-leicestershire-53959130. As of April 29, 2022, the Digitally Altered Body Images Bill was in its second reading in the UK House of Commons (https://bills.parliament.uk/bills/3093).

46. Sophia Choukas-Bradley, "Norway's New Social Media Law: Is It Supported by Research?," *Psychology Today*, July 8, 2021, https://www.psychologytoday.com/us/blog/psychology-adolescence/202107/norway-s-new-social-media-law-is-it-supported-research.

47. Cohen et al., "#BoPo on Instagram"; Tiggemann and Anderberg, "Social Media Is Not Real."

48. Ito et al., *Social Media and Youth Wellbeing*.

49. There's reason to believe this proportion would be even greater had the Gallup poll included younger members of Generation Z, since they found that younger generations are considerably more likely to identify as LGBT than older generations. Jeffrey M. Jones, "LGBT Identification in U.S. Ticks Up to 7.1%," *Gallup.com*, February 17, 2022, https://news.gallup.com/poll/389792/lgbt-identification-ticks-up.aspx.

50. Gardner and Davis, *The App Generation*.

51. Brianna Dym, Jed R. Brubaker, Casey Fiesler, and Bryan Semaan, "'Coming Out Okay': Community Narratives for LGBTQ Identity

Recovery Work," *Proceedings of the ACM on Human-Computer Interaction* 3, (November 7, 2019): 154:1–28, https://doi.org/10.1145/3359256; Lauren B. McInroy, "Building Connections and Slaying Basilisks: Fostering Support, Resilience, and Positive Adjustment for Sexual and Gender Minority Youth in Online Fandom Communities," *Information, Communication & Society* 23, no. 13 (November 9, 2020): 1874–1891.

52. Aragon and Davis, *Writers in the Secret Garden*; Brianna Dym and Casey Fiesler, "Vulnerable and Online: Fandom's Case for Stronger Privacy Norms and Tools," *Companion of the 2018 ACM Conference on Computer Supported Cooperative Work and Social Computing* (2018): 329–332; Dym et al., "'Coming Out Okay'"; Lauren B. McInroy, Ian Zapcic, and Oliver W. J. Beer, "Online Fandom Communities as Networked Counterpublics: LGBTQ+ Youths' Perceptions of Representation and Community Climate," *Convergence: The International Journal of Research into New Media Technologies* (July 25, 2021): 13548565211032376.

53. Aragon and Davis, *Writers in the Secret Garden*.

54. Ito et al., *Social Media and Youth Wellbeing*; Naezer and Ringrose, "Adventure, Intimacy, Identity, and Knowledge"; Catherine V. Talbot, Amelia Talbot, Danielle J. Roe, and Pam Briggs, "The Management of LGBTQ+ Identities on Social Media: A Student Perspective," *New Media & Society* (December 17, 2020): 1461444820981009.

55. Aragon and Davis, *Writers in the Secret Garden*; Dym et al., "'Coming Out Okay'"; McInroy, "Building Connections and Slaying Basilisks"; McInroy, Zapcic, and Beer, "Online Fandom Communities as Networked Counterpublics."

56. Trevor Boffone and Sarah Jerasa, "Toward a (Queer) Reading Community: BookTok, Teen Readers, and the Rise of TikTok Literacies," *Talking Points* 33, no. 1 (2021): 10–16.

57. Unfortunately, safety and acceptance aren't guaranteed in online fan communities. Youth sometimes encounter prejudice and discrimination, including from internet trolls and other LGBTQ+ people with more normative identities. McInroy, Zapcic, and Beer, "Online Fandom Communities as Networked Counterpublics"; Adam Bates, Trish Hobman, and Beth T. Bell, "'Let Me Do What I Please with It . . .

Don't Decide My Identity for Me': LGBTQ+ Youth Experiences of Social Media in Narrative Identity Development," *Journal of Adolescent Research* 35, no. 1 (January 1, 2020): 51–83; Michael Ann DeVito, Ashley Marie Walker, and Julia R. Fernandez, "Values (Mis)Alignment: Exploring Tensions Between Platform and LGBTQ+ Community Design Values," *Proceedings of the ACM on Human-Computer Interaction* 5 (April 22, 2021): 88:1–27, https://doi.org/10.1145/3449162; Jacqueline Nesi, "The Impact of Social Media on Youth Mental Health: Challenges and Opportunities," *North Carolina Medical Journal* 81, no. 2 (April 2020): 116–121; Ellen Selkie, Victoria Adkins, Ellie Masters, Anita Bajpai, and Daniel Shumer, "Transgender Adolescents' Uses of Social Media for Social Support," *Journal of Adolescent Health* 66, no. 3 (March 1, 2020): 275–280.

58. Erik H. Erikson, *Identity: Youth and Crisis* (New York: Norton, 1969); Moin Syed and Kate C. McLean, "Understanding Identity Integration: Theoretical, Methodological, and Applied Issue," *Journal of Adolescence* 47 (February 2016): 109–118.

59. Weinstein and James, *Behind Their Screens*.

60. Bates, Hobman, and Bell, "'Let Me Do What I Please with It."

61. Bates, Hobman, and Bell, "'Let Me Do What I Please with It."

62. Alexander Cho, "Default Publicness: Queer Youth of Color, Social Media, and Being Outed by the Machine," *New Media & Society* 20, no. 9 (September 1, 2018): 3183–3200; Sander De Ridder and Sofie Van Bauwel, "The Discursive Construction of Gay Teenagers in Times of Mediatization: Youth's Reflections on Intimate Storytelling, Queer Shame and Realness in Popular Social Media Places," *Journal of Youth Studies* 18, no. 6 (2015): 777–793; Oliver L. Haimson and Anna Lauren Hoffmann, "Constructing and Enforcing 'Authentic' Identity Online: Facebook, Real Names, and Non-Normative Identities," *First Monday* (June 10, 2016); Talbot et al., "The Management of LGBTQ+ Identities."

63. Weinstein and James, *Behind Their Screens*.

64. McInroy, Zapcic, and Beer, "Online Fandom Communities as Networked Counterpublics."

65. Cho, "Default Publicness"; Haimson and Hoffmann, "Constructing and Enforcing 'Authentic' Identity Online."

66. David Kirkpatrick, *The Facebook Effect: The Inside Story of the Company That Is Connecting the World* (New York: Simon and Schuster, 2011).

67. Cho, "Default Publicness."

68. Tiidenberg, Hendry, and Abidin, *Tumblr*.

69. Benjamin Hanckel, Son Vivienne, Paul Byron, Brady Robards, and Brendan Churchill, "'That's Not Necessarily for Them': LGBTIQ+ Young People, Social Media Platform Affordances and Identity Curation," *Media, Culture & Society* 41, no. 8 (November 1, 2019): 1261–1278; Jeanna Sybert, "The Demise of #NSFW: Contested Platform Governance and Tumblr's 2018 Adult Content Ban," *New Media & Society* (February 26, 2021): 1461444821996715.

70. Tiidenberg, Hendry, and Abidin, *Tumblr*.

71. This positive ethos has suffered since the company announced a ban on adult content in December 2018. The policy change had the effect of pushing away marginalized communities, including artists, fandom communities, and transgender users. See Oliver L. Haimson, Avery Dame-Griff, Elias Capello, and Zahari Richter, "Tumblr Was a Trans Technology: The Meaning, Importance, History, and Future of Trans Technologies," *Feminist Media Studies* 21, no. 3 (April 3, 2021): 345–361; Sybert, "The Demise of #NSFW."

72. Cho, "Default Publicness."

73. Bivens notes that even with Facebook's expansion of gender categories in 2014, gender options other than male or female are made visible to users only after they click on a "custom" category, positioning nonbinary and trans genders as a single mass that stands in relation to the dominant and "normal" binary of male/female. Moreover, in the deep level of the Facebook database, nonbinary users are recoded into a binary system: if they are neither male nor female, the database returns no specific gender information about them at all. See Rena Bivens, "The Gender Binary Will Not Be Deprogrammed: Ten Years of Coding Gender on Facebook," *New Media & Society* 19, no. 6 (June 1, 2017): 880–898.

74. Cho, "Default Publicness"; Tiidenberg, Hendry, and Abidin, *Tumblr*.

75. Haimson discusses the importance to individuals of being able to maintain separation across different networks and platforms in his work on trans identity disclosure on Tumblr vs. Facebook. See Oliver Haimson, "Social Media as Social Transition Machinery," *Proceedings of the ACM on Human-Computer Interaction* (November 1, 2018): 63:1–21, https://doi.org/10.1145/3274332.

76. Caroline Pitt, Ari Hock, Leila Zelnick, and Katie Davis, "The Kids Are / Not / Sort of All Right," *Proceedings of the 2021 CHI Conference on Human Factors in Computing Systems* (May 7, 2021): 352:1–14, https://doi.org/10.1145/3411764.3445541.

77. Pitt et al., "The Kids Are / Not / Sort of All Right." Consistent with our research, other researchers found that teens turned to networked technologies, particularly social media, as a lifeline and coping mechanism during the pandemic; see Verolien Cauberghe, Ini Van Wesenbeeck, Steffi De Jans, Liselot Hudders, and Koen Ponnet, "How Adolescents Use Social Media to Cope with Feelings of Loneliness and Anxiety during COVID-19 Lockdown," *Cyberpsychology, Behavior, and Social Networking* 24, no. 4 (2021): 250–257, https://doi.org/10.1089/cyber.2020.0478; Michelle F. Wright and Sebastian Wachs, "Self-Isolation and Adolescents' Friendship Quality: Moderation of Technology Use for Friendship Maintenance," *Youth & Society*, March 7, 2022, https://doi.org/10.1177/0044118X221080484.

78. Rideout et al., *Common Sense Census.*

79. Pitt et al., "The Kids Are / Not / Sort of All Right."

80. Tran et al., "Modeling the Engagement-Disengagement Cycle."

81. Geiger and Davis, "A Growing Number of American Teenagers;" Richtel, "Surgeon General Warns of Youth Mental Health Crisis"; Schaeffer, "In CDC Survey"; Thompson, "Why American Teens Are So Sad."

82. Holland and Tiggemann, "A Systematic Review of the Impact of the Use of Social Networking Sites"; Jarman et al., "Direct and Indirect Relationships between Social Media Use and Body Satisfaction"; Nesi and Prinstein, "Using Social Media for Social Comparison and Feedback-Seeking."

83. To add further confusion to the inconclusive results across studies, researchers working with the same datasets have come to different

conclusions about the relationship between teens' social media use and well-being; see Patti M. Valkenburg, Adrian Meier, and Ine Beyens, "Social Media Use and Its Impact on Adolescent Mental Health: An Umbrella Review of the Evidence," *Current Opinion in Psychology* 44 (April 2022): 58–68, https://doi.org/10.1016/j.copsyc.2021.08.017.

84. Laura Marciano, Charles C. Driver, Peter J. Schulz, and Anne-Linda Camerini, "Dynamics of Adolescents' Smartphone Use and Well-Being Are Positive but Ephemeral," *Scientific Reports* 12, no. 1 (2022), https://doi.org/10.1038/s41598-022-05291-y; Tijana Milosevic, Niamh Ní Bhroin, Kjartan Ólafsson, Elisabeth Staksrud, and Sebastian Wachs, "Time Spent Online and Children's Self-Reported Life Satisfaction in Norway: The Socio-Ecological Perspective," *New Media & Society* (April 6, 2022), https://doi.org/10.1177/14614448221082651; Nesi, "The Impact of Social Media on Youth Mental Health"; Candice L. Odgers and Michaeline R. Jensen, "Annual Research Review: Adolescent Mental Health in the Digital Age: Facts, Fears, and Future Directions," *Journal of Child Psychology and Psychiatry* 61, no. 3 (2020): 336–348; Amy Orben, "Teenagers, Screens and Social Media: A Narrative Review of Reviews and Key Studies," *Social Psychiatry and Psychiatric Epidemiology* 55, no. 4 (April 2020): 407–414; Amy Orben and Andrew K. Przybylski, "The Association between Adolescent Well-Being and Digital Technology Use," *Nature Human Behaviour* 3, no. 2 (2019): 173–182.

85. Amy Orben, Andrew K. Przybylski, Sarah-Jayne Blakemore, and Rogier A. Kievit, "Windows of Developmental Sensitivity to Social Media," *Nature Communications* 13 (2022): 1649, https://doi.org/10.1038/s41467-022-29296-3.

86. Robin Achterhof, Olivia Kirtley, Maude Schneider, Noëmi Hagemann, Karlijn Hermans, Anu P. Hiekkaranta, Aleksandra Lecei, Ginette Lafit, and Inez Myin-Germeys, "Adolescents' Real-Time Social and Affective Experiences of Online and Face-to-Face Interactions," *PsyArXiv* (May 21, 2021); Michaeline Jensen, Madeleine J. George, Michael R. Russell, and Candice L. Odgers, "Young Adolescents' Digital Technology Use and Mental Health Symptoms: Little Evidence of Longitudinal or Daily Linkages," *Clinical Psychological Science* 7, no. 6 (2019): 1416–1433; Marciano et al., "Dynamics of Adolescents' Smartphone Use and Well-Being Are Positive but Ephemeral"; Nesi, "The Impact of Social Media on Youth Mental Health"; Odgers and Jensen, "Annual Research Review"; Candice L. Odgers, and Michael B.

Robb, "Tweens, Teens, Tech, and Mental Health: Coming of Age in an Increasingly Digital, Uncertain, and Unequal World" (San Francisco: Common Sense Media, 2020); Jessica Taylor Piotrowski and Patti M. Valkenburg, "Finding Orchids in a Field of Dandelions: Understanding Children's Differential Susceptibility to Media Effects," *American Behavioral Scientist* 59, no. 14 (2015): 1776–1789; Pitt et al., "The Kids Are / Not / Sort of All Right"; Mitchell J. Prinstein, Jacqueline Nesi, and Eva H. Telzer, "Commentary: An Updated Agenda for the Study of Digital Media Use and Adolescent Development—Future Directions Following Odgers & Jensen (2020)," *Journal of Child Psychology and Psychiatry* 61, no. 3 (2020): 349–352; Patti Valkenburg, Ine Beyens, J. Loes Pouwels, Irene I. van Driel, and Loes Keijsers, "Social Media Use and Adolescents' Self-Esteem: Heading for a Person-Specific Media Effects Paradigm," *Journal of Communication* 71, no. 1 (February 1, 2021): 56–78; Valkenburg, Meier, and Beyens, "Social Media Use and Its Impact on Adolescent Mental Health"; Patti Valkenburg and Jochen Peter, "The Differential Susceptibility to Media Effects Model," *Journal of Communication* 63, no. 2 (2013): 221–243.

87. J. Beyens Ine, Loes Pouwels, Irene I. van Driel, Loes Keijsers, and Patti M. Valkenburg, "The Effect of Social Media on Well-Being Differs from Adolescent to Adolescent," *Scientific Reports* 10, no. 1 (2020): 1–11.

88. Researchers often distinguish between passive and active social media use. Passive social media use involves scrolling through one's feed, reading posts but not posting oneself. Active social media use involves posting, liking, or commenting on posts, or engaging in direct communication with other users of the platform.

89. In a subsequent paper, the researchers observe that even greater specificity than active versus passive social media use is needed, for instance, by distinguishing how positively or negatively a teen experiences a social media interaction; see Patti M. Valkenburg, Irene I. van Driel, and Ine Beyens, "The Associations of Active and Passive Social Media Use with Well-Being: A Critical Scoping Review," *New Media & Society* 24, no. 2 (2022): 530–549, https://doi.org/10.1177/14 614448211065425.

90. National Academies of Sciences, Engineering, Medicine, *Promoting Positive Adolescent Health Behaviors and Outcomes*; Somerville, "The Teenage Brain."

91. Geiger and Davis, "A Growing Number of American Teenagers"; Richtel, "Surgeon General Warns of Youth Mental Health Crisis"; Schaeffer, "In CDC Survey"; Thompson, "Why American Teens Are So Sad."

92. Cohen, Newton-John, and Slater, "The Relationship between Facebook and Instagram"; Holland and Tiggemann, "A Systematic Review of the Impact of the Use of Social Networking Sites"; Kleemans et al., "Picture Perfect."

93. Brough, Literat, and Ikin, "'Good Social Media?'"; Kennedy, "'If the Rise of the TikTok Dance."

94. Marciano et al., "Dynamics of Adolescents' Smartphone Use and Well-Being Are Positive but Ephemeral"; Nesi, "The Impact of Social Media on Youth Mental Health"; Odgers and Jensen, "Annual Research Review"; Orben, "Teenagers, Screens and Social Media"; Orben and Przybylski, "The Association between Adolescent Well-Being and Digital Technology Use;" Valkenburg, Meier, and Beyens, "Social Media Use and Its Impact on Adolescent Mental Health."

95. Orben, "Teenagers, Screens and Social Media."

96. Beyens et al., "The Effect of Social Media"; Pitt et al., "The Kids Are / Not / Sort of All Right."

97. Pitt et al., "The Kids Are / Not / Sort of All Right."

98. McInroy, Zapcic, and Beer, "Online Fandom Communities as Networked Counterpublics."

99. Cho, "Default Publicness."

100. boyd, *It's Complicated*.

101. In 2018, Tumblr announced it would start banning "adult" content, which was seen by many users as a prioritization of the company's bottom line over community values; see Sybert, "The Demise of #NSFW."

102. Kai Lukoff, Ulrik Lyngs, Himanshu Zade, J. Vera Liao, James Choi, Kaiyue Fan, Sean A. Munson, and Alexis Hiniker, "How the Design of YouTube Influences User Sense of Agency," *Proceedings of the 2021 CHI Conference on Human Factors in Computing Systems* (May 7, 2021): 1–17, https://doi.org/10.1145/3411764.3445467.

103. Sybert, "The Demise of #NSFW."

104. TikTok admitted to suppressing videos by disabled, queer, and fat creators in an effort to prevent bullying of vulnerable people; see Elena Botella, "TikTok Admits It Suppressed Videos by Disabled, Queer, and Fat Creators," *Slate*, December 4, 2019, https://slate.com /technology/2019/12/tiktok-disabled-users-videos-suppressed.html; Ellen Simpson and Bryan Semaan, "For You, or For 'You'?: Everyday LGBTQ+ Encounters with TikTok," *Proceedings of the ACM on Human-Computer Interaction* (January 5, 2021): 252:1–34, https://doi .org/10.1145/3432951.

CHAPTER 8

1. Adele Diamond, "Normal Development of Prefrontal Cortex from Birth to Young Adulthood: Cognitive Functions, Anatomy, and Biochemistry," *Principles of Frontal Lobe Function* 466 (2002): 503; Susan M. Sawyer, Peter S. Azzopardi, Dakshitha Wickremarathne, and George C. Patton, "The Age of Adolescence," *The Lancet Child & Adolescent Health* 2, no. 3 (March 1, 2018): 223–228; Daniel J. Simmonds, Michael N. Hallquist, Miya Asato, and Beatriz Luna, "Developmental Stages and Sex Differences of White Matter and Behavioral Development through Adolescence: A Longitudinal Diffusion Tensor Imaging (DTI) Study," *NeuroImage* 92 (May 15, 2014): 356–368.

2. Mary Helen Immordino-Yang, Joanna A. Christodoulou, and Vanessa Singh, "Rest Is Not Idleness: Implications of the Brain's Default Mode for Human Development and Education," *Perspectives on Psychological Science* 7, no. 4 (July 1, 2012): 352–364; Sawyer, Azzopardi, Wickremarathne, and Patton, "Age of Adolescence."

3. Parissa J. Ballard and Emily J. Ozer, "The Implications of Youth Activism for Health and Well-Being," in *Contemporary Youth Activism: Advancing Social Justice in the United States: Advancing Social Justice in the United States*, ed. Jerusha Conner and Sonia M. Rosen (Santa Barbara, CA: ABC-CLIO, 2016), 223–244; William Damon, Jenni Menon, and Kendall Cotton Bronk, "The Development of Purpose During Adolescence," *Applied Developmental Science* 7, no. 3 (July 1, 2003): 119–128; William Damon and Heather Malin, "The Development of Purpose: An Interdisciplinary Perspective," in *The Oxford Handbook of Moral Development: An Interdisciplinary Perspective*, ed. Lene Arnett Jensen (Oxford: Oxford University Press, 2020), 110–132; Erikson,

Identity; Constance Flanagan and Peter Levine, "Civic Engagement and the Transition to Adulthood," *The Future of Children* 20, no. 1 (2010): 159–179.

4. Mizuko Ito and Remy Cross, *Asset and Action-Based Approaches to Civic Learning: A Review of Frameworks, Evidence and Approaches* (Irvine, CA: Connected Learning Alliance, 2022), https://clalliance.org/wp-content/uploads/2022/02/Asset-and-Action-Based-Approaches-to-Civic-Learning-A-Review-of-Frameworks-Evidence-and-Approaches-1.pdf; Nkemka Anyiwo, Gordon J. M. Palmer, Janay M. Garrett, Jordan G. Starck, and Elan C. Hope, "Racial and Political Resistance: An Examination of the Sociopolitical Action of Racially Marginalized Youth," *Current Opinion in Psychology, Social Change (Rallies, Riots and Revolutions)* 35 (October 1, 2020): 86–91; Ballard and Ozer, "Implications of Youth Activism for Health and Well-Being"; Weinstein and James, *Behind Their Screens*.

5. Kristian Lundberg, "Despite Pandemic, Civically Engaged Youth Report Higher Well-Being," Center for Information & Research on Civic Learning and Education (CIRCLE), accessed November 1, 2021, https://circle.tufts.edu/latest-research/despite-pandemic-civically-engaged-youth-report-higher-well-being.

6. John Della Volpe, *Fight: How Gen Z Is Channeling Their Fear and Passion to Save America* (New York: St. Martin's Press, 2022).

7. Anyiwo et al., "Racial and Political Resistance"; Alec Tyson, Brian Kennedy, and Cary Funk, "Gen Z, Millennials Stand Out for Climate Change Activism, Social Media Engagement with Issue," Pew Research Center Science & Society, May 26, 2021, https://www.pewresearch.org/science/2021/05/26/gen-z-millennials-stand-out-for-climate-change-activism-social-media-engagement-with-issue/.

8. Flanagan and Levine, "Civic Engagement and the Transition to Adulthood"; Robert D. Putnam, "Bowling Alone: America's Declining Social Capital," in *Culture and Politics: A Reader*, ed. Lane Crothers and Charles Lockhart (New York: Palgrave Macmillan US, 2000), 223–234.

9. Henry Jenkins, Sangita Shresthova, Liana Gamber-Thompson, Neta Kligler-Vilenchik, and Arely Zimmerman, *By Any Media Necessary: The New Youth Activism* (New York: New York University Press, 2016); Ethan Zuckerman, "New Media, New Civics? My Bellwether Lecture at the Oxford Internet Institute," . . . *My Heart's In Accra*

(blog), December 6, 2013, https://ethanzuckerman.com/2013/12/06/new-media-new-civics-my-bellweather-lecture-at-the-oxford-internet-institute/.

10. Cynthia Cho and Anna Gorman, "Massive Student Walkout Spreads across Southland," *Los Angeles Times*, March 28, 2006, https://www.latimes.com/archives/la-xpm-2006-mar-28-me-protests28-story.html.

11. Liana Gamber-Thompson and Arely Zimmerman, "DREAMing Citizenship: Undocumented Youth, Coming out, and Pathways to Participation," in Jenkins et al., *By Any Media Necessary*, 186–218.

12. Gamber-Thompson and Zimmerman, "DREAMing Citizenship."

13. Gamber-Thompson and Zimmerman, "DREAMing Citizenship."

14. Jenkins et al., *By Any Media Necessary*.

15. Jenkins et al., *By Any Media Necessary*, 32.

16. Neta Kligler-Vilenchik, "'Decreasing World Suck': Harnessing Popular Culture for Fan Activism," in Jenkins et al., *By Any Media Necessary*, 102–148.

17. Jenkins et al., *By Any Media Necessary*, 29.

18. Henry Jenkins, *Convergence Culture: Where Old and New Media Collide* (New York: NYU Press, 2006); Henry Jenkins, *Fans, Bloggers, and Gamers: Exploring Participatory Culture* (New York: NYU Press, 2006); Henry Jenkins, "Rethinking 'Rethinking Convergence/Culture,'" *Cultural Studies* 28, no. 2 (2014): 267–297; Jenkins, *Confronting the Challenges of Participatory Culture*; Jenkins et al., *By Any Media Necessary*.

19. Ioana Literat and Neta Kligler-Vilenchik, "Youth Collective Political Expression on Social Media: The Role of Affordances and Memetic Dimensions for Voicing Political Views," *New Media & Society* 21, no. 9 (2019): 1988–2009; Ioana Literat and Neta Kligler-Vilenchik, "How Popular Culture Prompts Youth Collective Political Expression and Cross-Cutting Political Talk on Social Media: A Cross-Platform Analysis," *Social Media + Society* 7, no. 2 (2021): 1–14, https://doi.org/10.1177/20563051211008821.

20. Aragon and Davis, *Writers in the Secret Garden*; Tiidenberg, Hendry, and Abidin, *Tumblr*.

21. Literat and Kligler-Vilenchik, "Youth Collective Political Expression on Social Media"; Regina Marchi and Lynn Schofield Clark, "Social Media and Connective Journalism: The Formation of Counterpublics and Youth Civic Participation," *Journalism* 22, no. 2 (2021): 285–302; An Xiao Mina, *Memes to Movements: How the World's Most Viral Media Is Changing Social Protest and Power* (Boston: Beacon Press, 2019).

22. Tiidenberg, Hendry, and Abidin, *Tumblr*.

23. Literat and Kligler-Vilenchik, "Youth Collective Political Expression on Social Media"; Marchi and Clark, "Social Media and Connective Journalism."

24. Tiidenberg, Hendry, and Abidin, *Tumblr*.

25. Sarah Jerasa and Trevor Boffone, "BookTok 101: TikTok, Digital Literacies, and Out-of-School Reading Practices," *Journal of Adolescent & Adult Literacy* 65, no. 3 (2021): 219–226.

26. Mizuko Ito, Elisabeth Soep, Neta Kligler-Vilenchik, Sangita Shresthova, Liana Gamber-Thompson, and Arely Zimmerman, "Learning Connected Civics: Narratives, Practices, Infrastructures," *Curriculum Inquiry* 45, no. 1 (January 1, 2015): 10–29.

27. Gamber-Thompson and Zimmerman, "DREAMing Citizenship."

28. Mina, *Memes to Movements*.

29. Zuckerman, "New Media, New Civics?"

30. Zuckerman, "New Media, New Civics?"

31. Sarah J. Jackson, Moya Bailey, and Brooke Foucault Welles, *#HashtagActivism: Networks of Race and Gender Justice* (Cambridge, MA: MIT Press, 2020); Watkins et al., *The Digital Edge*.

32. Victoria Rideout and S. Craig Watkins, *Millennials, Social Media, Politics* (Austin: The University of Texas at Austin Insitute for Media Innovation, February 2019). At the same time, youth of color are less likely to have civic learning experiences in school; see Cathy Cohen, Joseph Kahne, and Jessica Marshall, *Let's Go There: Making a Case for Race, Ethnicity and a Lived Civics Approach to Civic Education* (Chicago: GenForward at the University of Chicago, 2018), https://www.civic survey.org/publications/lets-go-there.

33. Emanuella Grinberg, "How the Parkland Students Pulled off a Massive National Protest in Only 5 Weeks," *CNN*, 2018, https://www.cnn.com/2018/03/26/us/march-for-our-lives/index.html.

34. Deen Freelon, Charlton D. McIlwain, and Meredith Clark, "Beyond the Hashtags: #Ferguson, #Blacklivesmatter, and the Online Struggle for Offline Justice," Center for Media & Social Impact, American University, February 29, 2016, https://dx.doi.org/10.2139/ssrn.2747066.

35. Jackson, Bailey, and Foucault Welles, *#HashtagActivism*.

36. André Brock, "From the Blackhand Side: Twitter as a Cultural Conversation," *Journal of Broadcasting & Electronic Media* 56, no. 4 (October 1, 2012): 529–549.

37. Freelon, McIlwain, and Clark, "Beyond the Hashtags."

38. Brad J. Porfilio, Debangshu Roychoudhury, and Lauren Gardner, "Ending the 'War Against Youth': Social Media and Hip-Hop Culture as Sites of Resistance, Transformation and (Re) Conceptualization," *Journal for Critical Education Policy Studies (JCEPS)* 11, no. 4 (2013): 85–105.

39. Anyiwo et al., "Racial and Political Resistance."

40. Freelon, McIlwain, and Clark, "Beyond the Hashtags."

41. Tiera Chante Tanksley, "Race, Education and #BlackLivesMatter: How Social Media Activism Shapes the Educational Experiences of Black College-Age Women," dissertation, University of California, Los Angeles, 2019.

42. Jackson, Bailey, and Foucault Welles, *#HashtagActivism*; Amy Stornaiuolo and Ebony Elizabeth Thomas, "Disrupting Educational Inequalities through Youth Digital Activism," *Review of Research in Education* 41, no. 1 (March 1, 2017): 337–357; Sherri Williams, "Digital Defense: Black Feminists Resist Violence with Hashtag Activism," *Feminist Media Studies* 15, no. 2 (2015): 341–344; Guobin Yang, "Narrative Agency in Hashtag Activism: The Case of #BlackLivesMatter," *Media and Communication* 4, no. 4 (January 1, 2016): 13–17.

43. Literat and Kligler-Vilenchik, "Youth Collective Political Expression on Social Media"; Stornaiuolo and Thomas, "Disrupting Educational Inequalities through Youth Digital Activism."

44. Jackson, Bailey, and Foucault Welles, *#HashtagActivism*.

45. Anna Foley, "Ready to Feel Old? The #Hashtag Turned 10 Today," August 25, 2017, https://www.refinery29.com/en-us/2017/08/169303/twitter-hashtag-10-anniversary.

46. Tanksley, "Race, Education and #BlackLivesMatter."

47. Freelon, McIlwain, and Clark, "Beyond the Hashtags."

48. Tanksley, "Race, Education and #BlackLivesMatter."

49. Tanksley, "Race, Education and #BlackLivesMatter."

50. Tiidenberg, Hendry, and Abidin, *Tumblr*.

51. Megan Lindsay Brown and Hanna Phifer, "The Rise of Belle from Tumblr," in *Microcelebrity Around the Globe*, ed. Crystal Abidin and Megan Lindsay Brown (Bingley, UK: Emerald Publishing Limited, 2018), 121–130.

52. A more recent example of white appropriation of Black dance moves is the Renegade, a widely popular dance on TikTok in 2020. Then fifteen-year-old Jalaiah Harmon, who is Black, choreographed the dance, but it was popularized primarily by white influencers.

53. Brown and Phifer, "The Rise of Belle from Tumblr."

54. Christian Fuchs, "Capitalism, Patriarchy, Slavery, and Racism in the Age of Digital Capitalism and Digital Labour," *Critical Sociology* 44, no. 4–5 (July 1, 2018): 677–702.

55. Tanksley, "Race, Education and #BlackLivesMatter."

56. Brough, Literat, and Ikin, "'Good Social Media?'"; Tiidenberg, Hendry, and Abidin, *Tumblr*; Lenhart and Owens, *The Unseen Teen*.

57. Rey Junco, Peter de Guzman, Kristian Lundberg, Abby Kiesa, and Alberto Medina, "Early Takeaways on What Worked to Reach Youth During the 2020 Election," Center for Information & Research on Civic Learning and Education (CIRCLE), January 25, 2021, https://circle.tufts.edu/latest-research/early-takeaways-what-worked-reach-youth-during-2020-election.

58. Weinstein and James, *Behind Their Screens*.

59. Weinstein and James, *Behind Their Screens*.

60. Weinstein and James, *Behind Their Screens*.

61. Patton et al., "Stop and Frisk Online."

62. Eli Pariser, *The Filter Bubble: How the New Personalized Web Is Changing What We Read and How We Think* (New York: Penguin, 2011).

63. Ellen Middaugh, Lynn Schofield Clark, and Parissa J. Ballard, "Digital Media, Participatory Politics, and Positive Youth Development," *Pediatrics* 140, suppl. 2 (November 1, 2017): S127–S131.

64. Rossini argues that it's intolerance and not incivility that poses the greatest threat to democracy. Whereas incivility may involve foul language or a harsh tone, intolerance singles out individuals or groups for attack. Patricia Rossini, "Beyond Incivility: Understanding Patterns of Uncivil and Intolerant Discourse in Online Political Talk," *Communication Research* 49, no. 3: 399–425, https://doi.org/10.1177/0093650220921314.

65. Literat and Kligler-Vilenchik, "How Popular Culture Prompts Youth Collective Political Expression."

66. Ashley A. Anderson, Dominique Brossard, Dietram A. Scheufele, Michael A. Xenos, and Peter Ladwig, "The 'Nasty Effect': Online Incivility and Risk Perceptions of Emerging Technologies," *Journal of Computer-Mediated Communication* 19, no. 3 (April 1, 2014): 373–387; Bryan T. Gervais, "Incivility Online: Affective and Behavioral Reactions to Uncivil Political Posts in a Web-Based Experiment," *Journal of Information Technology & Politics* 12, no. 2 (April 3, 2015): 167–185; Meredith Y. Wang and David E. Silva, "A Slap or a Jab: An Experiment on Viewing Uncivil Political Discussions on Facebook," *Computers in Human Behavior* 81 (2018): 73–83; Moran Yarchi, Christian Baden, and Neta Kligler-Vilenchik, "Political Polarization on the Digital Sphere: A Cross-Platform, Over-Time Analysis of Interactional, Positional, and Affective Polarization on Social Media," *Political Communication* 38, no. 1–2 (2021): 98–139.

67. Anderson et al., "The 'Nasty Effect'"; Gervais, "Incivility Online."

68. Brough, Literat, and Ikin, "'Good Social Media?'"; Merrill and Oremus, "Five Points for Anger, One for a 'Like'"; Wang and Silva, "A Slap or a Jab."

69. Although users may be more engaged by emotional or provocative online content, there are limits. Extremism and hate speech seem to disengage a lot of users. See Casey Newton, "The Platforms

Witness a Crime," May 17, 2022, https://www.platformer.news/p/the
-platforms-witness-a-crime.

70. Amanda Baughan, Justin Petelka, Catherine Jaekyung Yoo, Jack
Lo, Shiyue Wang, Amulya Paramasivam, Ashley Zhou, and Alexis
Hiniker, "Someone Is Wrong on the Internet: Having Hard Conversa-
tions in Online Spaces," *Proceedings of the ACM on Human-Computer
Interaction* 5, no. CSCW1 (April 22, 2021): 156:1–22, https://doi.org
/10.1145/3449230.

71. Bryan Semaan, Heather Faucett, Scott P. Robertson, Misa
Maruyama, and Sara Douglas, "Designing Political Deliberation
Environments to Support Interactions in the Public Sphere," *Proceedings of the 33rd Annual ACM Conference on Human Factors in Computing* Systems (April 18, 2015): 3167–3176, https://doi.org/10.1145
/2702123.2702403.

72. Baughan et al., "Someone Is Wrong on the Internet"; Semaan et
al., "Designing Political Deliberation Environments."

73. Brough, Literat, and Ikin, "'Good Social Media?'"; Kennedy, "'If
the Rise of the TikTok Dance."

74. Baughan et al., "Someone Is Wrong on the Internet."

75. Yarchi, Baden, and Kligler-Vilenchik, "Political Polarization."

76. Farnaz Irannejad Bisafar, Brooke Foucault Welles, Catherine
D'Ignazio, and Andrea G. Parker, "Supporting Youth Activists? Strategic Use of Social Media: A Qualitative Investigation of Design
Opportunities," *Proceedings of the ACM on Human-Computer Interaction*
4, no. CSCW2 (October 15, 2020): 109:1–25, https://doi.org/10.1145
/3415180.

77. Although such information holds promise to support youth with
their online civic engagement, Parker and her colleagues did identify
potential pitfalls with their visualization tools. For instance, some
youth inferred that the lack of certain hashtags, such as #BlackLives-
Matter, in a user's list of commonly used hashtags meant they didn't
support that particular societal issue, failing to realize that the user
may indeed use this hashtag, but just not as frequently as others.

78. Jenkins, *Confronting the Challenges of Participatory Culture*; Jenkins et al., *By Any Media Necessary*; Literat and Kligler-Vilenchik,
"Youth Collective Political Expression on Social Media"; Literat and

Kligler-Vilenchik, "How Popular Culture Prompts Youth Collective Political Expression."

79. Jenkins et al., *By Any Media Necessary*.

80. Tiidenberg, Hendry, and Abidin, *Tumblr*.

81. Weinstein and James, *Behind Their Screens*.

82. Tanksley, "Race, Education and #BlackLivesMatter."

83. Jackson, Bailey, and Foucault Welles, *#HashtagActivism*.

84. Tanksley, "Race, Education and #BlackLivesMatter."

85. Weinstein and James, *Behind Their Screens*.

86. Tanksley, "Race, Education and #BlackLivesMatter."

87. Tiidenberg, Hendry, and Abidin, *Tumblr*.

88. Gervais, "Incivility Online"; Yarchi, Baden, and Kligler-Vilenchik, "Political Polarization."

89. Brough, Literat, and Ikin, "'Good Social Media?'"; Kennedy, "'If the Rise of the TikTok Dance."

90. Baughan et al., "Someone Is Wrong on the Internet."

91. Zuckerman, "New Media, New Civics?"

92. Bisafar et al., "Supporting Youth Activists?"

CHAPTER 9

1. Deci and Ryan, "The 'What' and 'Why' of Goal Pursuits"; Ryan and Deci, "Intrinsic and Extrinsic Motivation from a Self-Determination Theory Perspective."

2. Researchers Jenny Radesky and Alexis Hiniker use the same term, *child-centered design*, in a 2021 vision article that calls for policies that encourage platforms to establish child-centered design as a default user interface. Though our viewpoints are complementary, they are distinct.

3. Radesky and Hiniker, "From Moral Panic to Systemic Change."

4. Radesky and Hiniker, "From Moral Panic to Systemic Change."

5. Rob Reich, Mehran Sahami, and Jeremy M. Weinstein, *System Error: Where Big Tech Went Wrong and How We Can Reboot* (New York: Harper, 2021).

6. *The Social Dilemma*, directed by Jeff Orlowski (Los Gatos, CA: Netflix, 2020), film. Indeed, there are a growing number of former big-tech employees who have gone on to found organizations and startups that focus explicitly on prioritizing individual well-being over company growth and profit; see Issie Lapowsky, "The Center for Humane Technology Wants to Spark a Grassroots Ethical Tech Revolution," *Wired*, February 18, 2008, https://www.wired.com/story /center-for-humane-technology-tech-addiction/; Deepa Seetharaman, "Former Facebook, WhatsApp Employees Lead New Push to Fix Social Media," *Wall Street Journal*, May 4, 2022, sec. Tec, https://www.wsj .com/articles/social-media-startups-take-aim-at-facebook-and-elon -musk-11651656600.

7. Lenhart and Owens, *The Unseen Teen."*

8. Lenhart and Owens, *The Unseen Teen.*

9. Lenhart and Owens, *The Unseen Teen.*

10. Radesky and Hiniker, "From Moral Panic to Systemic Change."

11. In May 2022, the U.S. Senate Judiciary Committee held a hearing to consider legislation that would force big tech companies to become more transparent by disclosing internal data to qualified researchers; see Casey Newton, "How Platform Researchers Convinced the Senate," May 5, 2022, https://www.platformer.news/p /how-platform-researchers-convinced. Meanwhile, the EU actually passed legislation in 2022 requiring big tech companies to provide vetted researchers with access to internal data and provide users with information about ads and recommender systems; see Daphne Keller, "What Does the DSA Say?," April 25, 2022, https://cyberlaw.stanford .edu/blog/2022/04/what-does-dsa-say-0; Casey Newton, "How Europe Could Thwart Elon Musk's Free-Speech Plans for Twitter," April 26, 2022, https://www.platformer.news/p/how-europe-could-thwart-elon -musks; Adam Satariano, "E.U. Takes Aim at Social Media's Harms With Landmark New Law," *New York Times*, April 22, 2022, sec. Technology, https://www.nytimes.com/2022/04/22/technology/european -union-social-media-law.html.

12. In April 2022, the EU passed the Digital Services Act, which governs how large tech companies such as Meta and Google handle users' content as well as the information they provide to users, researchers, and regulators. For instance, the law requires these companies

to avoid dark patterns nudges, label deepfakes, remove hate speech within twenty-four hours, and notify users when their content has been taken down, among other requirements; see Keller, "What Does the DSA Say?"; Newton, "How Europe Could Thwart Elon Musk's Free-Speech Plans for Twitter."

13. Casey Newton, "How the American Internet Is Turning European," October 27, 2021, https://www.platformer.news/p/how-the -american-internet-is-turning; UK Information Commissioner's Office, "Introduction to the Age Appropriate Design Code," ICO, September 2, 2021, https://ico.org.uk/for-organisations/guide-to-data-protection/ico -codes-of-practice/age-appropriate-design-code/.

14. Newton, "How the American Internet Is Turning European."

15. Liza Lin, "TikTok to Adjust Its Algorithm to Avoid Negative Reinforcement," *Wall Street Journal*, December 16, 2021, sec. Tech, https://www.wsj.com/articles/tiktok-to-adjust-its-algorithm-to-avoid -negative-reinforcement-11639661801; Casey Newton, "TikTok's Safety Dance," February 9, 2022, https://www.platformer.news/p/tik toks-safety-dance.

16. David McCabe, "Anonymity No More? Age Checks Come to the Web," *New York Times*, October 27, 2021, sec. Technology, https:// www.nytimes.com/2021/10/27/technology/internet-age-check-proof .html; Newton, "How the American Internet Is Turning European."

17. Bacon, "All Along."

18. Lenhart and Owens, *The Unseen Teen*.

19. Weinstein and James, *Behind Their Screens*.

20. Carrie James and Megan Cotnam-Kappel, "Doubtful Dialogue: How Youth Navigate the Draw (and Drawbacks) of Online Political Dialogue," *Learning, Media and Technology* 45, no. 2 (2020): 129–150.

21. James, Weinstein, and Mendoza, "Teaching Digital Citizens in Today's World."

22. Gutiérrez and Rogoff, "Cultural Ways of Learning"; Nasir et al., "Rethinking Learning."

23. Rose and Meyer, *Teaching Every Student in the Digital Age*.

24. Ames, "Charismatic Technology"; Reich, *Failure to Disrupt*.

25. Reich, *Failure to Disrupt*.

26. Christina Pazzanese, "Experts Consider the Ethical Implications of New Technology," *Harvard Gazette* (blog), October 16, 2020, https://news.harvard.edu/gazette/story/2020/10/experts-consider-the-ethical-implications-of-new-technology/.

27. Radesky and Hiniker, "From Moral Panic to Systemic Change." In addition to the examples provided by Radesky and Hiniker, the World Economic Forum has developed a toolkit designed to help companies develop trustworthy artificial intelligence for children and youth (https://www.weforum.org/reports/artificial-intelligence-for-children). As part of its AI for children project, UNICEF developed recommendations for building AI policies and systems that uphold children's rights (https://www.unicef.org/globalinsight/reports/policy-guidance-ai-children). In 2021, the United Nations Committee on the Rights of the Child launched their General Comment No. 25 on children's rights in relation to the digital environment; Ge Wang, Jun Zhao, Max Van Kleek, and Nigel Shadbolt, "Informing Age-Appropriate AI: Examining Principles and Practices of AI for Children," *CHI Conference on Human Factors in Computing Systems* (April 29, 2022): 536:1–29, https://doi.org/10.1145/3491102.3502057.

28. Radesky and Hiniker, "From Moral Panic to Systemic Change."

29. Radesky and Hiniker, "From Moral Panic to Systemic Change."

30. Lucas Colusso, Cynthia L. Bennett, Gary Hsieh, and Sean A. Munson, "Translational Resources: Reducing the Gap between Academic Research and HCI Practice," *Proceedings of the 2017 Conference on Designing Interactive Systems* (June 10, 2017): 957–968, https://doi.org/10.1145/3064663.3064667.

31. Saba Kawas, "Supporting Developmentally Responsive Design in Children's Technologies," dissertation, University of Washington, Seattle, 2021.

INDEX